LEADERSHIP AND DECISION-MAKING

VICTOR H. VROOM and PHILIP W. YETTON

LEADERSHIP AND DECISION-MAKING

UNIVERSITY OF PITTSBURGH PRESS

Library of Congress Cataloging in Publication Data

Vroom, Victor Harold, date
   Leadership and decision-making.

   Bibliography: p. 221
   1. Decision-making. 2. Organization.
3. Leadership. I. Yetton, Philip W., date
joint author. II. Title.
HM131.V69   301.18'32   72-94068
ISBN 0-8229-3266-0

To Derek, Jeffrey, and Jason

Contents

Figures

Preface

This book really began during the fall semester of 1968. Vic was teaching a graduate seminar on organizations in the Carnegie-Mellon Graduate School of Industrial Administration. He had recently completed a review of the literature on participation in decision-making in connection with a chapter he wrote for the *Handbook in Social Psychology.* In discussing his conclusions in that chapter he indicated his intention to work during the remainder of the year on the construction of a normative model that would organize the empirical evidence concerning the multiple consequences of participation in a form that would be both understandable and useful to the practicing manager.

Phil was one of the students taking the seminar. He had just recently arrived from England to work on a Ph.D. in organizational behavior and expressed interest in working on the problem. Before long we were both engaged in reading the literature and drawing decision trees that we thought reflected the principal implications of that literature for the practicing manager. It is encouraging to look back on those early models and to see how far we have come. The early models were far simpler than those to be presented in this book, and they ignored considerations that we have subsequently come to regard as quite important.

We were not too far into this work before we began speculating about how close our models were to how leaders actually behave. Within a few weeks we began some empirical research on the situational factors that influence managers to adopt one leadership style or another, work that will be reported in chapter 4.

The work, both normative and descriptive, was in high gear when in the fall of 1970 Vic was granted a sabbatical year, which he decided to spend at the University of California at Irvine. It appeared that the collaboration would be ended, but with the financial support of the Ford Foundation and the Graduate School of Industrial Administration it became possible for Phil to go to California to continue the work.

While in California, we developed the concept of using standardized problems to explore further the descriptive questions. Phil decided to base his thesis on this aspect of the problem, and much of his time became devoted to the issues presented in chapter 5. It was at that time that we began to become aware of the potential use of the data collection methods in leadership development.

On our return to Carnegie, Phil set about finishing his thesis while Vic started the task of writing up the research in the form taken in this book. Thus, matters of organization and writing style are items for which Vic must bear the principal responsibility. On the other hand, decisions regarding the content of the model and of the appropriate data analysis were matters that we jointly decided.

This book has been written with two audiences in mind. The principal group to which it is addressed is the set of scholars and researchers who share with us an interest in leadership, decision-making, and organizational behavior. The second group is made up of those in managerial or administrative positions—including those who have participated in the research and who, since the first days of the project, have been asking where they could find a written exposition of these ideas.

It is not an easy task to write simultaneously for these two audiences. Inclusion of the detail and documentation required by the first group runs the risk of "losing" the second. An attempt has been made to organize the book in such a way that the practicing manager can extract what he wishes without the necessity of going into a detailed examination of research findings. Such a person should read chapters 1–3 and 7–10 and examine the introductions and conclusions of the three more technical middle chapters.

An undertaking of this magnitude clearly cannot be completed without substantial financial support. We are grateful to the McKinsey Foundation, which looked kindly on the original idea and provided financial support during the critical early days of the project. We are also indebted to the Smith Richardson Foundation and the General Electric Foundation for their financial support during the interim period, and to the Office of Naval Research, which has supported the work since December of 1971. We must also acknowledge our gratitude to Carnegie-Mellon University for

granting Vic his sabbatical leave and to the Ford Foundation for
making it possible for Phil to go to California.

Our intellectual debts are many, but there is one person, Norman
R. F. Maier, who deserves special mention for having contributed
not only to Vic's general development as a psychologist interested
in behavior in organization but also to our way of thinking about
the specific problems dealt with in this book. The frequent cita-
tions of his work on the pages to follow are but a small indication
of his influence.

Of the many individuals who have assisted at some point or other
during the four years of work on this book, there are three whose
contributions should be explicitly noted. First, we would like to
acknowledge our debt to Vic's wife, Ann, who put in countless
hours reading the manuscript, correcting the English, and helping
us to clarify our thinking. Second, we must acknowledge the help
of Evelyn Hart, who typed the manuscript more times than we care
to mention. Her willingness to work long hours, even during her
vacation, in our final days at Carnegie-Mellon have earned our un-
ending gratitude. Finally, we would like to thank Phil's wife, Maria,
for enduring all the trials and tribulations that are part of his
simultaneously completing a Ph.D. and working on a research
project such as this one.

VICTOR H. VROOM
PHILIP W. YETTON

LEADERSHIP AND DECISION-MAKING

CHAPTER 1

Introduction

Few problems of interest to behavioral scientists have as much potential relevance to the problems of society as the study of leadership. The effective functioning of social systems ranging in size from the local PTA to the United States of America is assumed to be dependent on the quality of their leadership. This assumption is reflected in our tendency to blame a football coach for a losing season and to credit a general for a military victory. While one can identify many factors influencing organizational effectiveness, some of which are outside the direct control of those in positions of leadership, the critical importance of executive functions and of those persons who carry them out to the survival and effectiveness of the organization cannot be denied. Any knowledge that the behavioral sciences could contribute to the identification, development, and enhancement of leadership in organized human endeavor would be of immense societal value.

For several decades sociologists and psychologists have carried out research on the process of leadership. Most textbooks in social psychology include at least one chapter on the subject, and the contents of the academic journals reflect a continued interest on the part of researchers. Opinions differ, however, on the social impact of this work. It would be hard to defend the thesis that leadership research and theory had a substantive impact on the behavior of leaders or the ways in which they were recruited, selected, and developed.

The probable reasons for this state of affairs include the inherent complexity of the processes involved, ambiguity in the conceptualization of leadership, difficulties in measuring behavior, and inevitable "value" questions concerning the standards by which leadership outcomes are to be assessed. In this book, a fresh look is taken at certain of the traditional problems of leadership, such as the conceptualization and measurement of differences in leadership style and specification of situations that require different styles. The approach to be taken is suggested by the second part of the title of the book—decision-making.

Decision-making is central to many scientific disciplines. Much of human behavior is simply a reflection of the decisions people make, and the processes that regulate and control these choices or decisions are central to any discipline that purports to understand and predict human behavior. Some disciplines, such as economics, statistics, and operations research, approach decision-making from a normative standpoint with a fundamental interest in how choices or decisions should be made. Others, including psychology, sociology, and political science, are fundamentally concerned with understanding and predicting human behavior, including those areas of behavior that are the result of human choices and decisions.

An understanding of the decision-making process is critical not only for the explanation of individual behavior but also for the behavior of complex organizations. March and Simon (1958) were the first scholars to attempt to explain the behavior of organizations in terms of their decision-making processes, and their effort was subsequently extended by Cyert and March (1963). A key concept in both analytical frameworks is that of a "program" (a term borrowed from computer science), which embodies the observed regularities in activities generated by a class of environmental stimuli. Receiving particular attention both by March and Simon and by Cyert and March are programs that govern the processes of problem-solving and decision-making within organizations. The mechanisms incorporated within such programs are largely borrowed from theories concerning information processing within individuals and include such activities as searching for alternative solutions, giving sequential attention to goals, and changing the level of aspiration.

It can be argued, however, that the processes of problem-solving and decision-making when carried out by organizations are different from the same processes carried out by individuals in at least one fundamental respect. Organizational decision-making involves both cognitive and social processes. The events that intervene between the identification of a problem (or occasion for decision-making) and a solution or decision are both intrapersonal and interpersonal. It is the interpersonal or social aspects of decision-making that are of most direct relevance to processes of leadership. The leader not only makes decisions but also designs, regulates, and selects social systems that make decisions.

The particular intersection of leadership and decision-making to be explored in this book can now be identified. We are interested in the way in which leadership is reflected in social processes utilized for decision-making, specifically in leaders' choices about how much and in what way to involve their subordinates in decision-making. Let us consider an example to illustrate this connection between leadership and decision-making. Assume that you are a manager who has five subordinates reporting to you. Each of these subordinates has a clearly defined and distinct set of responsibilities. One of them resigns to take a position with another organization. Due to a cost-cutting program recently initiated within the organization, which makes it impossible to hire new employees, you cannot replace him with someone else. It will be necessary for you to find some way of reallocating the departing subordinate's responsibilities among the remaining four in such a way as to maintain the present workload and effectiveness of the unit.

The situation described is representative of many faced by persons in positions of leadership. There is some need for action—a problem exists and a solution or decision must be forthcoming. You, as leader, have some area of freedom or discretion (there are a number of possible ways in which the work can be reallocated), but there are also some constraints on your actions. For example, you cannot solve the problem by hiring someone from outside the organization. Furthermore, the solution adopted is going to have effects on people other than yourself. Your subordinates are going to have to carry out whatever decision is reached.

One could examine your behavior when confronted with this problem in purely cognitive terms. Normatively, one could "arm you" with a set of rules for solving problems of this kind. These rules may take the form of an algorithm that would assure selection of the optimal set of work assignments from the total set of possibilities, or it could take the form of heuristics for reaching a satisfactory solution to the problem. Descriptively, one could obtain from you a protocol of your thoughts as you generated and evaluated alternative solutions to this problem and from such observations attempt to formulate a model of your decision-making processes that could subsequently be tested against your behavior in other similar situations.

Underlying such cognitive approaches is the conviction that a leader is a problem-solver or decision-maker—that the task of translating problems into solutions is inevitably *his* task. Alternatively, one can view the leader's task as one of determining the mechanism or process by which the problem is to be solved. A major portion of his job is to determine what person or persons should take part in the solution of the problem.

In the situation described, one can envision a number of possible decision-making processes that could be employed. You could make the decision by yourself and announce it to your subordinates; you could obtain additional information from your subordinates and then make the decision; you could consult with them either individually or collectively before making the decision; or you could convene them as a group, share the problem with them, and attempt to reach agreement on the solution to the problem. These alternatives vary in terms of not cognitive but social processes—specifically, the amount and form of opportunity afforded subordinates to participate in the decision.

Two theoretically distinct sets of questions can be asked concerning the manager's choice of a decision process. One contains the normative questions as to which process *should* be used to make the decision. The other consists of the descriptive questions concerning which decision-making process *would* actually be used.

It should be emphasized that we are separating two issues that have seldom been clearly differentiated by those studying leadership behavior. The first is the evaluation of the consequences for the organization of a leader adopting a particular behavior or leadership style, and the second is the study of processes that generate the behavior of the incumbents of leadership roles. In the former, the outcome could be a normative model in which the leader's behavior is the independent variable and the organizational consequences of this behavior are the dependent variables. An outcome of the latter could be the development of a descriptive model in which the leader's behavior is the dependent variable and individual characteristics and situational factors are the independent variables.

The main body of the literature on participation addresses itself to the normative question of what is effective managerial behavior. Most social psychologists and other behavioral scientists who have turned their attention toward the implications of psychological and social processes for the practice of management have called for greater participation by subordinates in the problem-solving and decision-making process. Pointing to evidence of restriction of output and lack of involvement under traditional managerial systems, they have argued for greater influence in decision-making on the part of those who are held responsible for decision execution.

The normative issues relevant to the effectiveness of participative management are the subject of chapters 2 and 3. Among the questions considered are the following: Should leaders adopt the same decision process regardless of the nature of the situation? If not, what situational properties should affect their choices among alternative decision processes? Chapter 2 begins with a brief review of the empirical evidence concerning the consequences of participation. Reconciliation of the discrepant findings reported there is not an easy task. It is made complex by different empirical interpretations of the term "participation" (Strauss 1963) and by great differences in the situations in which the word is applied. From the evidence considered, it appears highly likely that an increase in the participation of subordinates in decision-making may increase productivity under some circumstances but decrease productivity under others.

To identify the situational conditions which determine the efficacy of participative management, it is necessary to specify the decision-making processes which it entails and to examine the various mechanisms by which it may influence the extent to which the formal objectives of the organization are attained. Accordingly, in chapter 2, a taxonomy of leadership behaviors is presented, with discrete alternatives expressed in terms of the extent to which subordinates have an opportunity to participate in decision-making. The same chapter includes the definitions of a set of situational variables that existing empirical evidence suggests should be considered in evaluating the alternative consequences of these decision procceses. Chapter 3 introduces a normative model, incorporating those situational variables, that purports to show which decision process should be used in different situations. We then apply the model to a set of specific cases to illustrate its operation.

In the next three chapters of the book (chapters 4, 5, and 6), we turn our attention from normative to descriptive issues. Our goal is an understanding of how leaders do behave. The approach adopted is different from that employed by previous investigators in the sense that leaders' behavior is assumed to be attributable to individual differences, situational variables, and the interaction between them (Cronbach 1957). Our empirical methods permit an examination of the relative contribution of these variables to the explanation of leaders' choices among different decision processes.

Chapter 4 presents evidence that leaders do use different decision-making processes for different situations, and it describes a set of studies designed to reveal some of the situational factors which affect how much the leaders' power is shared with their subordinates. In these studies, leaders were asked to describe a problem they recently had to solve, to answer a set of questions designed to reveal specific properties of the problem and its social context, and to indicate which decision-making process they used in solving the problem.

Chapter 5 deals with the same issue but uses a different methodology. Managers were asked how they would behave in each of a standard set of situations presented in the form of case studies. Each of the case studies contained different situational characteristics, and the selection of cases conformed to the specifications of an experimental design. This procedure provided considerable methodological advantages over that used in chapter 4 and permitted the determination of the relative importance of individual and situational differences in managers' choices of decision processes. In chapter 6 the possibility of using the set of case studies as a test of leadership style is examined. The scores that can be obtained from a person's responses to the case studies are described and compared with other tests of leader behavior.

Since the situational variables used in the descriptive analysis of leader behavior are identical to those used in the normative model, it is possible to compare the behavior of any given leader or set of leaders with that of the model. This comparison is made in chapter 7. Similarities and differences between the model's behavior and that of industrial managers are presented in an effort to determine the changes in leader behavior that would occur if these managers voluntarily used the normative model as the basis for selecting their methods of making decisions. We have developed as part of this analysis a number of comparative individual-difference measures that indicate the degree to which the individual's behavior correlates with that of the normative model.

Discrepancies between how a leader does behave and how he should behave are potentially relevant to the development of technologies for leadership improvement. Chapter 8 deals with one of the technological "by-products" of the research program. It describes a new approach to leadership development that includes a method of providing individuals with feedback concerning their leadership style from their reports of how they would behave in standardized cases. Initial evidence concerning the effects of the leadership-development program is presented.

In chapter 9 we reexamine the normative model in the light of our findings and present a revised model that encompasses a wider range of decision-making situations. Alternatives for further elaboration and development of models of this type are discussed in the context of their potential uses.

Central to all the research reported in this book is the role of situational differences as determinants of the choice of a decision process. In this emphasis we have departed from the mainstream, which has focused on individual differences as determinants of actual behavior and has advocated a highly participative decision style as optimal for all situations. For this reason, in a concluding statement in chapter 10, we have attempted not only to summarize our major findings but also to relate them to other approaches to the study of leadership.

CHAPTER 2

Basic Considerations
Underlying the Normative Model

One of the most persistent and controversial issues in the study of management is that of participation in decision-making by subordinates. Traditional models of the managerial process have been autocratic in nature. The manager makes decisions on matters within his area of freedom, issues orders or directives to his subordinates, and monitors their performance to ensure conformity with these directives. Scientific management, from its early developments in time and motion study to its contemporary manifestations in mathematical programming, has contributed to this centralization of decision-making in organizations by focusing on the development of methods by which managers can make more rational decisions, substituting objective measurements and empirically validated methods for casual judgments.

In contrast, social psychologists and other behavioral scientists who have turned their attention toward the implications of psychological and social processes for the practice of management have called for greater participation by subordinates in the problem-solving and decision-making processes. The empirical evidence provides some, but not overwhelming, support for beliefs in the efficacy of participative management. Field experiments on rank-and-file workers by Coch and French (1948), Bavelas (reported in French 1950), and Strauss (reported in Whyte 1955) indicate that impressive increases in productivity can be brought about by giving workers an opportunity to participate in decision-making and goal-setting. In addition, several correlational field studies (Katz, Maccoby, and Morse 1950; Vroom 1960) indicate positive relationships between the amount of influence supervisors afford their subordinates in decisions that affect them and individual or group performance.

On the other hand, in an experiment conducted in a Norwegian factory, French, Israel, and Ås (1960) found no significant differences in production between workers who did and those who did not participate in decisions regarding the introduction of changes in work methods. To complicate the picture further, Morse and Reimer (1956) compared the effects of two programs of change, each of which was introduced in two divisions of the clerical operations of a large insurance company. One of the programs involved increased participation in decision-making by rank-and-file workers, while the other involved increased hierarchical control. The results show a significant increase in productivity under both programs, with the hierarchically controlled program producing the greater increase.

The investigations cited constitute only a small portion of those which are relevant to the effects of participation. The reader interested in a more comprehensive review of that evidence should consult Lowin (1968), Vroom (1970), and Wood (1974). We conclude, as have other scholars who have examined the evidence, that participation in decision-making has consequences that vary from one situation to another. Given the potential importance of this conclusion for the study of leadership and its significance to the process of management, social scientists should begin to develop some definitions of the circumstances under which participation in decision-making may contribute to or hinder organizational effectiveness. These could then be translated into guidelines to help leaders choose leadership styles to fit the demands of the situations they encounter.

In this and the following chapter, one approach to dealing with this important problem will be described. A normative model is developed which is consistent with existing empirical evidence concerning the consequences of participation and which purports to specify a set of rules that *should* be used in determining the form and amount of participation in decision-making by subordinates in different classes of situations. This chapter presents the basic assumptions that have guided the development of the normative model and the situational attributes that are contained within it.

BASIC ASSUMPTIONS

1. The normative model should be constructed in such a way as to be of potential value to managers or leaders in determining which leadership methods they should use in each of the various situations that they encounter in carrying out their formal leadership roles. Consequently, it should be operational in that the behaviors required of the leader should be specified unambiguously.

To be operational, a prescriptive statement must permit the person to determine whether or not he is acting in accordance with the statement. The statement "in case of headache, take one aspirin tablet at intervals of four hours" is quite operational in this sense. It specifies the activities to be performed and the conditions under which they are to be performed. On the other hand, the statement "to maintain one's health, one should lead a clean life" is not operational. The activities subsumed by "leading a clean life" are subject to many differences in interpretation, and there is no clear indication in the statement of the conditions under which the activities are to be carried out.

Many of the prescriptions of behavioral scientists are far closer in operationality to the second statement than to the first. Leaders are told to exhibit maximum concern for people and for production or to develop relationships with subordinates that are supportive. Such prescriptions have some informational value but fall short of the degree of operationality that we believe could be achieved.

2. There are a number of discrete social processes by which organizational problems can be translated into solutions, and these processes vary in terms of the potential amount of participation by subordinates in the problem-solving process.

The term participation has been used in a number of different ways. Perhaps the most influential definitions have been those of French, Israel, and Ås (1960) and Vroom (1960), who define participation as a process of joint decision-making by two or more parties. The amount of participation of any individual is the amount of influence he has on the decisions and plans agreed upon. Given the existence of a property such as participation that varies from high to low, it should be possible to define leader behaviors representing clear alternative processes for making decisions that can be related to the amount of participation each process affords the managers' subordinates.

TABLE 2.1. Decision Methods for Group and Individual Problems

Group Problems	Individual Problems
AI. You solve the problem or make the decision yourself, using information available to you at the time.	AI. You solve the problem or make the decision by yourself, using information available to you at the time.
AII. You obtain the necessary information from your subordinates, then decide the solution to the problem yourself. You may or may not tell your subordinates what the problem is in getting the information from them. The role played by your subordinates in making the decision is clearly one of providing the necessary information to you, rather than generating or evaluating alternative solutions.	AII. You obtain the necessary information from your subordinate, then decide on the solution to the problem yourself. You may or may not tell the subordinate what the problem is in getting the information from him. His role in making the decision is clearly one of providing the necessary information to you, rather than generating or evaluating alternative solutions.
CI. You share the problem with the relevant subordinates individually, getting their ideas and suggestions without bringing them together as a group. Then *you* make the decision, which may or may not reflect your subordinates' influence.	CI. You share the problem with your subordinate, getting his ideas and suggestions. Then you make a decision, which may or may not reflect his influence.
CII. You share the problem with your subordinates as a group, obtaining their collective ideas and suggestions. Then you make the decision, which may or may not reflect your subordinates' influence.	GI. You share the problem with your subordinate, and together you analyze the problem and arrive at a mutually agreeable solution.
GII. You share the problem with your subordinates as a group. Together you generate and evaluate alternatives and attempt to reach agreement (consensus) on a solution. Your role is much like that of chairman. You do not try to influence the group to adopt "your" solution, and you are willing to accept and implement any solution which has the support of the entire group.	DI. You delegate the problem to your subordinate, providing him with any relevant information that you possess, but giving him responsibility for solving the problem by himself. You may or may not request him to tell you what solution he has reached.

A taxonomy of decision processes created for normative purposes should distinguish among methods that are likely to have different outcomes but should not be so elaborate that leaders are unable to determine which method they are employing in any given instance. The taxonomy to be used in the normative model is shown in table 2.1.

The table contains a detailed specification of several alternative processes by which problems can be solved or decisions made. Each process is represented by a symbol (AI, CI, GII, DI) which will be used throughout this book as a convenient method of referring to each process. The letters in this code signify the basic properties of the process (A stands for autocratic; C, for consultative; G, for group; and D, for delegated). The roman numerals that follow the letters constitute variants on that process. Thus AI represents the first variant on an autocratic process; AII, the second variant; and so on.

It should be noted that the methods are arranged in two columns corresponding to their applicability to problems which involve the entire group or some subset of it (hereafter called group problems) or a single subordinate (hereafter called individual problems). If a problem or decision clearly affects only one subordinate, the leader would choose among the methods shown in the right-hand column; if it had potential effects on the entire group (or subset of it) he would choose among the methods shown in the left-hand column. Those in both columns are arranged from top to bottom in terms of the opportunity for subordinates to influence the solution to the problem. The distinction between group and individual problems can be illustrated with the following examples.

GROUP PROBLEMS

A. Sharply decreasing profits for the firm has resulted in a directive from top management that makes it impossible to take on any new personnel even to replace those who leave. Shortly after this directive is issued, one of your five subordinates resigns to take a job with another firm. Your problem is how to rearrange the work assignments among the remaining four subordinates without reducing the total productivity of the group.

B. You have been chosen by your firm to attend a nine-week senior executive program at a famous university. Your problem is to choose one of your subordinates to take your place during your absence.

C. You have two main projects under your direction with three subordinates assigned to each. One of these projects is three months behind schedule with only six months remaining before the work *must* be completed. Your problem is to get the project back on schedule to meet the completion date.

INDIVIDUAL PROBLEMS

D. As principal of an elementary school, you often handle disciplinary cases. Over the last six months, one of your fifteen teachers has referred an inordinately large number of cases to your attention. This fact, combined with other information you have received, leads you to believe that there is a serious breakdown of discipline within that teacher's classroom.

E. The cost figures for section B have risen faster than those of the other three similar sections under your direction. The manager of section B is your immediate subordinate.

F. You have the opportunity to bid on a multi-million-dollar government contract. While the decision will be made by top management, you have to formulate a recommendation that has a high probability of being accepted. You have only one subordinate who is a specialist in the area in which the contract is to be granted, and you will have to rely heavily on him to present and defend the recommendation to top management. As you see it, there are at least three options: to bid as prime contractor; to bid as subcontractor for another firm planning to bid as prime contractor; or to do nothing.

The person in the leadership position could presumably employ any one of the alternatives on the left-hand side of table 2.1 (AI, AII, CI, CII, GII) for problems A, B, and C and could employ any one of the alternatives on the right-hand side of table 2.1 (AI, AII, CI, GI, DI) for problems D, E, and F. Since the two sets of alternatives have three common decision processes (AI, AII, CI), this categorization effectively eliminates from consideration *GI* and *DI* as relevant decision processes for group problems (like *A*, *B*, and *C*) and eliminates CII and GII for individual problems (like *D*, *E*, and *F*). The reader can verify for himself the appropriateness of these exclusions.

Table 2.2 shows the relationship between the methods shown in table 2.1 and those described in prior taxonomies. Our methods appear as row headings, and the names of other authors or researchers appear as column headings. If there seems to be correspondence between the definition of one of our methods and that used by a given author, his term appears in the intersection of row and column. A vacant cell, defined by the intersection of a column and row, indicates that the investigator whose name heads the column does not recognize any style corresponding to that in the row heading. If a column is partitioned within a row, it means that the investigator uses a finer breakdown than that employed in the model. Similarly, if a column entry cuts across two or more rows, it indicates that the model employs a finer breakdown than that made by the investigator. The relationships presented in table 2.2 are matters of judgment and are merely intended to suggest the correspondence or lack of correspondence existing between the taxonomy that is used here and those which were previously employed.

3. No one leadership method is applicable to all situations; the function of a normative model should be to provide a framework for the analysis of situational requirements that can be translated into prescriptions of leadership styles.

The fact that the most effective leadership method or style is dependent on the situation is becoming widely recognized by behavioral scientists interested in problems of leadership and administration. A decision-making process that is optimal for a quarterback on a football team making decisions under severe time constraints is likely to be far from optimal when used by a dean introducing a new curriculum to be implemented by his faculty. Even the advocates of participative management have noted this "situational relativity" of leadership styles. Thus, Argyris (1962) writes:

> No one leadership style is the most effective. Each is probably effective under a given set of conditions. Consequently, I suggest that effective

TABLE 2.2. Correspondence Between Decision Processes Employed in the Model and Those of Previous Investigators

	Lewin, Lippitt, and White (1939)	Maier (1955)	Tannenbaum and Schmidt (1958)			Heller (1971)	Likert (1967)
AI	Autocratic leadership	Autocratic management	Manager makes decision and announces it	Manager sells decision	Manager presents ideas and invites questions	Own decision with detailed explanation	Exploitive authoritative (system 1)
AII						Own decision without detailed explanation	Benevolent authoritative (system 2)
CI		Consultative management	Manager presents tentative decision, subject to change	Manager presents problem, gets suggestions, makes decision		Prior consultation with subordinate(s)	Consultative (system 3)
CII							
GI						Joint decision-making with subordinate(s)	
GII	Democratic leadership	Group decision	Manager defines limits, asks group to make decision	Manager permits group to make decisions within prescribed limits			Participative group (system 4)
DI	Laissez-faire leadership					Delegation of decision to subordinate(s)	

leaders are those who are capable of behaving in many different leadership
styles, depending on the requirements of reality as they and others perceive it. I call this "reality-centered" leadership. (1962, p. 81)

We must go beyond noting the importance of situational factors
and begin to move toward a road map or normative models that
attempt to prescribe the most appropriate leadership style for different kinds of situations. The most comprehensive treatment of
situational factors as determinants of the effectiveness and efficiency of participation in decision-making is found in the work of
Tannenbaum and Schmidt (1958). They discuss a large number of
variables, including attributes of the manager, his subordinates,
and the situation, which ought to enter into the manager's decision about the degree to which he should share his power with his
subordinates. But they stop at this inventory of variables, and do
not show how these might be combined and translated into different forms of action.

4. *The most appropriate unit for the analysis of the situation is
the particular problem to be solved and the context in which the
problem occurs.*

While it is becoming widely recognized that different situations
require different leadership methods, there is less agreement concerning the appropriate units for the analysis of the situation. One
approach is to assume that the situations that determine the effectiveness of different leadership styles correspond to the environment of the system. Thus, Bennis (1966) argues that egalitarian
leadership styles work better when the environment of the organization is rapidly changing and the problems with which it has to
deal are continually being altered. If this position were extended
to provide the basis for a comprehensive normative model, one
would prescribe different leadership styles for different systems
but make identical prescriptions for all leadership roles within a
system.

Alternatively, one might assume that the critical features of the
situation concern the role of the leader, including his relations
with his subordinates. Examples would include Fiedler's (1967)
three dimensions of task structure, leadership position power, and
leader-member relations. Implicit is the assumption that all problems or decisions made within a single role require a similar leader-

ship style. Normatively, one might prescribe different amounts or forms of participation for two different leaders but prescribe identical amounts or forms of participation for all problems or decisions made by a single leader within a single role.

The approach taken here is to select the properties of the problem to be solved as the critical situational dimensions for determining the appropriate form or amount of participation. Different prescriptions would be made for a given leader for different problems within a given role. It should be noted that constructing a normative model with the problem rather than the role or any organizational differences as the unit of analysis does not rule out the possibility that different roles and organizations may involve different distributions of problem types that, in aggregate, may require different modal styles or levels of participation.

5. *The leadership method used in response to one situation should not constrain the method or style used in other situations.*

Implicit in the use of the attributes of the particular problem to be solved or decision to be made as the unit of analysis is the assumption that problems can be classified such that the relative usefulness of each alternative decision process is identical for all problems in a particular classification. A corollary to this assumption is that the process or method used on problems of one type does not constrain that used on problems of a different type. It is only in this way that prescriptions could be made for a given problem without knowing the other problems encountered by a leader or his methods for dealing with them.

This assumption is necessary to the construction of a normative model founded on problem differences. It may seem inconsistent with the view, first proposed by McGregor (1944), that consistency in leadership style is desirable because it enables subordinates to predict their superiors' behavior and to adapt to it. However, predictability does not preclude variability. There are many variable phenomena which can be predicted quite well because the rules or processes that govern them are understood. The antithesis of predictability is randomness, and, if McGregor is correct, a normative model to regulate choices among alternative leadership styles should be deterministic rather than stochastic. The model to be developed here is deterministic; the normatively prescribed method for a given problem type is a constant.

CONCEPTUAL AND EMPIRICAL BASIS OF THE MODEL

A model designed to regulate, in some rational way, choices among the decision methods shown in table 2.1 should be based on sound empirical evidence concerning their likely consequences. The more complete the empirical base of knowledge, the greater the certainty with which one can develop the model and the greater will be its usefulness. In this section we will restrict ourselves to the development of a model concerned only with group problems and, hence, will use only the methods shown in the left-hand column of table 2.1. A comparable model for individual problems will be discussed in chapter 9.

We will now consider the empirical evidence that can at present be brought to bear on such a normative model. You will note that much of the evidence is incomplete, and future research should prove helpful in providing a firmer foundation for a model. In this analysis it is important to distinguish three classes of outcomes that influence the ultimate effectiveness of decisions. These are: (1) the quality or rationality of the decision, (2) the acceptance of the decision by subordinates and their commitment to execute it effectively, and (3) the amount of time required to make the decision.

The evidence regarding the effects of participation on each of these outcomes or consequences has been reviewed elsewhere (Vroom 1970). He concluded that

> the results suggest that allocating problem solving and decision-making tasks to entire groups as compared with the leader or manager in charge of the groups, requires a greater investment of man hours but produces higher acceptance of decisions and a higher probability that the decisions will be executed efficiently. Differences between these two methods in quality of decisions and in elapsed time are inconclusive and probably highly variable. . . . It would be naive to think that group decision-making is always more "effective" than autocratic decision-making, or vice versa; the relative effectiveness of these two extreme methods depends both on the weights attached to quality, acceptance and time variables and on differences in amounts of these outcomes resulting from these methods, neither of which is invariant from one situation to another. The critics and proponents of participative management would do well to direct their efforts toward identifying the properties of situations in which different decision-making approaches are effective rather than wholesale condemnation or deification of one approach. (Vroom 1970, pp. 239–40)

Stemming from this review, an attempt has been made to identify these properties of the situation, which will be the basic elements in the model. These problem attributes are of two types: (1) those which specify the importance for a particular problem of quality and acceptance (see A and E below), and (2) those which, on the basis of available evidence, have a high probability of moderating the effects of participation on each of these outcomes (see B, C, D, G, and H below). The following are the problem attributes used in the present form of the model.

A. The importance of the quality of the decision. According to Maier (1955, 1963), decision quality refers to the "objective or impersonal" aspects of the decision. For groups embedded within formal organizations with specifiable goals, the relative quality of a set of alternative decisions can be expressed in terms of their effects, if implemented with equal expenditure of energy, on the attainment of those goals.

The first attribute refers to what Maier (1963) has termed the quality requirement for the decision. There are some problems for which the nature of the solution reached within identifiable constraints is not at all critical. The leader is (or should be) indifferent among the possible solutions since their expected value is equal, provided that those who have to carry them out are committed to them. Typically, the number of solutions that meet the constraints is finite, and the alternatives are obvious or do not require substantial search. In such instances, there is no technical, rational, or analytic method of choosing among the alternatives.

In Maier's new-truck problem (Maier 1955), the issue of which of the five truck drivers should get the new truck has no quality requirement. The foreman is (or should be) indifferent among the various possible alternatives provided they are accepted by the men. On the other hand, the problem of which truck should be discarded to make way for the new one does have a quality requirement. The five present trucks vary in age and condition, and a decision to discard other than the poorest truck in the set would be irrational.

While on a consulting assignment, the senior author encountered another problem which may help to illustrate the meaning of the term "quality requirement." A plant manager and his staff were about to move into a new plant. On inspecting the plans, he discovered that there were insufficient reserved parking places (directly in front of the building) to accommodate all six of his department heads. The design of the building permitted only four such parking places with all other cars having to park across the street in a large parking lot. There was no possible way to increase the number of parking spaces without modifying the design of the structure, and the costs would be prohibitive. Any solution to the parking-space allocation problem would have satisfied the plant manager provided it had the support of his department heads, each of whom, incidentally, expected to receive a reserved parking place. The problem had no quality requirement since he was indifferent among all possible solutions which met the constraints.

In both of the examples given, the constraints were imposed on the leader by forces outside him. The foreman had only one new truck to allocate among his drivers, and the plant manager could do nothing to increase the size of the reserved parking lot. In other instances, the quality requirement can be eliminated from the problem if the leader *imposes* constraints on the possible solutions. By attaching suitable constraints, quality requirements can be eliminated from such problems as the choice of personnel to be assigned to work on each shift, the design of a vacation schedule showing when each person should take his vacation, and the selection of a time at which to hold a meeting.

At the other end of the dimension specified by this attribute are so-called strategic decisions (Ansoff 1965), which involve the allocation of scarce resources and are not easily reversible. At what level should we price our products? What new businesses should we acquire? Where should we locate our plants? What is the most effective advertising policy? These are just a few of the problems and decisions which have marked consequences for the effectiveness of the organization. No leader should be indifferent among possible alternative courses of action. Even though the relative consequences of the alternatives may not be known at any given point in time, the specific course chosen is going to make a difference in the degree to which the system attains its goals. In such instances, the variance in contribution to organizational objectives of alternative courses of action is large, and the rational quality of the decision is of central importance.

The function of this attribute in the model is to determine the relevance to the choice of decision process of such considerations as the nature and location of information or expertise necessary to generate and evaluate alternatives. If the quality of the decision is unimportant, then attributes *B*, *C*, *D*, and *G* below can be shown to be irrelevant to the prescription of that process.

B. The extent to which the leader possesses sufficient information/expertise to make a high quality decision by himself. The quality of the decisions reached by any decision-making process is dependent on the resources the leader is able to utilize. One of the most critical of these resources is information. If a rational solution to the problem is to be obtained, alternatives must be generated and evaluated in terms of their organizational consequences. Any such activities require the use of the relevant information and expertise by participants in the decision process.

It is possible to distinguish two different kinds of information that are potentially relevant to problem-solving in an organizational setting. One is information necessary to the task of evaluating the relative quality or rationality of different alternatives. The other is information concerning the preferences of subordinates and their feelings about the alternatives.

These two kinds of information and associated expertise need not be correlated. One leader may be extremely knowledgeable about the terrain to be traversed and its possible pitfalls, and he may have worked out an elegant means of attaining the external objective. However, he may be completely unaware of the preferences of his men. Another may be uninformed about the external environment but highly sensitive to the attitudes and feelings of his subordinates. A low correlation between these two components of information is suggested by research on role differentiation in problem-solving groups. Task facilitative leadership tends to be carried out by different persons than socio-emotional leadership (Bales and Slater 1955).

The information referred to in attribute *B* deals with the external goals and the consequences of actions on the part of the system for their attainment. In other words, we are interested only in the degree to which the leader possesses facts and skills relevant to the quality of the decision. Thus, in evaluating the level of this attribute in the case of a head dietician in a hospital faced with the task of preparing the week's menus, one would be concerned with such things as her knowledge of the components of a balanced diet, the availability and cost of different food products, and the existence of special dietary requirements among the patient load.

One would not be concerned with the kinds of foods that her staff liked to consume, prepare, or deliver. Similarly, in evaluating the information possessed by a university department chairman faced with the problem of selecting a text to be used by members of his department in teaching the introductory course, the relevant questions would concern his knowledge of the alternatives as they relate to the goal of education and not his information regarding the preferences of those assigned to teach the course.

In defining this attribute solely in terms of information or expertise in matters relating to the quality of the decision, we intend not to render unimportant the task of having decisions accepted by subordinates, but rather to recognize the conceptual and empirical independence of the two kinds of information. As will be seen later in the description of other problem attributes, acceptance requirements are an integral part of the framework being developed.

The decision-making processes shown in table 2.1 differ in terms of the amount of information and expertise that can be brought to bear on the problem. For example, in AI, only information available to the leader may be utilized in problem-solving, whereas in GII the information base extends to all group members including the leader.

There has been little research on the determinants of whether the leader's information is adequate to deal with the problems he encounters. Since he has been selected by somewhat different criteria, may have received special training, and has access to different information, there is strong *a priori* reason to believe that his information base will be different from (and in most cases superior to) that of the average group member. However, its absolute level must be assumed to be variable with the nature of the problem. There are undoubtedly some situations in which the leader possesses all of the necessary information and others for which his information is critically deficient. In the model, this attribute determines the importance of choosing a decision-making process that augments the information base of the decision.

Kelley and Thibaut (1969) have reviewed the literature on group and individual problem-solving and have advanced a set of hypotheses concerning the conditions in which a group solution is likely to be higher than, equal to, or lower in quality than that of the best member of the group. The studies were conducted principally on ad hoc leaderless groups in laboratory settings, so it is not clear that the best member would always have been a formal leader. However, their hypotheses may ultimately prove fruitful in relating variation on the attribute defined above to problem differences.

Kelley and Thibaut (1969) suggest that: (1) group decisions are likely to be above the level of the most proficient member when the problem has multiple parts and when group members have uncorrelated (complementary) deficiencies and talents; (2) groups are likely to perform at the level of the most proficient member when the problem is simple (very few steps are required for its solution) and the solution is highly verifiable by all persons in possession of the original facts; and (3) groups are likely to do less well than the best member when the solution requires thinking through a series of interrelated steps or stages, applying a number of rules at each point, and always keeping in mind conclusions reached at earlier points.

C. The extent to which subordinates, taken collectively, have the necessary information to generate a high quality decision. This attribute is similar to *B* above except that it deals with the resources of subordinates rather than the leader. There are some situations in which these resources may in fact be very small. For example, the problem may be a highly technical one, and the subordinates may lack any of the knowledge needed to deal with it. On the other hand, in problems with multiple parts and where the level of information needed to deal with these parts is uncorrelated, the potential contribution of subordinates may be very high. This attribute is relevant to the choice of a decision process only when the information available to the leader is deficient. It determines whether the information search activities can be conducted within the group as part of the decision-making activity or whether, in order to obtain a high quality decision, it will be necessary to go outside the group for the necessary information.

D. The extent to which the problem is structured. A distinction is frequently made between problems or decisions that are structured or programmed and those which are unstructured or nonprogrammed (Simon 1960). Structured problems are those for which the alternative solutions or methods for generating them and the parameters for their evaluation are known. There are typically specific procedures within the organization for handling them. Under these circumstances, the decision is made once all the necessary information has reached a central source, in this case the leader. The process is essentially that of the "wheel" in communication net experiments, which has been found to be more efficient for the solution of simple problems than less centralized networks (Shaw 1964).

However, if the problem is unstructured and the relevant information widely dispersed among persons, the organizational task is somewhat different. Under these circumstances it is less clear what information is relevant, and empirical evidence appears to favor a less centralized network which permits those with potentially relevant information to interact with one another in the course of solving the problem. This process is more akin to that in the circle networks, which have been found to be more effective in solving complex problems (Shaw 1964). Within the model, this attribute bears on the relative efficiency of information collection activities that involve interaction among subordinates (that is, CII and GII) and those which do not involve such interaction (AII and CI).

E. The extent to which acceptance or commitment on the part of subordinates is critical to the effective implementation of the decision. In most situations, the effectiveness of an organizational decision is influenced both by its quality or rationality and by the extent to which it is accepted by subordinates. A decision can be ineffective because it did not utilize all of the available information concerning the external environment or because it was resisted and opposed by those who had to implement it.

The distinction between quality and acceptance is reminiscent of Bales's (1949) distinction between problems of the group involving goal achievement and adaptation to external demands and problems involving internal integration and expression of emotional tensions. Bales divides problems into two groups, adaptive-instrumental problems and integrative-expressive problems. In the framework being developed, quality and acceptance requirements are seen not as discrete types or even as opposite ends of a single continuum but rather as two separable dimensions. Just as the quality of the decision varies in importance from one problem to another, so also does the acceptance of the decision by subordinates, and there is no necessary correlation between these two dimensions.

There are two classes of situations in which acceptance of the decision by subordinates may be regarded as irrelevant to its effective implementation. One of these is what Maier (1970) has termed "outsider problems." In an "outsider problem," the subordinates are not involved in the execution of the decision. One may still desire their participation in order to enhance the quality of the solution, but the decision will be implemented by the leader or some other group. Acceptance by this particular set of persons is not critical to the ultimate success or failure of the decision.

The second type of situation in which acceptance or commitment to the decision by subordinates is not critical is that in which subordinates will be required to execute the decision but its nature is such that compliance on their part, rather than acceptance or commitment, is sufficient. Typically in such situations, subordinates' actions necessary for implementation of the decision are specific; the leader is able to monitor or observe these actions, and he controls rewards and punishments, which he is able to mete out accordingly. Both in the larger society and in organizations, people carry out directives to which they feel no personal commitment and, in fact, may be strongly opposed. The forces operating on them are "induced" forces rather than "own" forces (Lewin 1935), and the conditions necessary for the successful induction of a force must be present. The actions must be observable by others who wish to see the directive carried out, and these others must control rewards and/or penalties, which are meted out in accordance with the degree of compliance observed.

Acceptance becomes more critical as the effective execution of the decision requires initiative, judgment, or creativity on the part of subordinates or when one or more of the conditions necessary for obtaining compliance breaks down; for example, the leader is unable to monitor subordinates' behavior and reward or punish deviations. Within the model, the interaction of this attribute with the following one determines the importance of attempting to develop subordinates' commitment to the final solution by employing a participative decision-making process.

F. The prior probability that the leader's autocratic decision will receive acceptance by subordinates. The relationship between participation in decision-making and the acceptance of decisions by subordinates is marked but probably not invariant with the nature of the problem and the context within which it occurs. Thus, Vroom (1960) found that the effects of participation varied with the subordinate's need for independence and authoritarianism. Similarly, in a field experiment in a Norwegian factory, French, Israel, and Ås (1960) discovered that the effects varied with subordinates' perceptions of the legitimacy of their participation, and Marrow (1964) has provided a brief account of some of the problems that occurred when the Harwood Manufacturing Company attempted to increase participation in decision-making, which had proved highly successful in their plants in the United States, in their newly acquired subsidiary in Puerto Rico.

It appears that participation is not a necessary condition for the acceptance of decisions. There are some circumstances in which the leader's decision has high prior probability of being accepted by subordinates. These circumstances are predictable from a knowledge of the relationship between the leader and his subordinates. French and Raven (1959) distinguish among five bases of power all of which are defined in terms of the relationship between the source and object of influence. Three of these bases (legitimate power, expert power, and referent power) are hypothesized to produce "own" forces on the object of influence to engage in the indicated action, thereby conforming to our definition of acceptance. Thus, the subordinates may accept the leader's decision because they believe that it is his legitimate right to make that decision by virtue of the position he occupies (legitimate power), because he is the acknowledged expert and the only one capable of taking all the necessary factors into consideration (expert power), or because he is strongly admired by them (referent power). In such situations, it is not at all difficult for the leader to "sell" his decision to his subordinates, thereby gaining the necessary acceptance.

There are many situations in which the prior probability of acceptance of a decision by subordinates will vary with the nature of the solution adopted. Some alternatives may be acceptable to subordinates and some may not. In effect, the prior probability of acceptance becomes a property of a solution rather than a property of the problem. To deal with the potential complexities introduced by this state of affairs, the following guidelines are suggested. For problems with a quality requirement (attribute A), the relevant prior probability of acceptance is that of the highest quality alternative known to the leader. Thus, if the leader had worked out a solution to a complex production scheduling problem using critical path analysis and were convinced that it would work and would be superior to the present method and other alternatives known to him, one would be interested in the prior probability that this new method would be accepted by his subordinates.

For problems without a quality requirement, the relevant prior probability of acceptance is the highest value for any of the solutions meeting the constraints specified. In a case described earlier in this chapter—that of the plant manager assigning four reserved parking places among his six department heads—the level specified for prior probability would be that of the most palatable alternative to his subordinates.

This attribute is relevant to the choice of method only where acceptance is required in order for the decision to be effectively implemented (attribute E). It, in turn, determines whether participation in decision-making is necessary in order to attain that acceptance.

G. *The extent to which subordinates are motivated to attain the organizational goals as represented in the objectives explicit in the statement of the problem.* In all problems, there are one or more goals to be achieved. Ultimately, it is the attainment of those goals that determines whether the problem is actually solved. In effect, the general goal of organizational effectiveness is replaced by surrogate and more operational goals such as improving the safety record, reducing costs by 30 percent, or reorganizing to adapt to a cut in manpower while maintaining volume.

It is assumed that the quality of the decision reached is dependent not only on the information or expertise of those participating in it, but also on their disposition to use their information in the service of the goals stated in the problem. This phenomenon has seldom been examined in laboratory experiments on group problem-solving, where participants are motivated to solve the problem as accurately and as quickly as possible. But in formal organizations, there are many situations in which the goals of the group members may be in conflict with those stated in the problem. For example, decisions concerning the wage levels or the work loads of the participants may be among those which personal rather than organizational goals might dominate the search for and evaluation of alternatives.

This problem attribute is similar to what Maier (1963) terms "mutual interest," and to the potential amount of trust that the leader can place in his subordinates to solve the problem in the best interest of the organization. It determines the potential risk to the quality of the decision of methods like GII in which the leader relinquishes his final control over the decision.

   H. The extent to which subordinates are likely to be in disagreement over preferred solutions. Conflicts or disagreements among group members over the appropriate solution are quite common features of decision-making in organizations. It is possible for group members to agree on a common goal but disagree over the best means of attaining it. Such disagreements can result from access to different information or from the fact that personal gains or losses from different solutions are negatively correlated.

   There is substantial evidence from the literature in social psychology (see Brown 1965) to indicate that interaction among people tends to increase their similarity in attitudes and opinions. Members of a group with initially wide variance in individual judgments will tend to converge on a common position. This process seems to be enhanced when the issue is relevant to their interaction and when the problem is of mutual interest. Thus, Kelley and Thibaut (1969) note in their review of the literature on group problem-solving that "group problem discussion generates pressures toward uniformity" (p. 71). This attribute determines the importance of choosing a decision-making process (CII and GII) in which subordinates interact in the process of solving the problem, as opposed to those (AII and CI) in which no such interaction takes place.

   Table 2.3 shows the same eight problem attributes expressed in the form of questions which might be used by a leader in diagnosing a particular problem before choosing his leadership method. In phrasing the questions, technical language has been held to a minimum. Furthermore, the questions have been phrased in yes-no form, translating the continuous variables defined above into dichotomous variables. For example, instead of attempting to determine how important the decision quality is to the effectiveness of the decision (attribute A), the leader is asked in the first question to judge whether there is any quality component to the problem. Similarly, the difficult task of specifying exactly how much information the leader possesses that is relevant to the decision (attribute B) is reduced to a simple judgment by the leader

TABLE 2.3. Problem Attributes

A. If decision were accepted, would it make a difference which course of action were adopted?

B. Do I have sufficient information to make a high quality decision?

C. Do subordinates have sufficient additional information to result in a high quality decision?

D. Do I know exactly what information is needed, who possesses it, and how to collect it?

E. Is acceptance of decision by subordinates critical to effective implementation?

F. If I were to make the decision by myself, is it certain that it would be accepted by my subordinates?

G. Can subordinates be trusted to base solutions on organizational considerations?

H. Is conflict among subordinates likely in preferred solutions?

---

concerning whether he has sufficient information to make a high quality decision.

Expressing what are obviously continuous variables in dichotomous form greatly simplifies the problem of incorporating these attributes into a model that can be used by leaders. It sidesteps the problem of scaling each problem attribute and reduces the complexity of the judgments required of leaders.

It has been found that managers can diagnose a situation quickly and accurately by answering this set of eight questions. But how can such responses generate a prescription for the most effective leadership method or decision process? What kind of normative model of participation in decision-making can be built from this set of problem attributes? These questions and our mode of resolving them will be taken up in chapter 3.

A Normative Model
of Leadership Styles

Let us assume that you are a manager faced with a concrete problem to be solved. We will also assume that you have judged that this problem could potentially affect more than one of your subordinates. Hence, it is what we have defined as a group problem, and you have to choose among the five decision processes (AI, AII, CI, CII, GII) shown at the left side of table 2.1.

On *a priori* grounds any one of these five decision processes could be called for. The judgments you have made concerning the status of each of the problem's attributes can be used to define a set of feasible alternatives. This occurs through a set of rules that eliminate decision processes from the feasible set under certain specifiable conditions.

The rules are intended to protect both the quality and the acceptance of the decision. In the present form of the model, there are three rules that protect decision quality and four that protect acceptance. The seven rules are presented here both as verbal statements and in the more formal language of set theory. In the set theoretic formulation, the letters refer to the problem attributes as stated in question form in table 2.3. The letter A signifies that the answer to question A for a particular problem is *yes*; $\overline{A}$ signifies that the answer to that question is *no*; $\cap$ signifies intersection; $\Rightarrow$ signifies "implies"; and $\overline{AI}$ signifies not AI. Thus $A \cap \overline{B} \Rightarrow \overline{AI}$ may be read as follows: when both the answer to question A is yes and the answer to question B is no, AI is eliminated from the feasible set.

1. The information rule. If the quality of the decision is important and if the leader does not possess enough information or expertise to solve the problem by himself, AI is eliminated from the feasible set. (Its use risks a low quality decision.)

$$(A \cap \overline{B} \Rightarrow \overline{AI})$$

2. The trust rule. If the quality of the decision is important and if the subordinates cannot be trusted to base their efforts to solve the problem on organizational goals, GII is eliminated from the feasible set. (Alternatives that eliminate the leader's final control over the decision may jeopardize its quality.)

$$(A \cap \overline{G} \Rightarrow \overline{GII})$$

3. The unstructured problem rule. When the quality of the decision is important, if the leader lacks the necessary information or expertise to solve the problem by himself, and if the problem is unstructured, that is, he does not know exactly what information is needed and where it is located, the method used must provide not only for him to collect the information but to do so in an efficient manner. Methods which involve interaction among all subordinates with full knowledge of the problem are likely to be both more efficient and more likely to generate a high quality solution to the problem. Under these conditions, AI, AII, and CI are eliminated from the feasible set. (AI does not provide for him to collect the necessary information, and AII and CI represent more cumbersome, less effective, and less efficient means of bringing the necessary information to bear on the solution of the problem than methods that do permit those with the necessary information to interact.)

$$(A \cap \overline{B} \cap \overline{D} \Rightarrow \overline{AI}, \overline{AII}, \overline{CI})$$

4. The acceptance rule. If the acceptance of the decision by subordinates is critical to effective implementation, and if it is not certain that an autocratic decision made by the leader would receive that acceptance, AI and AII are eliminated from the feasible set. (Neither provides an opportunity for subordinates to participate in the decision, and both risk the necessary acceptance.)

$$(E \cap \overline{F} \Rightarrow \overline{AI}, \overline{AII})$$

5. The conflict rule. If the acceptance of the decision is critical, an autocratic decision is not certain to be accepted, and subordinates are likely to be in conflict or disagreement over the appropriate solution, AI, AII, and CI are eliminated from the feasible set. (The method used in solving the problem should enable those in disagreement to resolve their differences with full knowledge of the problem. Accordingly, under these conditions, AI, AII, and CI, which involve no interaction or only "one-on-one" relationships and therefore provide no opportunity for those in conflict to resolve their differences, are eliminated from the feasible set. Their use runs the risk of leaving some of the subordinates with less than the necessary commitment to the final decision.)

$$(E \cap \overline{F} \cap H \Rightarrow \overline{AI}, \overline{AII}, \overline{CI})$$

6. The fairness rule. If the quality of decision is unimportant, and if acceptance is critical and not certain to result from an autocratic decision, AI, AII, CI, and CII are eliminated from the feasible set. (The method used should maximize the probability of acceptance as this is the only relevant consideration in determining the effectiveness of the decision. Under these circumstances AI, AII, CI, and CII, which create less acceptance or commitment than GII, are eliminated from the feasible set. To use them will run the risk of getting less than the required acceptance of the decision.)

$$(\overline{A} \cap E \cap \overline{F} \Rightarrow \overline{AI}, \overline{AII}, \overline{CI}, \overline{CII})$$

7. The acceptance priority rule. If acceptance is critical, not assured by an autocratic decision, and if subordinates can be trusted, AI, AII, CI, and CII are eliminated from the feasible set. (Methods which provide equal partnership in the decision-making process can provide greater acceptance without risking decision quality. Use of any method other than GII results in an unnecessary risk that the decision will not be fully accepted or receive the necessary commitment on the part of subordinates.)

$$(E \cap \overline{F} \cap G \Rightarrow \overline{AI}, \overline{AII}, \overline{CI}, \overline{CII})$$

It should be noted that some rules are nested within other rules such that violating one rule is a special case of violating another.

Consider an unstructured problem in which the leader does not have sufficient information on which to make a high quality decision. Rule 1 excludes the use of AI (no opportunity to collect data), and rule 3 excludes AI, AII, and CI (no opportunity for group problem-solving). If rule 1 is violated in a problem for which rule 3 is applicable, then rule 3 is also violated. Since the applicability of rule 1 to the problem is a necessary but not sufficient condition for the applicability of rule 3, one can view rule 3 as "nested within" rule 1. Similarly, rules 5, 6, and 7 are nested within rule 4. Rule 4 is the basic acceptance rule which excludes AI and AII when acceptance is necessary and unlikely to exist for an autocratic decision. Rules 5, 6, and 7 further limit the feasible set as a function of additional properties of the problem. Thus, in the same way as the applicability of rule 1 is a necessary but not sufficient condition for the applicability of rule 3, rule 4 is necessary but not sufficient for rules 5, 6, and 7.

In applying these rules to a problem, you will find that it helps to represent them pictorially in the form of a decision tree. Figure 3.1 shows a simple decision tree that serves this purpose. The problem attributes are arranged along the top of the figure. To apply the rules to a particular problem, one starts at the left-hand side and works toward the right, asking oneself the question immediately above any box that is encountered. When a terminal node is reached, the number designates the problem type which in turn designates a set of methods that remain feasible after the rules have been applied.[1] It can be seen that this method of representing the decision tree generates fourteen problem types. Problem type is a nominal variable designating classes of problems generated by the paths that lead to the terminal nodes. Thus, all problems that have no quality requirement and in which acceptance is not critical are defined as type 1; all problems that have no quality requirement, in which acceptance is critical, but the prior probability of acceptance of the leader's decision is high, are defined as type 2, and so on.

An inspection of the structure of the flow diagram reveals that three problem types (6, 7, and 8) can be further subdivided. To each of these three terminal nodes, there are two alternative paths,

---

1. Rule 2 has not been applied to problem types 4, 9, 10, 11, and 14. This rule eliminates GII from the feasible set when the answer to question G is no. Thus, we can distinguish two variants of each of these types.

A. If decision were accepted, would it make a difference which course of action were adopted?

B. Do I have sufficient info to make a high quality decision?

C. Do subordinates have sufficient additional info to result in high quality decision?

D. Do I know exactly what info is needed, who possesses it, and how to collect it?

E. Is acceptance of decision by subordinates critical to effective implementation?

F. If I were to make the decision by myself, is it certain that it would be accepted by my subordinates?

G. Can subordinates be trusted to base solutions on organizational considerations?

H. Is conflict among subordinates likely in preferred solutions?

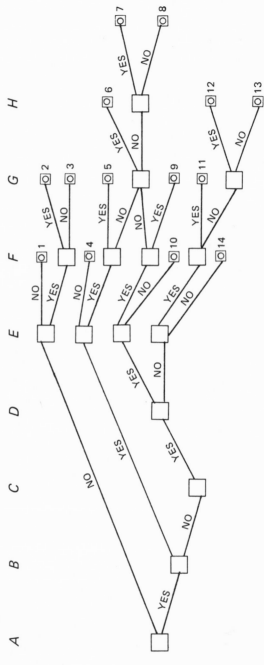

FIGURE 3.1. Problem Types

which diverge at attribute B (leader's information). Thus, one could broaden the classification of problem types, differentiating those of types 6, 7, and 8 into subcategories, making a total of seventeen problem types. For some purposes in this book, we will use this broadened classification scheme, referring to problems of type 6, 7, and 8 in which the leader has sufficient information as $6a$, $7a$, or $8a$ and to those in which he does not have sufficient information as $6b$, $7b$, or $8b$.

The feasible set for each of the fourteen problem types is shown in table 3.1. It can be seen that there are some problem types for

TABLE 3.1. Problem Types and the Feasible Set of Decision Methods

Problem Type	Acceptable Methods
1	AI, AII, CI, CII, GII
2	AI, AII, CI, CII, GII
3	GII
4	AI, AII, CI, CII, GII*
5	AI, AII, CI, CII, GII*
6	GII
7	CII
8	CI, CII
9	AII, CI, CII, GII*
10	AII, CI, CII, GII*
11	CII, GII*
12	GII
13	CII
14	CII, GII*

*Within the feasible set only when the answer to question G is yes

which only one method remains in the feasible set, others for which two methods remain feasible, and still others for which five methods remain feasible. It should be recalled that the feasible set is defined as the methods that remain after all those which violate rules designated to protect the quality and acceptance of the decision have been excluded.

CHOOSING AMONG ALTERNATIVES IN THE FEASIBLE SET

When more than one method remains in the feasible set, there are a number of alternative decision rules which might dictate the choice among them. One, which will be examined in greater depth, utilizes the number of man-hours required to solve the problem as the basis for choice. Given a set of methods with equal likelihood of meeting both quality and acceptance requirements for the decision, it selects the method that requires the least investment in man-hours. This is deemed to be the method furthest to the left within the feasible set. Thus, if AI, AII, CI, CII, and GII are all feasible, as in problem types 1 and 2, AI would be the method chosen. This decision rule acts to minimize man-hours, subject to quality and acceptance constraints.

Figure 3.2 shows the decision tree with methods prescribed for each of the problem types. In addition, two other attributes have been added to cover cases in which the group does not have sufficient information to make a decision. The attributes regulate predecisional activities such as problem identification and prior information collection. They do not affect choice of method except insofar as the net result of these activities is to affect the status of the situational attributes for that problem.

This decision rule for choosing among alternatives in the feasible set results in the prescription of each of the five decision processes in some situations. Method AI is prescribed for four problem types (1, 2, 4, and 5); AII is prescribed for two problem types (9 and 10); CI is prescribed for only one problem type (8); CII is prescribed for four problem types (7, 11, 13, and 14); and GII is prescribed for three problem types (3, 6, and 12). The relative frequency with which the five decision processes would be prescribed for any leader would, of course, be dependent on the distribution of problem types in his role.

It should be noted that the order of problem attributes is irrelevant to the final specification of the decision-making process. The order shown in figure 3.2 was selected because it minimizes the number of branches and terminal nodes necessary to determine the process in accordance with the rules given. Any other order would increase the complexity of the decision tree and increase the number of terminal nodes. For example, if conflict were switched from position H to position A and each other attribute advanced by one position, the number of terminal nodes would be increased from fourteen to twenty-six.

THE COMPOSITION OF THE GROUP

In phrasing the attributes in the model for group problems, the term subordinates has been used frequently. Attribute C deals with the information possessed by subordinates, attribute F with

A. If decision were accepted, would it make a difference which course of action were adopted?
B. Do I have sufficient info to make a high quality decision?
C. Do subordinates have sufficient additional info to result in high quality decision?
D. Do I know exactly what info is needed, who possesses it, and how to collect it?
* Is necessary additional info to be found within my entire set of subordinates?
† Is it feasible to collect additional info outside group prior to making decisions?
E. Is acceptance of decision by subordinates critical to effective implementation?
F. If I were to make the decision by myself, is it certain that it would be accepted by my subordinates?
G. Can subordinates be trusted to base solutions on organizational considerations?
H. Is conflict among subordinates likely in preferred solutions?

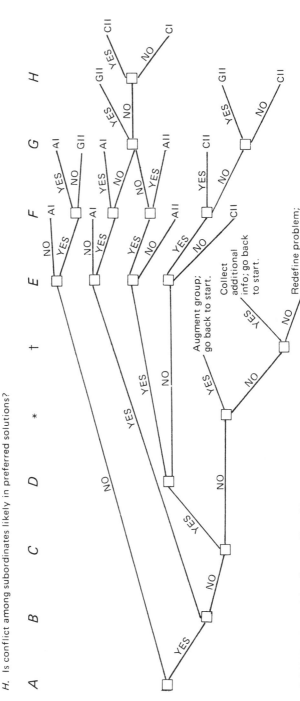

FIGURE 3.2. Decision-Process Flow Chart

the prior probability of acceptance of the leader's decision by sub-ordinates, and so on. The choice of the term subordinate to refer to other potential participants in the decision-making process should not be taken to mean that the members of the group are necessarily those defined by the organization chart as reporting to the leader. Many problems cut across organizational boundaries, and the groups, task forces, or committees set up to solve them are made up of persons from many different parts of the organization. Such problem-solving units typically have a leader, chairman, or head, and we consider the attributes as being equally relevant for this leader's choice of decision-making process as in the more tra-ditional case of a formal organizational unit. Thus, the subordi-nates referred to in the problem attributes can be taken more broadly to mean members of the group formally established to deal with that problem.

But what of the case in which the group of potential participants is ambiguous and not defined by any existing organizational unit, even one with temporary membership? Does the model have any implications for the composition of the group where none has ex-isted in the past? These questions are potentially separable from the model, which deals primarily with the choice of decision-making process given a specified leader, problem, and group. The follow-ing mechanisms are, however, consistent with the basic framework and may be useful as a point of departure for future thinking and research on the subject. Let us begin by defining as the group that set of persons or their representatives who are potentially affected by the decision. This set of persons may be the entire set of subor-dinates reporting to the leader; they may be a subset of those sub-ordinates; or they may be persons from different parts of the for-mal organization. In the event that this group, including the leader, does not have the necessary information and expertise, the model shown in figure 3.2 provides a means of augmenting the size of the group (see pre-decisional mechanism) until such time as the necessary information is represented within the group. It is only at that time when the decision-making process can be determined through the use of the model.

APPLICATION OF THE MODEL

To illustrate how the model might be applied in actual adminis-trative situations, a set of four cases will be presented and analyzed with the use of the model. Following the description of the case, the authors' analysis will be given including a specification of problem type, feasible set, and solution indicated by the model shown in figure 3.2. While an attempt has been made to describe these cases as completely as necessary to permit the reader to make the judgments required by the model, there may remain some room for subjectivity. The reader may wish to analyze the case himself using the model and then to compare his analysis with that of the authors.

Case I

You are general foreman in charge of a large gang laying an oil pipeline. It is now necessary to estimate your expected rate of progress in order to schedule material deliveries to the next field site.

You know the nature of the terrain you will be traveling and have the historical data needed to compute the mean and variance in the rate of speed over that type of terrain. Given these two variables it is a simple matter to calculate the earliest and latest times at which materials and support facilities will be needed at the next site. It is important that your estimate be reasonably accurate. Underestimates result in idle foremen and workers, and an overestimate results in tying up materials for a period of time before they are to be used.

Progress has been good and your five foremen and other members of the gang stand to receive substantial bonuses if the project is completed ahead of schedule.

Analysis

Questions—A (Quality?) = yes
B (Leader's information?) = yes
E (Acceptance?) = no

Problem type—4
Feasible set—AI, AII, CI, CII, GII
Minimum man-hours solution (from figure 3.2)—AI

Rule violations—none

Case II

You are supervising the work of twelve engineers. Their formal training and work experience are very similar, permitting you to use them interchangeably on projects. Yesterday, your manager informed you that a request had been received from an overseas affiliate for four engineers to go abroad on extended loan for a period of six to eight months. For a number of reasons he argued, and you agreed, that this request should be met from your group.

All your engineers are capable of handling this assignment, and, from the standpoint of present and future projects, there is no particular reason why any one should be retained over any other. The problem is somewhat complicated by the fact that the overseas assignment is in what is generally regarded in the company as an undesirable location.

Analysis

Questions—A (Quality?) = no
     E (Acceptance?) = yes
     F (Prior probability of acceptance?) = no

Problem type—3
Feasible set—GII
Minimum man-hours solution (from figure 3.2)—GII

Rule violations—AI and AII violate rules 4, 5, and 6.
      CI violates rules 5 and 6.
      CII violates rule 6.

Case III

You are the head of a staff unit reporting to the vice-president of finance. He has asked you to provide a report on the firm's current portfolio including recommendations for changes in the selection criteria currently employed. Doubts have been raised about the efficiency of the existing system in the current market conditions, and there is considerable dissatisfaction with prevailing rates of return.

You plan to write the report, but at the moment you are quite perplexed about the approach to take. Your own specialty is the bond market, and it is clear to you that a detailed knowledge of the equity market, which you lack, would greatly enhance the value of the report. Fortunately, four members of your staff are specialists in different segments of the equity market. Together they possess a vast amount of knowledge about the intricacies of investment. However, they seldom agree on the best way to achieve anything when it comes to the stock market. While they are obviously conscientious as well as knowledgeable, they have major differences when it comes to investment philosophy and strategy.

You have six weeks before the report is due. You have already begun to familiarize yourself with the firm's current portfolio and have been provided by management with a specific set of constraints that any portfolio must satisfy. Your immediate problem is to come up with some alternatives to the firm's present practices and select the most promising for detailed analysis in your report.

Analysis

Questions—A (Quality?) = yes
B (Leader's information?) = no
C (Subordinates' information?) = yes
D (Structured?) = no
E (Acceptance?) = no

Problem type—14
Feasible set—CII, GII
Minimum man-hours solution (figure 3.2)—CII

Rule violations—AI violates rules 1 and 3.
AII violates rule 3.
CI violates rule 3.

Case IV

You are on the division manager's staff and work on a wide variety of problems of both administrative and technical nature. You have been given the assignment of developing a universal method to be used in each of the five plants in the division for manually reading equipment registers, recording the readings, and transmitting the scorings to a centralized information system. All plants are located in a relatively small geographical region.

Until now there has been a high error rate in the reading and/or transmittal of the data. Some locations have considerably higher error rates than others, and the methods used to record and transmit the data vary between plants. It is probable, therefore, that part of the error variance is a function of specific local conditions rather than anything else, and this will complicate the establishment of any system common to all plants. You have the information on error rates but no information on the local practices that generate these errors or on the local conditions that necessitate the different practices.

Everyone would benefit from an improvement in the quality of the data, as it is used in a number of important decisions. Your contacts with the plants are through the quality-control supervisors who are responsible for collecting the data. They are a conscientious group committed to doing their jobs well, but they are highly sensitive to interference on the part of higher management in their own operations. Any solution that does not receive the active support of the various plant supervisors is unlikely to reduce the error rate significantly.

Analysis

Questions—A (Quality?) = yes
B (Leader's information?) = no
C (Subordinates' information?) = yes
D (Structured?) = no
E (Acceptance?) = yes
F (Prior probability of acceptance?) = no
G (Trust?) = yes

Problem type—12
Feasible set—GII
Minimum man-hours solution (figure 3.2)—GII

Rule violations—AI violates rules 1, 3, 4, and 7.
AII violates rules 3, 4, and 7.
CI violates rules 3 and 7.
CII violates rule 7.

SHORT- VERSUS LONG-TERM MODELS

The model shown in figure 3.2 seeks to protect the quality of the decision, to create any necessary acceptance of the decision, and to expend the lowest number of man-hours in the process. In view of its attention to conditions surrounding the making and implementation of a particular decision rather than any long-term considerations, it could be termed a short-term model.

It seems likely, however, that the leadership methods that may be optimal for short-term results may be different from those which would be optimal when executed over a longer period of time. Consider a leader who has been uniformly pursuing an autocratic style (AI or AII) and, perhaps as a consequence, has subordinates who cannot be trusted to pursue organizational goals (attribute G) and who have little additional knowledge or experience to bring to bear on the decisions to be made (attribute C). An examination of the structure of the model shown in figure 3.2 reveals that with few exceptions, the leader would be instructed by the model to continue his present autocratic style.

It appears likely, however, that the use of more participative methods would, in time, change the status of these problem attributes (that is, increase the extent to which subordinates would have information relevant to the solution of problems in the future, increase the extent to which their goals are congruent with those of the organization) and ultimately develop a more effective problem-solving team. In the example given above, an autocratic approach would be indicated to maximize short-run benefits, but a higher degree of participation might maximize performance aggregated over a longer period.

One promising approach to the development of a long-term model places less weight on man-hours as the basis for choice of method within the feasible set. Given a long-term orientation, one would be interested in the trade-off between man-hours and team development, both of which increase with participation. Viewed in these terms, the model shown in figure 3.2 places maximum relative weight on man-hours and no weight on development and hence chooses the method furthest to the left within the feasible set. A model that places no weight on man-hours and maximum weight on development would, if these assumptions are correct, choose the method furthest to the right within the feasible set.

SUBJECTIVE FACTORS IN PROBLEM CODING

To use the model, a leader must make judgments about the characteristics of problems with which he is faced. His judgments are guided by definitions of the attributes, but they are still judgments on his part, with unknown correspondence to the actual properties of the situation. A leader may think he has the necessary information to solve the problem by himself, only to discover later that there were critical facts to which he did not have access; or he may believe that subordinates will be certain to accept his decision, only to discover later that they actively opposed it. The model is at best a vehicle for subjective rationality that purports to help a leader to select a decision process that is rational given his view of the situation. Insofar as their judgments are imperfectly related to the actual state of affairs, deviations from objective rationality might be expected.

In some cases, the leader's view of the situation may cause him to select a decision process that he may find unworkable in practice. He discovers that his judgments of the situation were in error, and a revision of those judgments causes him to substitute another process. Let us consider the following example.

A newly appointed chairman of a university department was faced with the task of assigning the courses to be taught among the members of his seven-man faculty. Using the model shown in figure 3.1 as a guide, he judged the problem to be of type 5.A: Quality—yes. ("It is important to match the requirements of the course with the competence and training of the faculty member.") B: Leader's info—yes. ("I know the course descriptions and the areas in which the faculty were trained and are currently doing research.") E: Importance of acceptance of decision by subordinates —yes. ("They are going to have to teach the courses, not me, and I have no means of controlling their behavior in the classroom.") F: Prior probability of acceptance of decision by subordinates— yes. ("I am the chairman of the department, and my faculty see it as my job to make course assignments.")

The model prescribes AI for type 5 problems: the leader should make the decision himself and announce it to his subordinates. The department chairman carried out this process by sending a memo to each faculty member concerned, containing the courses he was expected to teach. Within two hours of distributing the memos, the chairman had received visits from three of the faculty, each of whom was opposed to his assignment. Their arguments seemed reasonable but differed from one case to another. "I don't know how to teach that course." "I have been teaching the course you assigned me for four years in a row and want to change." "I am trying to complete a book based on my research, and the demands of grading and meeting with students in the introductory course you have assigned me will prevent my finishing it."

Throughout the visits from the first two faculty members, the chairman found himself trying to figure out what modifications he could make in his plan that would be acceptable to the person to whom he was talking. He was reluctant to make any final concessions however, since a change in any one person's assignment required a change in the assignments of others, and satisfying these three might have simply shifted the discontent to the others.

After the third visit, the chairman concluded that his method of making that decision was incorrect. He had altered his view of the situation. It had become more complicated than he thought. He had thought he had enough information, but did he really? He had thought his subordinates would accept his decision, but it was now apparent that they had not.

The chairman then reexamined the model and reassessed the problem with which he was faced. This time he judged that he did not have enough information to solve the problem by himself and that it was not certain that his subordinates would accept the decision were he to make it. He pondered for a few seconds when he encountered the question about whether his subordinates could be trusted but, after reading a more complete specification of that attribute, concluded that they could be. He was more uncertain as to whether the problem should be classified as structured or unstructured, but on examining the model, he saw that it made no difference in the decision process recommended. The problem was either of type 6 or type 12 and both specified GII.

Accordingly, he invited his seven faculty members to a meeting, explaining that there were unforeseen problems with his previous decision regarding course assignments. He then gave the problem to the group to solve. The meeting took about an hour and a half, but at the end of the meeting everyone seemed satisfied with his assignment, and, in the chairman's judgment, the decision was of higher quality and certainly received more acceptance than his previous AI decision.

In the preceding case, the leader was able to alter his decision-making process as he acquired new information that caused him to reassess his previous view of the situation. The feedback he received was sufficiently rapid that the decision process could be altered before it was too late. It seems likely that assessments of problem attributes related to the acceptance of the decision tend to have relatively short feedback cycles connected with them, permitting the leader, if he so chooses, to adjust his decision-making process.

To be sure, not all leaders receive the rapid feedback concerning the acceptance of their decisions that the department chairman received in the previous example. Apathy and passive resistance seem more likely consequences of more extended exposure to the AI decision-making process. The critical point to be made is that conditions can be created that will provide leaders with feedback concerning the acceptability of particular decisions in time to modify the decision-making process. On the other hand, incorrect assessments of problem attributes related to the quality of the decision can have much longer feedback cycles. In the automobile industry, the design for a new automobile has to be determined several years before manufacturers begin to get information concerning appeal in the marketplace. Even more critical is the fact that empirical testing of the quality of the decision typically requires its implementation. The definitive test of the quality of a decision made by a football quarterback concerning the next play is the number of yards gained. The definitive test of the quality of a surgeon's decision to operate is improvement in the patient's condition. Information obtained regarding the external consequences of a decision may cause one to reevaluate one's view of the situation and decision-making process on the next occasion but can seldom modify that decision.

The potential usefulness of the model shown earlier (or any other model based on leaders' judgments concerning situational properties) is in direct proportion to the veridicality of those judgments. To know how the model will work in practice, we need to understand the factors affecting the inferences that leaders draw about the attributes contained in the model and the accuracy of the inferences themselves. If one were interested in judgments of attributes of simple stimuli such as heaviness, loudness, or brightness, it would be a relatively simple matter to design a psychophysical experiment to investigate this question. But the attributes of interest in the model do not correspond to measurable physical properties and are embedded in the context of a problem taking place in an organizational setting.

It is necessary to have standardized situations so that they can be presented to a number of leaders. The situations should be representative of the kinds of problems with which leaders are confronted in organizational life. Cues should be provided with each situation that would permit one to draw reasonably reliable inferences concerning each attribute, but the cues should be typical of those normally available to a leader, and the inferences from these cues should be similar in nature to those encountered in actual situations.

Accordingly, a group of over a thousand managers were asked to write cases depicting actual problems they had recently encountered in their jobs. From these a set of thirty were selected by the authors on the basis of diversity on each of the attributes. The cases were rewritten by the authors to protect the identity of the firm and to achieve comparable writing style and detail. A more complete account of the method of developing these cases will be found in chapter 5.

The cases ranged in length from 100 to 400 words. The written description of each case avoided the terms used in phrasing the questions in the model. For instance, there was no mention of the fact that the quality of the decision was important (or unimportant) or that subordinates could be trusted (or could not be trusted). However, there was sufficient information given about the facts in each case to draw reasonably reliable inferences concerning each attribute. The two authors had independently coded each case, and their agreement was perfect. The set of thirty cases contained examples of each of the fourteen problem types.

The set of cases was given to three groups of subjects. The three groups differed in a number of respects including the amount of training that they had been given in the use of the model. Group I was made up of eight British managers from a variety of firms and government departments. They had received a short lecture concerning the model, and each had a copy of the model and a handout regarding the definitions of each attribute, but had no practice in applying it to problems.[2] Group II consisted of thirteen managers from a division of a large public utility engaged in basic research. Like group I, they had received a copy of the model and the handout and in addition had received approximately two hours of instruction regarding the model, including practice in applying it to four written cases. Group III consisted of nineteen undergraduate students in a course in elements of administration. They did not have copies of the model or the handout but had received about five hours of instruction in the problem attributes, including practice in making judgments on a large number of cases other than those contained in the thirty-case problem set. It can be seen that the three groups differed in the amount of training in the use of the model, with group I having the least and group III having the most training. There were, however, other differences

2. See appendix 1 for a copy of the handout.

both in procedure and population which may have affected the results.

Subjects in all three groups were asked to read each case and to code it by making the judgments required by the model. Two questions can be examined with the use of these data. The first concerns the extent of agreement in coding among persons exposed to the same case. The greater the extent to which people see the problems in the same way, the less the extent to which solutions obtained from using the model are reflections of idiosyncratic differences among managers. A related question concerns the amount of agreement with the coding of the two experts trained in the use of the model. The greater the agreement with experts' coding, the more the application would be free from subjective influences.

No problem was coded in exactly the same way by all persons in any one of the three groups. This finding confirms the belief that problem coding is in part a subjective process with different persons drawing different inferences from the same information. However, both internal consistency in coding and agreement with expert coding greatly exceeded chance levels for all groups. Table 3.2 shows the percentage of cases for each group in which the sub-

TABLE 3.2. Internal and External Agreement in Problem Coding

Agreement with	Group I	Group II	Group III
1. Expert coding	30.0%	54.9%	63.1%
2. Modal coding	42.5	56.1	63.1

jects' coding agreed with expert coding and the percentage of cases in which the subjects' coding agreed with the modal problem type assigned by members of each group to each problem. The former is a measure of agreement with an external criterion (expert coding); the latter is a measure of internal agreement.

The fact that internal agreement exceeds agreement with expert coders in groups I and II indicates that the problem type specified by the experts was not always the most frequent judgment of the managers. This occurred for fifteen out of the thirty cases for group I, but only three cases for group II and none for group III.

There is substantial evidence that the groups with more training produced judgments that were both more internally consistent and more in agreement with the experts than did those with less training. Group III exceeded group II, and group II in turn exceeded group I on both criteria. The poor performance of group I implies that the model cannot be used reliably without training, whereas the improved performance of groups II and III probably indicates the effects of the training on eliminating errors in judgments.

However, even group III had a substantial number of inconsistencies with expert coding and disagreements among themselves. Thirty-seven percent of their judgments of problem type were at variance with those of the experts and with their own modal judgment. These figures are of course overestimates of the likelihood that leaders would arrive at the "wrong" decision process when using the model. Minor differences in coding, as for example between problem types 1 and 2 or 4 and 5, make no difference in either the feasible set or the model. When one considers the percentage of the time that a subject trained in the use of the model would arrive at the same decision process (AI, AII, etc.) as experts using the model, the percentage increases to 69 percent for group II and 78 percent for group III.

On what kinds of problems were discrepancies in problem coding between experts and managers most likely to appear? On theoretical grounds, it would seem likely that discrepancies would increase as a function of the number of judgments required by that problem type. The number of correct judgments required for accurate coding of problem type varies from two in problems of type 1 to eight in problems of type 7b. If the probability of a person making a correct judgment of each problem attribute were as high as .9, and if these probabilities were independent across attributes, the probability of his coding a type 1 problem accurately would be $.9^2$ or .81 (81 percent), and the probability of his coding a 7b problem accurately would be $.9^8$ or .43 (43 percent).

Table 3.3 shows the expected percentages of agreement based on the assumption of independent errors across attributes and a .9 probability of accurate coding for each attribute. It also contains actual percentages of agreement with problem coding for each group for problems requiring different numbers of judgments. The data from group III provide a remarkably good fit to the expected values. However, the percentage of correct codes assigned by groups I and II is essentially invariant with the number of required judgments. This finding suggests that, in the groups with lesser

TABLE 3.3. Relationship Between Number of Correct Judgments Required and Percentage of Correct Problem Coding

Number of Judgments	Problem Type	Number of Problems	Percentage of Correct Codings			Expected Percentage
			Group I	Group II	Group III	
2	1	2	25%	88%	80%	81%
3	2, 3, 4	8	28	55	70	73
4	5	4	28	47	66	66
5	6a, 10, 14	6	35	49	61	59
6	7a, 9, 11, 8a	6	25	55	58	53
7–8	6b, 7b, 12, 13	4	44	50	48	47

amounts of training, attributes do not have equal probabilities of being judged correctly. It also suggests that those which appear late in the sequence tend to have higher probabilities of being reliably assessed than those appearing earlier in the sequence.

The data from all three groups have been analyzed to determine the attributes on which there was greatest and poorest agreement between expert coders and subjects and the types of "errors" in judgments which were made. Table 3.4 presents the results. The first three columns of figures contain the percentage of cases in which the subjects' judgments of each attribute were at variance with those of the experts. The figure shown for each attribute is equal to the number of "errors" divided by the total number of problems judged. Thus for attribute A, quality requirement, there was a total of 31 discrepancies between experts and the managers in group II out of a total of 390 judgments, yielding a total error rate of 7.9 percent.

An inspection of the results shown in the first three columns of the table indicates the expected differences among the three groups in accuracy of coding virtually all attributes. However, there are also wide differences among attributes within groups. Structure is the most poorly coded attribute by all three groups with error rates ranging from 39 percent in group I to 19 percent in group III. Trust is poorly coded by groups I and II (38 percent and 23 percent) but quite accurately by group III (9 percent). Prior probability shows the least improvement with training, with error rates decreasing from 22 percent in group I to 13 percent in group III.

TABLE 3.4. Coding Errors on Attributes

	Total Error Percentage			False Positives			False Negatives		
	Group I	Group II	Group III	Group I	Group II	Group III	Group I	Group II	Group III
A. Quality requirement	28%	8%	7%	67%	6%	9%	19%	8%	7%
B. Leader's information	32	4	7	49	1	5	13	7	8
D. Structure in problem	39	30	19	75	43	34	6	17	4
E. Importance of acceptance	28	12	12	46	18	16	19	9	10
F. Prior probability of acceptance	22	21	13	17	8	11	28	33	15
G. Trust	38	23	9	23	12	3	55	39	15
H. Conflict	42	8	12	56	11	10	25	6	13

It is instructive to look at the types of "errors" that are made in judgments of each attribute. The errors have been broken down into two types. A false positive, shown in the three center columns, refers to an instance in which the experts coded an attribute as absent (that is, their response to the question shown in table 2.3 was no) but the respondent saw it as present (his response to the question was yes). A false negative, shown in the three right-hand columns, refers to instances in which the experts saw the attribute as present but a manager saw it as absent. Thus for attribute A, there were 24 problems judged by the experts as having a quality requirement. Of the 312 (24 $\times$ 13) judgments by group II of problems deemed by the experts to have a quality requirement, 26 were in error, resulting in a false negative rate of 8.3 percent. Similarly, of 78 judgments of problems deemed to have no quality requirement, 5 were in error, producing a false positive rate of 6.4 percent.

If the probabilities of the two types of errors are roughly of the same order of magnitude, it would seem to signify confusion as to the nature of the attribute or lack of care in making judgments. On the other hand, large differences in the probabilities of these two types of errors are indicative of different thresholds for judging presence or absence of attributes used by managers and experts.

The errors for three attributes (D, F, and G) stand out as being highly asymmetrical. On attribute D, all three groups had substantially higher probabilities of seeing problems as structured than did the experts. Apparently the problem is one of different thresholds and is potentially altered by more precise instructions and more training in this attribute.

With regard to attribute F, prior probability of acceptance, the errors occur in the opposite direction with false negatives exceeding false positives. The discrepancies between managerial and expert judgments of this attribute occurred overwhelmingly in cases in which the experts responded yes to the question and the managers responded no. Once again the difference is one of the threshold for judgments and is probably induced by the wording of the question, "Is it certain that an autocratic decision would be accepted by subordinates?" The managers were undoubtedly taking the word "certain" more literally than were the experts. As one manager remarked when asked to explain the reasoning behind his judgments on this attribute, "There isn't anything which is certain in this world." Revised wording of this question would probably serve to bring judgments closer to those intended.

Like prior probability, attribute G (trust in subordinates) produces an inordinately large number of false negatives. All three groups tended to judge subordinates as untrustworthy when the experts' judgment was the reverse. From discussions with managers, it appears likely that the word "trust" was the source of the confusion. To the experts, it meant congruence between organizational goals as represented in the problem and the goals of group members. This definition is apparent from the written exposition contained in appendix 1. But some managers interpreted this attribute and the question pertaining to it as meaning "can subordinates be trusted to come up with my solution to the problem?" Quite clearly, there can be agreement on goals and disagreement between leader and his subordinate on the mechanism for their attainment, giving rise to the large number of false negatives that are found here.

The results reported in this section have indicated that making judgments of the status of problem attributes from written case studies is in part a subjective process. The degree of subjectivity varied markedly among groups I, II, and III, in an inverse relationship to the amount of training they had received. The attributes were not judged equally reliably and in three of the attributes, structure, prior probability, and trust, there was substantial evidence of asymmetry in the "errors." In comparison with the experts, subjects in all three groups were more likely to classify problems as structured, less likely to see autocratic decisions as "certain" to be accepted, and less likely to judge subordinates as trustworthy. This asymmetry was interpreted as reflecting different thresholds used by subjects and experts for judging the presence or absence of an attribute. Further analysis of the data from group III, not reported here, shows that a subset of the subjects from that group contribute a much larger proportion of the false negatives on prior probability and trust and of false positives on structure than would be expected under the assumption that each person has the same error rates for these attributes. It can be inferred that the training this group received did not produce identical thresholds among subjects for judging presence or absence of these attributes.

The findings reported in this section suggest strongly that the model presented earlier cannot be used reliably without training in the attributes and practice with feedback in making the judgments required. Such training serves markedly to reduce but not to eliminate the number of errors. An analysis of the types of errors has suggested some ways in which the wording of questions can be altered to minimize the judgmental errors made. These ideas will be incorporated into a modified version of the model to be presented in chapter 9.

It should be pointed out that the judgmental processes examined in this section are judgments of written cases rather than situations in which the subject was actually involved. While every effort was made to make the cases realistic and representative of the types of problems actually confronting leaders in organizations, there is no way to estimate whether the findings are applicable to judgments made by leaders in real situations in which they are involved. It seems likely that leaders would have much more data on which to judge the status of problem attributes than can be presented in a short written case, thereby reducing the number of errors far below those presented here. On the other hand, it is possible that the leader's emotional involvement in actual situations might affect his judgments of certain of the attributes such as leader's information and trust in subordinates, which could increase certain errors.

SUMMARY

In this and the preceding chapter, a normative model of leadership style has been developed. The model attempts to deal with the complexities of the processes involved in leadership by specifying: (1) a set of alternatives among which a choice is to be made, (2) the general nature of the processes which they affect, (3) the principal variables governing the effects of the alternatives on each process, and (4) explicit rules for decision-making based on estimates of the outcome of each process.

Some might argue that it is premature for social scientists to attempt to be prescriptive. Our knowledge is too little and the issues too complex to warrant explicit normative models dealing with matters such as leadership style. It is also true, however, that leaders are facing daily the task of selecting decision-making processes which in turn reflect their leadership style. Is it likely that a model which encourages them to deal analytically with the forces impinging upon them and which is consistent with an admittedly imperfect research base would produce more rational choices than those which they do make? The criterion for social utility is not perfection but improvement over present practice.

Furthermore, social scientists are increasingly having an influence not only on people's leadership style but also on such matters as job design, training methods, and compensation systems. Too frequently, in the view of the present authors, their prescriptions for action, whether it be job enrichment, sensitivity training, or group decision-making, are not based on a systematic analysis of the situation in a manner which would point to the costs and benefits of available alternatives.

Perhaps the most convincing argument for the development of normative models is the fact that in developing and using them their weaknesses can be identified. Insofar as these weaknesses stem from lack of basic knowledge, this deficiency can be remedied through further research. A strong case can be made for the continued interplay between the worlds of practice and social science on the basis of their mutual contributions to one another.

Is the model in its present form an adequate guide to practice? Would managers make fewer errors in their choices of decision processes if they were to base them on the model? We would be less than honest if we said we knew the answer to such questions. Later in the book we will examine some data that bear on them. For example, in chapter 7, we will examine the ways in which the behavior of managers is similar to or different from the model, and in chapter 9 we will present some results relevant to the difficult problem of assessing the validity of a model such as this one. But the reader should be prepared for the fact that the issues surrounding the evaluation of normative or prescriptive models are complex, and the methodology for answering questions of validity through empirical research is not well developed.

But perhaps it would be premature to attempt to perform a definitive evaluation of this particular model. It represents the sixth version of models for the same purpose developed in the course of the research, and the evolutionary process is far from complete. In fact, in chapter 9 we will reexamine the normative model on the basis of research reported in the intervening chapters and will present what we believe to be an improved version.

In the next three chapters we turn away from the normative questions pursued in this section to descriptive questions pertaining to the factors that influence leaders to share power or retain it. We will return to the normative model again in chapters 7, 8, and 9.

CHAPTER 4

Some Descriptive Studies of Participation in Decision-Making

Imagine that you are manufacturing manager in a large electronics plant. The company's management have always been searching for ways of increasing efficiency. They have recently installed new machines and put in a new simplified work system, but to the surprise of everyone, including yourself, the expected increase in productivity has not been realized. In fact, production has begun to drop, quality has fallen off, and the number of employee separations has risen.

You do not believe there is anything wrong with the machines. You have had reports from other companies who are using them, and they confirm this opinion. You have also had representatives from the firm that built the machines go over them, and they report that the machines are operating at peak efficiency.

You suspect that some parts of the new work system may be responsible for the change, but this view is not widely shared among your immediate subordinates, who are: four first-line supervisors, each in charge of a section, and your supply manager. The drop in production has been variously attributed to poor training of the operators, lack of an adequate system of financial incentives, and poor morale. Clearly, this is an issue about which there is considerable depth of feeling and potential disagreement among your subordinates.

This morning you received a phone call from your division manager. He had just received your production figures for the last six months and was calling to express his concern. He indicated that the problem is yours to solve in any way you think best but that he would like to know within a week what steps you plan to take.

You share your division manager's concern with the falling pro-

ductivity and know that your men are also concerned. The problem is to decide what steps to take to rectify the situation.

What decision process would you adopt in this case? Would you
sit down and, using your best judgment, draw up a plan to resolve
the problem of falling productivity and then present it to both
your subordinates and your division manager? Would you send a
memo to each of your subordinates asking them for the weekly
records covering the periods before and after the introduction of
the new machines, for the purpose of helping you draw up the
plan of action requested by your division manager? Would you
invite your subordinates into your office, either individually or
together, to obtain their ideas before you drew up the plan? Or
would you invite them to a meeting, present them with the problem, and together attempt to reach agreement on the plan of action to be undertaken?

The reader will recognize these decision processes as specific
manifestations of AI, AII, CI, CII, and GII, the five methods that
are used in the normative model. But the focus in this and the
following two chapters is not normative but descriptive. The
question concerns not what one *should* do in that situation, but
what leaders *would* do if faced with that situation.

Of course, it is not only the particular problem just described
that is of interest, but the whole family of such situations defined
in chapter 2 as group problems. Among the questions that will be
guiding the inquiry in this and the following two chapters are the
following: Do leaders adopt the same decision process regardless of
the situation? If not, what situational properties affect leaders'
choices among decision processes? Are these properties the same
for all leaders or do leaders vary in the factors to which they
respond?

Insofar as empirical investigations of leadership have addressed
themselves to descriptive questions, they have tended to focus on
variables that can be used to describe differences among leaders.
In a substantial number of studies, such differences are reduced to
a single dimension, or a highly limited set of categories that might
be located on one dimension. Thus, leadership styles are characterized as autocratic, democratic, and laissez-faire (Lewin, Lippitt,
and White 1939; Baumgartel 1956) or employee-centered and
production-centered (Katz, Maccoby, Gurin, and Floor 1951).
Similarly, one finds leaders distinguished in terms of their esteem
for their least preferred co-worker (Fiedler 1967).

A more frequent approach, however, has been to represent such differences in two dimensions. Such concepts as consideration and initiating structure, the dimensions which emerged from the factor analytic work of the Ohio State group (Halpin and Winer 1957), and the similar concepts, concern for production and concern for people, used by Blake and Mouton (1964) as the basis for the managerial grid approach to organizational development, are the best known examples of two-dimensional frameworks.

This approach is convenient to apply, particularly if one is principally interested in using the measures to account for differences in the effectiveness of the units that the leaders manage. It is not, however, without its problems. It is reasonable to assume that any leader encounters, in the course of a day, month, or year, a number of different kinds of situations, ranging in character from a breakdown in the production line under his direction to a request from a subordinate for time off to go to a funeral. In each of these situations he exhibits some behavior and it is these behaviors that researchers have sought to represent by locating the position of the leader in one or two dimensions. To say that a leader is at the tenth percentile on consideration and at the ninetieth percentile on initiating structure (assuming the construct validity of the measures) presumably indicates something about his aggregate behavior compared with that of other leaders.

However, to summarize in one or two dimensions the multitude of ways in which leaders can differ from one another requires one to treat as equivalent, behaviors that are clearly different and may have different effects. Thus, the behaviors—"doing a personal favor for subordinates" and "putting suggestions made by subordinates into operation"—are clearly distinguishable and could have quite different consequences even though both contribute to a high score on consideration (Fleishman, Harris, and Burtt 1955).

Similarly, such representations of leader behavior also require one to treat situations in which a given behavior is exhibited as equivalent. The behavior—"letting others do the work in the way they think best"—contributes to a low score on initiating structure even though it may be a highly functional leadership method in some situations and highly dysfunctional in others.

To the extent that behaviors "lumped together" in the same category have different effects and the same behavior has effects that vary with the properties of the situation, measures of leadership style of the type we have been describing will tend to be less useful in accounting for criteria of effectiveness. This process could account for the fact that such correlations tend to be quite low and highly variable from one study to another (Vroom 1964).

Just as typical measures of leader behavior have limitations in accounting for significant amounts of variance in criteria of effectiveness, they also have shown limited usefulness in the kind of question in which we are interested in this chapter—What determines leader behavior? From other behavioral research, there is strong reason to believe that behavior is explained in terms of individual difference variables, situational variables, and the interaction between them (Cronbach 1957). In spite of this fact, there is a strong tendency to think that scores on such variables as consideration and initiating structure represent properties or traits of the leader. One is not likely to ask, let alone receive answers to, such questions as "What situations cause leaders to show consideration or lack of consideration for their subordinates?"

Ultimately, we wish to be able to predict not only the organizational consequences of specific leader actions but also the determinants of those actions. The fact that traditional approaches to the description of leader behavior aggregate over both behavior and situations greatly limits their suitability to the latter purpose. To what extent could one predict, for example, a leader's behavior in the situation with which we began this chapter by knowing his LPC score (Fiedler 1967) or his score on consideration and initiating structure (Halpin and Winer 1957)?

An alternative to the prevailing tendency to measure behavioral differences among leaders is to focus on behavioral differences within a single leader in different situations. No leader behaves in exactly the same manner in every situation. A more accurate representation would be to say that he has programs (Simon 1960) by which he analyzes the features of situations with which he is confronted and which generate actions on his part. The critical differences among leaders may lie in the structure of their programs or the decision rules they employ rather than in their aggregated behavior.

An exception to the predominant tendency to average over situations in describing leader behavior may be found in the work of Heller (1971). Heller concludes that "managers do not use one preferred style of decision irrespective of the nature of the decision" (1971, p. 27). Studying senior managers, he obtained judgments of the decision process they employed in making various classes of decisions. The taxonomy of decision processes is similar to that shown in chapter 2 for individual problems. The classes of decisions included those affecting (1) the entire department under the direction of the manager (for example, to purchase a necessary piece of equipment costing over $100), (2) a single subordinate reporting to the manager (to change an operating procedure followed by your subordinates), and (3) an employee reporting to a single subordinate (to give a merit increase to one of your subordinate's employees). The first category conforms to our definition of group problems, and the latter two conform to our definition of individual problems (see chapter 2).

Heller presents evidence of a substantial difference in the degree to which managers share power on decisions in categories 2 and 3 above. Managers are more likely to employ delegation (corresponding to DI in the classification used in chapter 2), joint decision-making (GI), and consultative (CI) methods in decisions affecting one of their subordinate's employees than in decisions affecting the subordinate himself.

The initial report of Heller's research (Heller and Yukl 1969) was published midway in the course of the research program on which this book is based, and the complete publication of results (Heller 1971) was received only during the write-up of results. Despite the lack of opportunity for coordination, the results of this investigation complement our research on the descriptive aspects of leadership styles. We will have several occasions in this and the following chapter to compare Heller's findings with our own.

If one is to develop a model capable of incorporating both interpersonal and intrapersonal variance, it is necessary to describe leadership behavior in terms of concrete and specifically defined acts that are exhibited in specific situations, rather than in terms of generalized dispositions or tendencies. A taxonomy or classification of acts is necessary so that one can begin to determine specific variables that influence the choices leaders make among these acts. The list of decision processes shown in table 2.1 constitutes such a taxonomy and provides a basis for illustrating and testing the fruitfulness of this approach. While originally developed for the normative model, these processes are equally useful in empirical studies aimed at the development of a descriptive model.

The balance of this chapter reports a set of four empirical investigations dealing with situational influences on the extent to which leaders encourage their subordinates to participate in decision-making. The studies are reported in the order in which they were conducted; the issues they address and the nature of the research designs become increasingly complex.

A CRUDE TEST OF INTRAPERSONAL VARIANCE: STUDY 1

The first study was principally concerned with testing the assumption on which the program of research is based; that is, there is variance in the decision processes used by a single leader in carrying out his job. If a leader invariably uses only one of the methods shown in table 2.1 then there is no within-person variance to be explained.

A simple test of this assumption was carried out in the following way. A total of 385 managers from over 100 different firms were given the written descriptions of the decision processes shown in table 2.1 and were asked to indicate the percentage of occasions in which they used each of these decision processes in solving problems and in making decisions in their jobs. They were free to allocate 100 percent to one method or to distribute the percentage across any number of methods. (The only constraint imposed on their judgments of frequency was that the sum of the total percentages allocated to the five styles equaled 100.)

The results show that 98.7 percent of the managers indicated that they employed each of the five decision processes some proportion of the time. Only five managers did not indicate some percentage for each of the five methods. Of these, three reported that they always employed a single process (two used CI and one used GII), one indicated he used four processes (eliminating GII), and one pointed out that he used only two of the five processes (CI and CII).

Even allowing for likely bias in reports of this kind, it is clear that an overwhelming proportion of managers see themselves as using different decision processes within a single role or job. This finding lends support to the basic idea of attempting to determine the situations that cause them to adopt each process.

The data also reveal substantial differences among managers in the frequency with which each style is used. For slightly over one half (54 percent) of the managers, CI was their most frequently chosen style, while 23 percent allocated their largest percentage to CII, 12 percent to GII, 8 percent to AI, and only 3 percent to AII.

Let us, for purposes of argument, take these data at face value and see what they tell us about managerial leadership. The data clearly show variance in behavior among managers. Some managers report predominant use of the participative styles like CII and GII; others report much more extensive use of autocratic styles (AI and AII). This is the variance among leaders which, we have argued, has been the starting point for most investigations of leadership. Leaders do differ in the predominant styles of leadership they employ, and these differences could have considerable bearing on their effectiveness. We do not know the source of these differences, the degree to which they are the reflection of relatively stable individual differences, or the degree to which they are the result of different situational demands. For some purposes, we may not need to know the source of the differences.

The data, however, also show variance of behavior within managers. It is likely that this variance is deterministic rather than random and that each manager uses different decision processes in different circumstances. It is not known, however, what circumstances cause managers to share their power or retain it, nor whether the circumstances that influence one leader to share power are the same as those for another leader. The variance within managers in their use of decision processes may be the result of situational variables (including interactions among them) or of interactions between situational and individual difference variables. The next three studies in this chapter and those to be reported in the next chapter will attempt to advance our understanding of such issues.

FINDING A METRIC FOR PARTICIPATION: STUDY 2

Early in the research it was realized that the development of a descriptive model would be greatly aided if it could be shown that the decision processes in table 2.1 could be arranged on a unidimensional scale and if nonarbitrary, scale values could be assigned to five alternatives. It would, of course, be possible to follow "standard practice" and assume all distances to be equal by assigning numbers such as 1, 2, 3, 4, and 5 to AI, AII, CI, CII, and

GII respectively. However, there is strong *a priori* reason for believing that the distances among them may not be equal.

The possibility of finding a more supportable metric for the five alternatives was suggested by visual inspection of the results of Study 1. From a knowledge of the style most frequently used, it was possible to predict with a high degree of accuracy the subsequent order of the four alternatives. This predictability was greatest if the most frequently used style was either AI or GII. Thus, in the former case the subsequent order had a high probability of being AII, CI, CII, GII, and in the latter case, CII, CI, AII, and AI. The managers appeared to be responding to the five discrete styles as though they fell along a unidimensional scale and to be ordering the alternatives in decreasing order of their distance from some ideal position.

The possibility of using rank order data as the basis for establishing the unidimensionality of a scale and assigning scale values is suggested by Coombs (1964). The logic may be illustrated with an example. Let us consider a set of showers, each set at a different temperature. Each shower can be characterized by a point on the centigrade scale, and with a thermometer it would be a simple procedure to estimate the location of the temperature of each shower on that scale.

Now assume that no thermometer exists. By what procedure can we locate these temperatures on an interval scale?[1] Let us assume that an individual's utility for a shower is proportional to the absolute difference between the temperature of the shower and the temperature of his ideal or perfect shower. Further assume that different individuals have different ideal shower temperatures. We could now ask a number of individuals to rank order the showers from most to least desirable. Differences in the temperature of the ideal shower would result in different preference orderings among showers. Coombs (1964) outlines a procedure that tests whether an underlying scale exists. If such a scale does exist, the procedure makes a numerical assignment to each of the showers.

Accordingly, a set of 597 managers were given a written description of the decision processes shown in table 2.1 and were asked to rank order them in accordance with the frequency with which they used them in their jobs. It should be noted that there

1. The procedure actually generates an ordered difference scale which has many of the properties of an interval scale.

are a total of 5! or 120 logically possible orders that could have been obtained. However, only 62 of the 120 possible rank orders occurred at all and many of these only once. Most of the choices were concentrated among a small subset of the possible orderings. Clearly, these judgments were not randomly distributed across the 120 possibilities.

If all of the orders were consistent with a single uniquely defined scale, 100 percent of the judgments would be concentrated on only 11 of the 120 possible orderings. This criterion is not satisfied here, and the problem becomes one of choosing the set of scale values that best fits the judgments obtained.

All alternative sets of eleven rank orders yielding a uniquely defined scale were compared to determine that one which conformed with the rank orders of the maximum number of managers. Using this criterion, one set dominated all others. The eleven orders are shown in table 4.1 along with the number of managers reporting each order. In total, they account for 55.1 percent of all judgments. By way of comparison, a scale allocating equal intervals between styles accounts for only 33.6 percent of the judgments. (Note only eight rank orders are possible using this scale.)

The concentration of orderings to such a small proportion of the total possible orders is particularly surprising when one considers that the subjects were not asked for preferences in some ideal situation but rather for estimates of relative frequency of use in highly complex roles. By rotating the styles in the fourth and fifth positions in the order (where the frequency estimates indicated that ties were common), the concentration of orders conforming to the eleven possibilities shown in table 4.1 increased to 64.4 percent.

The two extreme styles, AI and GII, were arbitrarily assigned scale values of 0 and 10, respectively. Through the use of the Goode Algorithm (see Coombs 1964), numerical assignments can be obtained for each of the three intervening methods. The ordered metric scale obtained by this procedure can be shown as follows:

AI	AII	CI	CII	GII
0	.625	5.0	8.125	10.0

The scale differs considerably from that which would occur if the values 1 through 5 were assigned to the alternatives. The distance between AI and AII is quite close; this is not surprising given the

TABLE 4.1. Frequency Distribution of Rank Orders Defining the Scale of Participation

Order					N	Percent	Ideal Point
AI	AII	CI	CII	GII	17	2.9%	0.00
AII	AI	CI	CII	GII	12	2.0	1.41
AII	CI	AI	CII	GII	10	1.7	2.66
CI	AII	AI	CII	GII	51	8.6	3.44
CI	AII	CII	AI	GII	27	4.6	4.22
CI	CII	AII	AI	GII	31	5.2	4.69
CI	CII	AII	GII	AI	18	3.0	5.16
CI	CII	GII	AII	AI	39	6.6	5.94
CII	CI	GII	AII	AI	35	5.9	7.03
CII	GII	CI	AII	AI	47	7.9	8.28
GII	CII	CI	AII	AI	39	6.6	10.00
Total					326	55.1%	

fact that, in the latter, the subordinates function only as sources of data for the leader. Similarly, CII and GII are located quite close together, with the larger distances occurring between AII and CI and between CI and CII.

Two other procedures were used to provide a crude check on the degree to which the values shown above correspond to estimates of the relative opportunities that the five decision processes provide to subordinates to influence the decisions made. A group of seventy-four students working for the master's degree in industrial administration were used as subjects. Each was familiar with the taxonomy of decision processes but totally unfamiliar with any of the empirical research reported in this or subsequent chapters. Each was provided with a single sheet of paper containing a line exactly ten inches long. At the extreme left-hand side appeared the symbol AI and the numerical value 0; at the extreme right appeared the symbol GII and the numerical value 100.

The instructions given on the sheet were as follows:

> Assume that the five decision styles (AI, AII, CI, CII and GII) vary in the amount of opportunity which they provide subordinates for participation in decision making. Also assume that AI represents zero opportunity, GII represents a value of 100 and the other three styles are located somewhere between these extremes. We would like you to locate these three intermediate styles (AII, CI and CII) on the scale drawn above in terms of your estimate of the degree to which they would provide an opportunity for subordinates to influence decisions. You should indicate your judgments in two ways: 1) by placing a dot on the line indicating where you think the

decision process should fall, clearly labeled with the symbol (AII, CI or CII) that you are referring to and 2) by indicating the scale value between 0 and 100 for each of these three intermediate processes.

The two types of judgments obtained for each process from each subject will be referred to as metric and numeric respectively. Median judgments for each decision process were obtained for judgments of each type and were used in calculations of the relative size of the distance perceived among the five decision processes. Since the distance between AI and GII was fixed, there remain only nine possible pairs for which distances can be calculated. Table 4.2 shows the relative size of the distances between these pairs shown on the ordered metric scale and reflected in the metric and numeric judgments. For comparison purposes the distances that would be exhibited on an equal interval scale partitioning the ten-point scale into four equal units are also shown.

The metric and numeric methods yield very similar results and both correspond quite closely with the intervals produced by the Coombs method. Of greatest interest are those cases in which the ordered metric scale denotes differences among intervals that would be assumed to be identical using an equal interval scale. In virtually all such instances the same differences are detected using the metric and numeric results. (There is only one exception and that is a reversal in the relative size of the CI–CII and AII–CI differences found only with the numeric measure.)

It is also interesting to note that the relatively small distance between AI and AII shown on the ordered metric scale is also ex-

TABLE 4.2. Comparison of Distances on Metric, Numeric, Ordered Metric, and Equal Interval Scales of Participation (N =74)

Interval	Equal Interval Scale	Ordered Metric Scale	Metric	Numeric
AI-AII	2.5	.625	1.25	1.50
CII-GII	2.5	1.875	2.50	2.00
CI-CII	2.5	3.125	3.00	3.50
AII-CI	2.5	4.375	3.25	3.00
AI-CI	5.0	5.000	4.50	4.50
CI-GII	5.0	5.000	5.50	5.50
AII-CII	7.5	7.500	6.25	6.50
AI-CII	7.5	8.125	7.50	8.00
AII-GII	7.5	9.375	8.75	8.50

hibited in the metric and numeric judgments. In all three cases it is the smallest distance in the entire set although the metric and numeric data imply that the distance perceived by the subjects is somewhat greater than that shown on the ordered metric scale. The only other major differences between these empirical results and the scale values previously shown stem from this difference in the location of AII.

The ordered metric scale has another property which we will capitalize on in the research to be described. Given a rank ordering that is consistent with the scale, it is possible to infer for the leader a range within which his ideal point on the scale must fall. The midpoints for this range for each of these orderings are also shown in table 4.1.

To test further the concentration of judgments in the eleven permutations shown in table 4.1 and the underlying scale values, a subset consisting of 207 managers used in a previous investigation was asked not only to rank order the methods in accordance with the frequency with which they employed them in their jobs, but also to rank order them in accordance with the frequency with which they were used by superiors. The judgments concerning one's superior should provide an independent estimate of the validity of the scale shown above and, in addition, indicate whether there are any consistent differences between managers' estimates of their own leadership style and that of the person to whom they report.

The results show that managers' superiors were typically seen as using much more autocratic styles than the managers themselves used. The three rank orders with the lowest ideal points shown in table 4.1 accounted for 23.1 percent of judgments concerning superiors' decision processes but only 8 percent of such judgments concerning managers themselves. This difference is further reflected in average ideal point scale values for the orderings that fall within the set of eleven shown in table 4.1. Descriptions of the superior yielded a mean ideal point score of 4.12 while descriptions of self by the 207 managers yielded a mean score of 5.79.

Despite differences in frequencies of occurrence of the eleven orders, the number of cases falling within them remained about the same, 54.8 percent. As was the case with judgments of one's own decision-making procedures, the scale values shown above provide the best fit to data concerning superiors' behavior.

The greater incidence of autocratic behavior on the part of one's superior seems to be a widely shared belief on the part of the managers studied. There are two possible explanations for this finding. If these perceptions are veridical, then it follows that an unbiased observer would find that leadership behavior tends to become increasingly autocratic as one moves up in the organizational hierarchy. This conclusion is inconsistent with Heller and Yukl's (1969) data showing that higher levels of management were more democratic. It seems more likely that the finding represents perceptual distortion on the part of the managers. While this study presents no direct data bearing on this point, it is possible that managers might describe themselves as more participative than they would be seen by their subordinates. If this were the case, managers' reports of the relative frequency with which they use the five methods would be biased toward the participative end of the scale. In addition, their reports of their superiors' behavior may be biased toward the autocratic end of the scale.

One should undoubtedly exercise extreme caution in making literal interpretations from the rank order data obtained in this study. The self-report data at this level of aggregation probably says more about a manager's ideal self than about his actual behavior, and his reports of his superior's behavior probably convey more about his attitude toward his superior than about his superior's actual behavior.

Neither of these considerations affects the usefulness of these data in estimating relative distances among points on the scale, and this is the principal use to which the findings of this study will be put. The scale developed in this study will be used in much of the research to be described in the rest of this book. Since support for these particular scale values is not perfect, all major findings reported in this book have been replicated against an equal interval scale.

PARTICIPATION AS A FUNCTION OF SELECTED PROBLEM ATTRIBUTES AND MANAGERS' PREFERRED STYLE: STUDIES 3 AND 4

Having established the fact that leaders do use different decision processes within a single role (Study 1), the problem becomes one of identifying the variables that influence this choice process and measuring the magnitude and direction of their effects. The reader will recall, from the presentation of the normative model in chapters 2 and 3, that the decision process it prescribed varied markedly with a set of situational variables, which were termed problem attributes. It remains to be seen if such problem attributes affect the choices which leaders do make among alternative decision processes. To what extent, if at all, are leaders' choices about sharing power with their subordinates affected by such situational variables as the importance of the quality of the decision, the existence of conflict among subordinates and so on. A principal function of Study 3 was to test a new methodology for determining the influence of situational variables on leader behavior and, at the same time, to attempt to assess the specific influence of certain of the situational variables contained in the normative model. Study 4 used the same methodology as Study 3 but extended the investigation to a larger number of situational variables.

A secondary purpose of both studies was to look at individual differences in leadership style. The normative model contains a set of rules for analyzing the problem and its context but has no role for individual differences. The prescribed decision process varied markedly in accordance with judgments of the problem attributes but was unaffected by such things as the process the leader prefers, a variable which may be expected to play some role in actual if not in prescribed behavior. In Studies 3 and 4, the leader's ideal point on the scale of participation measured by the procedures developed in Study 2 was used along with the situational variables, to determine its relative predictive value.

The subjects for Study 3 were 342 managers attending various management development programs. They represented a variety of different firms and a number of different nationalities. The data were collected by questionnaire preceded by a short lecture introducing the purposes of the research (understanding how people choose their leadership styles). The decision processes shown in table 2.1 were described and illustrations of each given. It was emphasized that no one process was best under all circumstances and that the researchers were interested in determining the situations which induce people to employ each one. Then the questionnaire was distributed and explained in detail to ensure that the managers understood the meaning of the questions.

The questionnaire began by asking each subject to choose a

problem that he had recently had to solve in his role as manager. He was cautioned that the problem selected should have three characteristics: (1) it must be a problem, not a solution, (2) it must have been within his area of freedom or discretion, and (3) it must have had effects on at least two of his subordinates. He was asked to provide a written description of that problem. After describing the problem, the manager was asked to choose from the list of decision processes shown in table 2.1 the one that came closest to describing his behavior in that situation. Next, he answered a set of six questions concerning the problem he had selected. These questions are shown below.

We are interested in characteristics of the problem which might affect your decision regarding *when* and *how* to involve your subordinates in the solution of this problem. Please circle the letter beside the phrase which best characterizes this problem:

1. The time within which a solution had to be found was . . .

   a. Less than 1 hour　　　　c. Less than 1 week
   b. Less than 1 day　　　　 d. More than 1 week

2. The quality of the solution reached was . . .

   a. Necessary　　　　　　　c. Probably beneficial
   b. Definitely beneficial to the　d. Irrelevant
      effectiveness of the solution

3. The information I possessed that was relevant to a solution of the problem was . . .

   a. Complete: I had the information necessary for reaching the optimal (best) solution to the problem.

   b. Sufficient: I had enough information to reach an adequate solution to the problem.

   c. Nearly sufficient: I had almost enough information to reach an adequate solution to the problem.

   d. Inadequate: I did not have enough information to reach an adequate solution to the problem.

4. The acceptance of the decision was . . .

   a. Necessary　　　　　　　c. Probably beneficial
   b. Definitely beneficial to the　d. Irrelevant
      effectiveness of the solution

5. Which of the following statements best describes your assessment of the degree to which your subordinates could be trusted to accept organizational goals (as opposed to personal goals related to self-interest) in their efforts to solve this problem?

   a. I was completely certain that they could be trusted.
   b. I was reasonably certain that they could be trusted.
   c. I was uncertain as to whether they could be trusted.
   d. I was reasonably certain that they could *not* be trusted.

6. In this problem the amount of disagreement or conflict to be expected among subordinates over the appropriate solution to the problem was . . .

   a. Strong   c. Weak
   b. Moderate   d. Non-existent

The subjects for Study 4 were 268 managers from a number of different firms who were also attending a series of management development programs. The data collection procedure was similar to that used in Study 3. Each manager was asked (1) to provide a written description of a problem that he had recently had to solve, (2) to select the decision process (AI, AII, CI, etc.) that he had employed in solving that problem, and (3) to answer a set of eight questions concerning that problem.

Selection of the eight questions to measure problem attributes in Study 4 was influenced by the development of the normative model (the present form of which was developed after the conclusion of Study 3) and by the results obtained in Study 3. The set of eight questions was identical to that previously shown in table 2.3 and subsequently used in the normative model. One of the questions from Study 3 concerning time constraints was eliminated since, as will be seen in the presentation of results, it produced relatively little variance and had no discernible relationship with decision process selected. Three new questions dealing with problem structure, additional information possessed by subordinates, and prior probability of acceptance of an autocratic decision were added. All questions asked were of the yes-no type, replicating the exact form and language given in table 2.3. The use of dichotomous responses was consistent with the finding from Study 3, reported later in this chapter, that no additional variance was explained by providing a larger number of response options. It has the additional desirable property of permitting a direct comparison of the behavior of managers with that of the normative model (see chapter 7).

In both studies, each manager was asked to rank order the five decision processes in accordance with the frequency with which he employed them in his job. His ideal point, which will be referred to as preferred level of participation (PLP), was then inferred in accordance with the procedure developed in Study 2. Interpretable ideal points were obtained for 305 of the 342 subjects in Study 3 and for 211 of the 268 managers in Study 4.

It should be noted that, in both studies, the data collection procedures produced a high level of involvement on the part of managers who served as subjects. Many reported that they liked the opportunity to reflect on the leadership methods they used. Their written problem descriptions ranged in length from one paragraph to two pages and covered virtually every facet of managerial decision-making. The problems shown in the previous chapter to illustrate the normative model are typical of the cases that were written and analyzed. In a subsequent session a lecture was given in which an earlier version of the normative model, incorporating either the six attributes or eight attributes used as independent variables, was introduced. Each manager was instructed in how to use his previous judgments to determine the model solution for his problem. Then the degree of agreement between the model and the managers was examined and the reasons for any differences were discussed.

Table 4.3 shows the problem attributes used in both Studies 3 and 4 and the distribution of judgments made by the managers concerning the problems that they described. From an inspection of this table a number of conclusions can be drawn about the characteristics of the problems reported by managers in each study.

In Study 3, few of the problems contained time constraints which might eliminate from consideration one or more of the methods shown in table 2.1. Less than 1 percent of the problems were described as having to be solved within one hour and the modal response to this attribute (representing 68.1 percent of the problems) was "more than one week." Time constraints may play a major role in dictating decision-making processes selected by military officers in battle conditions and leaders in timed athletic contests but do not appear to be sufficiently frequent in managerial

TABLE 4.3. Distribution of Judgments Concerning Problem Attributes: Studies 3 and 4

	Time Constraints	Quality	Leader's Information	Subordinate's Information	Structure in Problem	Importance of Acceptance	Prior Probability of Acceptance	Trust	Conflict
Study 3									
a	0.9%	35.4%	12.3%	—	—	43.4%	—	37.7%	20.8%
b	5.8	49.4	33.1	—	—	46.9	—	43.5	42.4
c	25.2	13.5	29.3	—	—	7.9	—	15.9	22.5
d	68.1	1.7	25.2	—	—	1.8	—	2.9	14.3
Study 4									
Yes	—	88.7	53.8	76.3%	69.9%	90.6	36.8%	66.2	43.5
No	—	11.3	46.2	23.7	30.1	9.4	63.2	33.8	56.5

decision-making to play a significant role in the choice of one process over another. At least that is true for the problems reported here.

The managers judged that most problems had a quality requirement. In Study 3, they judged the quality of the solution as necessary or definitely beneficial to its effectiveness 84.8 percent of the time; whereas, in Study 4, managers responded yes to the question "Given acceptance, does it make a difference which course of action is adopted?" 88.7 percent of the time.

Acceptance of the decision by subordinates is also seen by the managers as important to the effectiveness of a large proportion of the problems reported. It was judged to be necessary or definitely beneficial an overwhelming 90.3 percent of the time by managers in Study 3 and was seen as critical to the successful implementation of the solution in 90.6 percent of the problems described by managers in Study 4. Thus, a typical problem faced by these managers possessed what Maier (1963) has described as both quality and acceptance requirements.

There was considerable variance in other properties of the problems reported. In Study 3, managers judged that they lacked some of the necessary information to achieve an adequate solution to the problem in 54.5 percent of the problems, a figure which can be compared to a 46.2 percent negative response to the question concerning this attribute (see table 2.3) for those in Study 4. Conflict also showed large variance in both studies. In Study 3 it was judged to be: strong 20.8 percent; moderate 42.4 percent; weak 22.5 percent and nonexistent 14.3 percent. Responses to the question concerning conflict from the managers in Study 4 were distributed quite evenly with 43.5 percent positive and 56.5 percent negative.

Putting the results of both studies together, one can get a picture of a typical problem as viewed by one of these managers. The quality of the decision was important and the problem was structured. The manager may or may not have had enough technical information to make a rational decision although his subordinates had additional information of value. Acceptance of the decision by his subordinates was critical to getting the decision implemented, and it was uncertain that his autocratic decision would be accepted. Time constraints imposed no limitation on the methods he could use. His subordinates could be trusted to base solutions on organizational considerations, and they might or might not have been in initial disagreement over which solution to adopt. The reader may recognize this pattern as defining a type 6 problem (either 6*a* or 6*b*) in the taxonomy of problem types used in the normative model.

The manager's judgments of the status of the problem he had selected on each of the attributes and his ideal style computed from his ranking of the frequency with which he employed the five methods constituted the independent variables in both Studies 3 and 4. The dependent variable was the decision process he reported using on the problem he described and analyzed.

TABLE 4.4. Distribution of Decision Styles in Studies 3 and 4

	AI	AII	CI	CII	GII
Study 3	5.9%	4.7%	34.4%	25.3%	29.7%
Study 4	10.8	9.3	22.0	29.5	28.4

The distribution of methods that the managers employed in the problems they selected are shown in table 4.4. Using the scale values for the five methods developed in Study 2, the distribution for Study 3 has a mean of 6.7 and a standard deviation of 3.0 while the distribution for Study 4 has a mean of 6.3 and a standard deviation of 3.5. Compared with the managers in Study 3, those in Study 4 reported a lower mean and higher variance in the level of participation. An X^2 test on the difference between the two samples showed a value of 18.5 ($p < .01$) indicating that the groups studied are different. An inspection of demographic characteristics of the two groups revealed several distinguishing characteristics of the samples that could account for the differences in behavior. For example, a larger proportion of the managers in Study 4 were of foreign (non-USA) nationality (24 percent compared with 15 percent in Study 3) and they were working in a larger number of different countries (thirteen as compared with eight).

VALIDITY OF MANAGERS' REPORTS
OF THEIR DECISION PROCESSES

It is important to examine the use of the manager's *report* of the decision process that he employed in a particular situation as an indication of his actual behavior. It is possible that these reports would be biased. For example, managers might report using *more* participative methods than they actually employed.

It was originally planned to get the subordinates' reports of their superiors' behavior on the same problem, but the procedural difficulties turned out to be immense. To obtain such data, it would have been necessary to locate one or more subordinates who reported to the manager, communicate the specific event or problem to them in such a way that they could recognize it, instruct them in the taxonomy of decision processes and obtain their report of their superior's behavior. For obvious reasons mailed questionnaires could not be used, and the costs of interviews with subordinates, because of their geographical dispersion, were definitely prohibitive.

There are, however, other studies which are of assistance in investigating this question. Heller's data (Heller 1971) shed some light on the consistency between managers' reports of their own behavior and subordinates' reports of their superior's behavior. He compared the methods which managers said they used on twelve classes of decisions with the reports of their immediate subordinates. He found a consistent discrepancy between the two sets of reports but in a direction opposite to that referred to above. Subordinates reported that their superiors made greater use of delegation and joint decision-making processes and less use of autocratic and consultative processes than did the managers themselves. The discrepancies in reports varied with the type of decision. They were greatest in magnitude for decisions affecting one of the subordinate's own employees but were nonsignificant for decisions affecting the entire department, such as the group problems studied here. Heller attributes his findings to a perceptual distortion on the part of subordinates stemming from wish fulfillment. They saw their superiors as providing them with a greater measure of control over the internal operation of their unit because that was the state of affairs that they wished to exist.

The reader may recall that earlier in this chapter evidence was presented to the effect that managers, asked to rank order decision processes in accordance with the frequency with which they used them in carrying out their jobs, described themselves as more participative than they described their superiors. The most plausible interpretations appeared to be either a tendency for managers to overestimate the participativeness of the methods they used or to underestimate the participativeness of their superiors.

How can this interpretation be reconciled with that of Heller? Both interpretations involve the element of bias but in opposite directions. Conceivably, the difference relates to Heller's focus on individual problems and the concentration of this study on group problems. It is possible that subordinates are likely to overestimate the extent to which their superior delegates authority to them and enters into joint decision making. To believe that one's superior controlled decisions affecting one's own employees is inconsistent with one's own image of oneself as a manager. But on matters affecting the entire department managed by the superior, one's own self image is not at stake and there would be little if any consistent bias in subordinates' reports. This mechanism would account for the difference between superiors' and subordinates' judgments on their "employee" and "subordinate" decisions but not on departmental decisions.

It is also possible that managers' reports of their own behavior would be biased in the direction of what they conceive to be an ideal leadership style. What the ideal represents may vary somewhat from subculture to subculture, but the findings of Haire, Ghiselli, and Porter (1966) point to a widespread belief in the efficacy of participative management, which we might expect would bias one's descriptions of one's own behavior in the direction of reporting more participative practices than one actually exhibits.

Let us now make the plausible assumption that the amount of both kinds of biases is a function of the level of aggregation and complexity of the inferences required. If a manager has to judge the degree to which he *typically* employs participative methods, his estimates are likely to contain a greater degree of bias than his report of the method he used in a particular decision. Thus, we would expect substantially greater bias in a direction of overestimating democratic methods in managers' judgments of the relative frequency with which they employ different methods in their jobs —the basis of the ideal point measurement—than in their reports of the method they used in solving a particular problem.

What implications does this analysis have for the confidence that can be placed in managers' reports of the methods they used? Heller's finding of no significant difference between superiors' and subordinates' reports of the decision process used by the superior on departmental decisions is perhaps most directly relevant. While biases in managers' reports of their own behavior are a likely part of the explanation of the mean difference in ideal points on the scale of participation described earlier in this chapter, the greater specificity of the reports used as the dependent variables in this study should operate in such a way as to hold that bias to a minimum. Even if some bias remains, it presents no problem to our investigation of the situational correlates of participation unless it is both variable across persons and correlated with the independent variables in the study.

RELATIONSHIPS BETWEEN SITUATIONAL VARIABLES AND DECISION PROCESSES

Let us return to the central question to which Studies 3 and 4 were addressed; that is, the effects of situational variables on the decision process used. Tables 4.5 and 4.6 contain the simple correlations among the situational variables and between each of them and the level of participation for Studies 3 and 4, respectively. In Study 3, only two of the situational variables, leader's information and trust, are significantly correlated with participation at the .05 level or better (two-tailed test). No such relationship was found between time, quality, or acceptance and participation. In Study 4, all but one of the eight situational variables are significantly correlated with participation at the .05 level or better. Four variables, quality, subordinate's information, importance of acceptance, and trust, are positively correlated with participation; three

TABLE 4.5. Correlations Among Managers' Judgments of Problem Attributes and Between These Judgments and the Level of Participation: Study 3 (N = 342)

	Time	Quality	Leader's Information	Acceptance	Trust-worthiness	Conflict
− Time	1.00					
A * Quality	.12	1.00				
B Leader's information	−.07	.03	1.00			
E Acceptance	.07	.38	.00	1.00		
G Trustworthiness	.01	.15	.11	−.04	1.00	
H Conflict	−.02	.00	−.14	.11	−.30	1.00
Y Participation	−.02	−.02	−.34	.02	.18	−.01

*These symbols refer to attributes used in the normative model (see table 2.3).

TABLE 4.6. Correlations Among Managers' Judgments of Problem Attributes and Between These Judgments and the Level of Participation: Study 4 (N = 268)

	A	B	C	D	E	F	G	H
A* Quality	1.00							
B Leader's information	−.12	1.00						
C Subordinates' information	.14	−.41	1.00					
D Structure	−.10	.08	.14	1.00				
E Acceptance	.17	−.04	.03	−.07	1.00			
F Prior probability	−.20	.11	−.07	.11	−.13	1.00		
G Trustworthiness	.02	.01	.18	.08	.07	.12	1.00	
H Conflict	.12	.03	.07	.09	.06	−.16	−.12	1.00
Y Participation	.12	−.36	.43	−.15	.24	−.23	.21	.08

*These symbols refer to attributes used in the normative model (see table 2.3).

variables, leader's information, structure, and prior probability of acceptance, are negatively correlated with participation; and one variable, conflict, is uncorrelated with participation.

The situational variable accounting for the greatest proportion of the variance in Study 3 is the leader's information (r = - .34). On those problems for which the managers stated that they had complete or sufficient information to solve the problem by themselves, the managers were less participative than when they did not have sufficient information. Apparently, for many of the managers, involving their subordinates in decision-making was a means of enlarging the information base to protect the rational quality of the decision.

The trustworthiness of subordinates was the other situational variable found to influence the subordinates' level of participation in Study 3 (r = .18). The managers, as might be expected, were more participative when they trusted their subordinates than when they did not. It appears that a manager reduced the level of participation and, hence, the amount of influence that his subordinates could have exerted when he believed that their influence was likely to be biased in favor of their own personal goals and against the interests of the organization.

In Study 4, the two attributes that pertain to the amount of information possessed by the manager and his subordinates are most highly predictive of the decision process used. When the manager has sufficient information to make the decision by himself, more autocratic decision processes are used than when he lacks that information ($r = -.36$). Similarly, additional information on the part of subordinates is associated with more participative processes ($r = .43$). These relationships corroborate Heller's finding (1971) that the degree to which a manager perceives a skill differential between himself and his subordinates is negatively correlated with the extent to which he shares power with them. The correlations between participation and importance of acceptance and prior probability of acceptance of an autocratic decision are smaller ($r = .24$ and $r = -.23$) implying that considerations of acceptance play a smaller role than informational considerations. Of the three remaining attributes that correlate significantly with participation, there was a slight tendency for more participative decision processes to be used when the quality of the decision was important ($r = .12$), when the problem was unstructured ($r = -.15$) and when subordinates could be trusted ($r = .21$).

It should be noted that the directions of the above relationships are consistent with the roles of these attributes in the normative model presented in chapter 3. The results might be interpreted as following from managers' attempts to protect the quality and acceptance of decisions in ways that are similar, at least in part, to the behavior prescribed by the normative model presented earlier. However, as will be seen in chapter 7, the normative model does not constitute a good descriptive model, its axioms being frequently violated.

In neither study is there any evidence of a main effect of conflict among subordinates. In Study 4, quality and acceptance were found to be positively correlated with participation while in Study 3, there was apparently no evidence of any such relationships. This difference may in part be attributable to the different procedures used in each study; that is, in Study 4 the variables were dichotomous while in Study 3 they were polychotomous. To investigate this possibility, the scores on each of the attributes measured in Study 3 were dichotomized in such a way as to maximize the variance in the dichotomized variable. On correlating these new scores with level of participation, it was found that acceptance was then positively correlated with participation ($r = .13$). No such relationship was found between quality and participation ($r = .04$). The findings provide some additional support for the existence of an acceptance main effect. However, any claim for the existence of a quality main effect must remain tentative.

Caution should be exercised against drawing causal inferences from the correlations reported in tables 4.5 and 4.6. Other interpretations are too numerous to be cited here but include possible correlations among the attributes themselves. The correlations between a given attribute and participation may be markedly altered when other attributes are held constant. It is apparent from both tables that the judgments of the problem attributes cannot be treated as statistically independent. The number of statistically significant correlations greatly exceeds what would be expected under the null hypothesis. Thus, in table 4.6, twelve of twenty-eight correlations among independent variables are significant at the .05 level or better compared with an expected number under the null hypothesis of 1.4.

The nature of these significant relationships among attributes is worth noting. When a manager (in Study 4) judged the problem as possessing a quality requirement, he was likely to have reported that he did not have the necessary information ($r = -.12$), that his subordinates had additional relevant information ($r = .14$), that the execution of the decision would have required their acceptance ($r = .17$), but that his autocratic decision would not have been accepted ($r = -.20$), and that conflict among his subordinates was likely ($r = .12$). If the leader reported that he lacked the necessary information to make a high quality decision, he was more likely to have perceived his subordinates as having had relevant additional information ($r = -.41$). Subordinate's information is positively correlated with both structure ($r = .14$) and trustworthiness ($r = .18$). Prior probability of selling an autocratic decision to subordinates was negatively related to the information possessed by subordinates ($r = -.13$) and to the importance of acceptance ($r = -.13$), while it was positively correlated with trust ($r = .12$) and negatively correlated with conflict ($r = -.16$). Finally, conflict was less likely to be perceived among subordinates if they were also perceived as trustworthy ($r = -.12$).

All of these attribute intercorrelations can be plausibly interpreted as relationships which might exist within problems rather than confusion on the part of the subjects. Indeed, there is no evidence that "yes" responses to the eight questions tended to go together such as might be expected from research on the acquiescence response set (Bass 1955, Messick and Jackson 1957). The distribution of the twenty-eight correlations among problem attributes in table 4.6 is approximately normal with a mean of .01 and a median of .04. However, the attribute intercorrelations are large enough to make causal interpretations of the correlation data potentially misleading, as will be seen in the following analysis.

The next step is to construct a model incorporating and integrating the above findings. To do this, a linear function of the problem attributes and their first order interactions was fitted to the data from Studies 3 and 4. Terms were retained in the model if, and only if, they made a significant marginal contribution to the proportion of the variance in level of participation explained.

The empirical model derived from Study 3 can be written

$$(4.1) \qquad Y = 6.5 - 1.0X_b + 0.8X_g + \epsilon,$$

where Y is level of participation and X_b and X_g refer to the manager's ratings of the amount of information he possessed and the degree to which his subordinates could be trusted respectively. (Note that $X_b = 4$ if the manager had complete information, and $X_b = 1$ if he had inadequate information. Similarly, $X_g = 4$ if the subordinates could have been completely trusted, and $X_g = 1$ if the manager was certain he could not have trusted them.)

The model predicts, for example, that on problems for which the manager had complete information and was certain he could not have trusted his subordinates, his level of participation would have been 3.3 units of participation or a style between AII and CI. However, on problems for which the converse held, his level of participation would have been 8.7 units or between CII and GII.

The values of t for the coefficients of leader's information and subordinates' trustworthiness are 5.52 and 4.30, respectively, indicating that both coefficients are significantly different from zero at the .05 level or better (two-tailed tests). The two variables, leader's information and subordinates' trustworthiness, together account for 16.4 percent of the variance or a multiple correlation coefficient of .41. It appears that both manager's information and subordinates' trustworthiness independently influenced the level of participation on the problems selected for Study 3.

A similar procedure was used to derive an empirical mcdel for Study 4. The resultant model can be written

$$(4.2) \quad Y = 3.9 - 1.5X_b + 2.5X_c - 1.2X_d + 1.9X_e - 1.2X_f + 1.4X_g + \epsilon,$$

where Y is level of participation and X_b, X_c, X_d, X_e, X_f, and X_g refer to ratings of the attributes of leader's information, subordinates' information, problem structure, acceptance, prior probability of acceptance for an autocratic decision, and subordinates' trustworthiness, respectively. For example, equation 4.2 predicts that managers are most participative on problems for which they have insufficient information, their subordinates have additional relevant information, the problem is unstructured, the acceptance of the solution is critical for its effective implementation, the prior probability of this acceptance existing for an autocratic decision is low, and the subordinates can be trusted. The predicted level of participation on such a problem is 9.7 or close to GII. From chapter 3, the reader may recognize the above as a type 12 problem for which the feasible set is GII.

In contrast to the behavior predicted for the problem considered above, equation 4.2 predicts that managers are most autocratic when they have sufficient information to make a decision, their subordinates have no additional relevant information, the problem is well structured, acceptance is irrelevant but likely to exist for an autocratic decision, and their subordinates cannot be trusted. Such a description fits some type 4 problems, for which the feasible set is AI, AII, CI, and CII, and for which the normative model prescribes AI. The predicted level of participation for such a problem is 0.0 or AI. A detailed comparison between actual and prescribed behavior is delayed until chapter 7.

The inclusion of the three attributes of subordinates' information, problem structure, and prior probability of acceptance in Study 4 increased the predictive power of the empirical model. Equation 4.2 accounts for 33.4 percent of the total variance in the level of participation in Study 4 or a multiple correlation coefficient of .58, while equation 4.1 accounts for only 16.4 percent of the variance in Study 3 or a multiple correlation coefficient of .41.[2]

The t statistics for the coefficients for all of the attributes con-

2. The amount of variance explained in Study 3 is not influenced by the fact that the judgments are polychotomous rather than dichotomous as in Study 4. When the attributes used in Study 3 are dichotomized, the multiple correlation coefficient is .42.

tained in equation 4.2 are significant at the .05 level or better (two-tailed test). The values of t are as follows: leader's information, $t = 3.81$, subordinates' information, $t = 5.32$, problem structure, $t = 2.94$, importance of acceptance, $t = 3.14$, prior probability of acceptance, $t = 3.02$, and subordinates' trustworthiness, $t = 3.46$. The fact that the importance of the quality of the decision does not appear in equation 4.2 even though it is significantly correlated with participation (table 4.6) merely indicates that it cannot, at the margin, increase the proportion of the variance explained in Study 4.

In all the preceding analysis, no account has been taken of individual differences. In both studies the manager was asked to rank order the frequency with which he used each of the five methods. This data was used to compute his preferred level of participation (PLP), in accordance with the procedure outlined in Study 2. This will be the only individual difference variable considered in this chapter. A more complete discussion of individual difference variables can be found in chapter 6.

In both Studies 3 and 4, PLP is positively correlated with the level of participation. The simple correlation coefficients are .45 and .55, respectively; managers with more participative PLP values reported using more participative procedures on the problems they selected than did those with more autocratic values. Expanding equations 4.1 and 4.2 to include PLP as an independent variable gives

(4.3) $Y = 2.9 - 0.8X_b + 0.7X_g + 0.4X_k + \epsilon,$

and

(4.4) $Y = 1.9 - 1.0X_b + 2.1X_c - 1.0X_d + 1.1X_e - 0.9X_f$
$$+ 0.8X_g + 0.5X_k + \epsilon,$$

where X_k is the manager's preferred level of participation (PLP) score.

Equations 4.3 and 4.4 account for 29.7 percent and 45.6 percent of the total variance in participation or multiple correlation coefficients of .54 and .67 for Studies 3 and 4, respectively. If PLP and the status of the problem attributes had been independent, the inclusion of PLP in equations 4.1 and 4.2 would have accounted for an additional 20.2 percent and 30.2 percent of the variance, respectively. The fact that the incremental change in the explained variance in the two studies is only 13.3 percent and 12.2 percent is indicative of significant relationships between PLP and at least some of the problem attributes. Furthermore, a comparison of the coefficients for attributes in equations 4.2 and 4.4 shows that all have declined. The actual correlations between PLP and judgments of problem attributes are shown in table 4.7.

TABLE 4.7. Correlations Between Manager's Preferred Style, Participation, and Problem Attributes: Studies 3 and 4

	Study 3 (N = 305)	Study 4 (N = 211)
Time	.12*	—
Quality	−.02	.07
Manager's information	−.23*	−.19*
Subordinates' information	—	.24*
Structure	—	−.04
Acceptance	.16*	.20*
Prior probability of acceptance	—	−.14*
Trustworthiness	−.01	.22*
Conflict	.13*	.14*
Participation	.45*	.55*

*Significantly different from zero at .05 level or better.

In Study 4, six of the correlations between problem attributes and PLP are significant at the .05 level. The more participative a manager's preferred level of participation, the more likely he was to describe the problem which he had reported thus: (1) he did not have sufficient information, (2) his subordinates did have significant additional information, (3) acceptance on the part of his subordinates was critical to the effective implementation of the decision, (4) his subordinates were *not* certain to accept his autocratic decision, (5) his subordinates could be trusted to base their efforts to solve the problem on organizational considerations, and (6) his subordinates were likely, at least initially, to be in disagreement concerning the solution. The results for Study 3 are consistent except for the relation between PLP and trust.

There are at least three plausible interpretations of these findings. The first is that they indicate long-term effects of leadership style on the feasibility of participative decision-making. The reader may recall that in chapter 3 a distinction was made between short-term and long-term models of leadership behavior. It was argued that participative methods while consuming more man-hours (a short-term consideration) might alter the values of situational attributes (increasing the amount of information that subordinates would have to bring to bear on future decisions and the extent to which they were committed to attaining the goals of the organization).

Following this line of reasoning, the correlations shown in table 4.7 may be interpreted as follows. The leader's use of a participative style makes it less likely that he will need to have all of the information for a rational decision, but it increases the likelihood that such information or expertise will be contained somewhere in his organizational unit. The positive correlation between PLP and trust is consistent with the view (Patchen 1964) that participation increases the degree to which an individual will identify with the organization. It could also be argued that use of a participative style makes it less necessary to adopt an external control system and more likely that members of the group will be involved in the execution of decisions made. Consequently, acceptance of decisions by subordinates becomes more critical under a system which, in the past, has emphasized participative processes. Also the negative correlations between PLP and prior probability of acceptance may indicate that subordinates, once accustomed to participative decision-making, are more likely to resist and oppose autocratic methods. Such an interpretation would be consistent with experimental evidence (Mulder 1959; Mulder, Veen, Hartsuiker, and Westerduin 1970) that the exercise of power results in a stronger desire for power. Finally, the positive correlation between conflict and PLP may arise from the fact that the subordinates of highly participative managers are more likely to express conflict than to repress it.

The results reported in table 4.7 are consistent with the view that leader behavior has long-term effects on the problem-solving system, effects that alter the nature of the demands made upon the leader. But this is by no means the only interpretation. The data are correlations and, inevitably, subject to more than one interpretation.

A second plausible interpretation rests on the fact that the information reported by the managers consists of their judgments rather than externally verified facts. Results presented in chapter 3 indicated that these judgments had substantial subjective components, particularly among managers who were untrained in making them. It is conceivable that the correlations reported in table 4.7 are indicative of different inference processes among managers with different PLP values. If a group of managers with different preferred levels of participation were confronted with exactly the same administrative problem to handle, those with participative styles would be more likely to conclude that they did not have the necessary information, that acceptance on the part of subordinates was critical, and so on. The cues could be identical, but the inferences drawn from these cues could be very different, with the particular inferences for a manager being directly related to his implicit "theory" of leadership.

The third plausible explanation of the correlations reported in table 4.6 stems from the fact that each manager could choose the problem on which he reported. It is presumed that each manager had a wide range of problems from which he could choose, and there is no reason to believe that the basis for the choice was identical in all managers. Conceivably, managers tended to choose problems for which their own preferred decision-making process would be appropriate. Thus, those with a participative PLP would tend to choose problems in which they lacked the necessary information but their subordinates possessed it and so on.

It is impossible to select among these three explanations on the basis of the data reported here. Additional research is needed to identify their relative value in accounting for the entire set of results.

SUMMARY

This chapter differs from the three previous ones in its focus on the descriptive as opposed to normative analysis of decision processes employed in organizations. The central thesis is that the aspects of leadership style, which are reflected in leaders' choices about the amount of opportunity provided their subordinates to participate in making decisions, vary not only among leaders, as has been suggested in existing literature, but also within a single leader. Accordingly, it should be possible to identify the sources of that variance and to construct a descriptive model of participation in decision-making.

A set of four studies relevant to this goal was reported in this chapter. The first study was concerned with testing the central assumption on which the entire set of studies was founded, namely, that leaders do employ more than one decision-making process in carrying out their formal leadership roles. The results are consistent with the view that an overwhelming proportion of managers employ all five leadership methods in the normative model. In the second study, evidence was provided to support the assumption that these five decision processes could be assigned positions on a unidimensional scale of participation. From analysis of these data, a metric was developed that permitted the location of these five methods along a scale of participation. The empirically determined intervals between pairs of decision processes resulted in a relatively small distance between AI and AII, a large distance to CI, a moderately large distance to CII, and a smaller distance to GII.

In the remaining two studies, a new method was utilized for identifying both situational and individual difference correlates of leadership style. Managers were asked to identify and describe a recent problem which they had to solve in carrying out their leadership roles. They reported the decision process that they had used and answered a set of questions designed to measure the properties of the problem and its immediate context. Responses to these questions constituted the situational variables, which, it should be noted, corresponded to perceived rather than objectively measured situational properties. As was reported in the previous chapter, these judgments or perceptions are imperfectly related to actual properties and are themselves influenced by individual differences.

All situational variables except conflict correlated significantly with participation in a direction that was consistent with their role in the normative model. Identification of effects of single situational variables on participation was impaired by limited variance on several variables and significant intercorrelations among many pairs of variables. In spite of these problems, multiple regression analysis provided evidence that variables pertaining to the location of information relevant to the rational properties of the decision (attributes B and C in the normative model), the extent to which the problem was structured (attribute D), the manager's trust in his subordinates (attribute G), the importance of acceptance of the decision by subordinates (attribute E), and the prior probability that an autocratic decision would be accepted (attribute F) all played a significant role in influencing the amount of opportunity provided subordinates to participate in decision-making. The direction of each attribute's influence was similar to that found in the normative model. However, there was at least one important difference between the descriptive models as represented in equations 4.1 and 4.2 and the normative model shown in the previous chapter. While the normative model contains many interactions among problem attributes (effects of specific attributes depend on the level of other attributes), there was no evidence of any such interactions in the data from Studies 3 and 4.

An individual difference variable, which has been termed preferred level of participation (PLP), was correlated not only with the decision process employed by the manager on the specific problem on which he reported but also with the judgments he made of the problem attributes. Three plausible explanations of these relationships were discussed.

The investigations reported in this chapter provide but a first step toward the development of a descriptive model of leadership style. They have produced evidence that there is intrapersonal variance in leadership style and have identified some of the major situational factors affecting leaders' choices of decision processes. However, limited variance on certain of the situational variables and intercorrelations among these variables have restricted the ability to measure these effects with a great deal of precision. Furthermore, the fact that only one observation or problem was obtained for each manager makes it impossible to identify interactions between individual difference and situational variables. In chapter 5, to which we now turn, we approach the same problem—the identification and measurement of joint effects of situational variables and individual differences on leader behavior—with another method, which holds promise of overcoming these methodological deficiencies.

Leadership Behavior
on Standardized Cases

The methods employed in the previous chapter constitute a rather crude first attempt to understand the role of situational variables, individual differences, and the interactions among them in leaders' decisions about sharing power with their subordinates. We have already discussed some of the weaknesses inherent in the methodology employed, most notably the possible confounding of individual differences and situational effects because subjects selected and scored their own problems. Furthermore, since only one problem was obtained from each person, it is difficult or impossible to identify interactions between person and situational variables, or idiosyncratic rules for deciding when and to what extent to encourage participation.

To remedy these deficiencies, another technique was developed to attain the same outcome—a descriptive model of this aspect of leadership behavior. The technique involves the development of a standardized set of administrative problems or cases, each of which depicts a leader faced with some organizational requirement for action or decision-making. People who had previously been exposed to the definitions of the five decision processes (AI, AII, CI, CII, and GII) were asked to place themselves in the role of the leader in each situation and to indicate which decision process they would employ.

This method shows promise of overcoming the limitations noted in connection with the research described in chapter 4. All subjects could be given the same set of problems, thus eliminating spurious effects stemming from the influence of uncontrolled variables on problem selection. In addition, the objective definition of stimulus materials could make it possible to attribute be-

havioral effects to objectively defined problem attributes, eliminating the possible contaminating influence of individual differences in judgments about such attributes.

This technique is useful in that one can design sets of cases that
vary in particular problem attributes. Thus if one is interested in
the effects of conflict among subordinates on leadership style, the
problems selected should vary in terms of the amount of such conflict depicted. Furthermore, if more than one situational variable
is to be studied, for example, conflict among subordinates and the
degree to which the leader possesses the technical information
needed to solve the problem, the cases should ideally be constructed such that the variation in one variable is independent of
the variation in each other variable.

EXPERIMENTAL DESIGN

The problem of construction of a set of cases is similar to that
of a multifactorial experimental design in which each case corresponds to a particular combination of the situational attributes
and the set of cases includes all logically possible combinations of
these attributes. In this manner, a complete experiment could be
performed on a single subject. For each subject, the main effects
of each of the situational variables on the behavior of the subject
could be identified. The role of individual differences and interactions between individual difference and situational variables
could be studied by comparing the experimental results for different subjects.

The effects of any set of situational variables can be examined in
this manner, given only that they be operational, so that administrative problems could be selected or designed to conform unambiguously to them. In this investigation, the variables selected for
examination were seven of the eight investigated in the previous
chapter and used in the construction of the normative model. For
convenience, they are listed here again:

A. The importance of the quality of the decision

B. The extent to which the leader possesses sufficient informa-
tion/expertise to make a high quality decision by himself

D. The extent to which the problem is structured

E. The extent to which acceptance or commitment on the part

of subordinates is critical to the effective implementation of the decision

F. The prior probability that the leader's autocratic decision will receive acceptance by his subordinates

G. The extent to which subordinates are motivated to attain the organizational goals as represented in the objectives explicit in the statement of the problem

H. The extent to which subordinates are likely to be in disagreement over preferred solutions

The notation used in this chapter is similar to that employed in the previous chapter. The dummy variables $X_a, \ldots, X_h$ refer to the seven attributes listed above, and take the value 1 when the attribute is present and 0 when it is absent. Thus, $X_a = 0$, $X_e = 1$, $X_f = 0$ and $X_h = 0$ signifies a case in which the quality of the decision was irrelevant, acceptance was critical, the prior probability that the leader's decision would be accepted was low, and conflict among subordinates was absent. From chapter 3, the reader will recognize this as a type 3 problem for which the feasible set is GII.

If each of these seven dichotomous attributes were varied independently of every other variable, 2^7 or 128 unique combinations of attribute characteristics could be generated. This number of cases proved much too large for use with a single subject. Preliminary investigation revealed that it took about five minutes for a subject to read a typical case and reach a decision as to how he would act. Extrapolating from this figure, a set of 128 cases would require almost eleven hours of time from a single person! Clearly, some method had to be found to reduce the number of cases to more manageable proportions.

Fortunately, there were a number of fairly obvious ways to reduce the number of cases by varying certain problem attributes only under particular values of other problem attributes. The applications of this practice of "nesting" were dictated largely by interrelationships among attributes that were either logically necessary or empirically demonstrated. Three principles convey the nesting procedures used.

Principle 1. Leader's information, problem structure, and trust in subordinates are varied only when there is a quality requirement to the problem.

By definition, when there is no quality requirement to a problem, the leader should be indifferent among all possible solutions that satisfy the constraints. On such problems certain of the problems attributes become meaningless and are incapable of variation. It is meaningless to ask whether the leader has the relevant information, since no information is required, and meaningless to ask whether subordinates can be trusted or whether the problem is structured. This principle is not a matter of convenience but rather a necessity stemming from logical relationships among problem attributes.

Principle 2: Problem structure is varied only when the leader does not have sufficient information to make a high quality decision.

If a leader possesses all the necessary information to make a high quality decision, the problem is considered to be structured. Under such circumstances, it is assumed that the leader knows the alternatives, the criteria by which they should be evaluated, and the approximate degree to which the alternatives conform to the criteria. These conditions comprise the definition of problem structure. To demonstrate this relationship between structure and information, consider the question used to measure the structure variable, "Do I know exactly what information is needed, who possesses it and how to collect it?" It would be meaningless to ask this question when the leader already possessed the needed information.

Principle 3: The prior probability of acceptance of an autocratic solution is varied only when acceptance of the decision by subordinates is critical for effective implementation of the solution.

The case for this instance of nesting rests not on necessary relationships among attributes stemming from their definition, but on normative and empirical grounds. Normatively, if it is truly irrelevant whether subordinates accept the decision, then an attribute that bears on the conditions that will generate that acceptance, such as prior probability, should have no bearing on the decision process used. Empirically, a negative correlation between these two attributes was reported in chapter 4 for self-selected problems, and a similar negative correlation has been observed between judgments for standardized problems.

These three principles reduced the number of problems required to forty-two. This number was reduced further to thirty by 50 percent sampling of the cells involving high and low problem structure. The cells chosen to represent structured and unstructured problems were balanced with respect to acceptance, prior probability, trustworthiness, and conflict. As a consequence of this rule, some higher-order interactions are confounded, but the study was made more tractable. The balancing minimizes the number of interactions that are confounded, while retaining the desirable property that certain main effects are orthogonal.

The final specification for the case studies and the experimental design are shown in figure 5.1. The two rows of numbers at the bottom of the figure are the problem type and problem order. The latter refers to the order in which the cases were administered to the subjects. This order was constant across subjects and was initially derived by randomly numbering the cases in the problem set from one to thirty. A blank indicates that the cell was excluded by the sampling procedure under which only 50 percent of the cases involving high and low structure were selected. The other row of numbers refers to the classification of the problem types presented in chapter 3.

DEVELOPING AND TESTING CASE MATERIALS

Administrative problems closely corresponding to each of the combinations of attributes indicated in figure 5.1 were selected from the written problem descriptions obtained from managers in the investigations described in the previous chapter. In most instances it was necessary to rewrite the original problem description, sometimes extensively, both to protect the identity of the respondent and his firm and to achieve the properties of the designated cell in the experimental design. The case studies selected span a wide range of managerial problems including production scheduling, research and development, quality control, portfolio management, and personnel allocation.[1]

To arrive at a final set of thirty cases, approximately eighty were selected from the over six hundred obtained in the previous re-

1. For examples of the type of cases used the reader is referred to chapter 3, pp. 41 to 44.

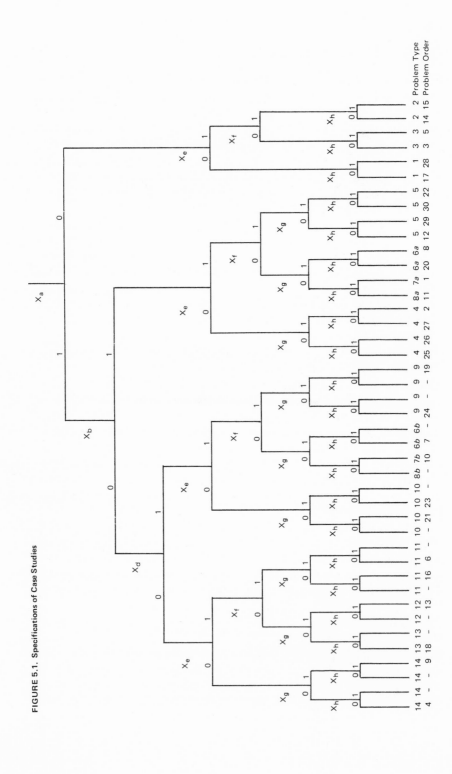

FIGURE 5.1. Specifications of Case Studies

search. Each case was rewritten by one of the authors to conform to a particular cell in the design. Care was taken to keep the cases authentic and concrete. It was then submitted to the other author and two trained observers who scored it on the seven attributes without knowledge of the intended classification. If all four raters coded the problem in the same manner, it was deemed acceptable and retained for possible inclusion in the final set. If there was disagreement, the case was rewritten. This iterative process was repeated until unanimous agreement was reached.

To determine if the authors' perceptions of the situations conform with those of actual or potential managers, a set of forty-two "acceptable" cases was given to forty middle-level managers and eighteen graduate students in administration, each of whom was asked to read each case and answer a set of seven yes-no questions concerning the presence or absence of each attribute used in the classification system. A criterion of 75 percent agreement with the authors' scoring on each attribute was established as the minimum level for retention in the acceptable category. Those cases not reaching this standard were revised further to eliminate all ambiguities.

From these forty-two problems, thirty were selected to conform with the experimental design described in figure 5.1. These were then given to nineteen management science students to be coded. In chapter 3 we presented the aggregate results for this group in connection with an examination of subjective factors in problem coding. Here we were interested in the accuracy of their coding by problem to ascertain the degree to which the experimental design had been achieved.

Each student made a total of 180 judgments. Of these only 170 were required to establish the correspondence between the problem set and the experimental design. The remaining 10 judgments, concerning the prior probability of acceptance of an autocratic decision that lacked an acceptance requirement, were obtained in order to ascertain the empirical basis for principle 3.

Table 5.1 reports the proportion of correct judgments for each of the thirty problems. Of the 170 judgments, only 18 did not meet the 75 percent criterion. All attributes appear to have been coded accurately with the exception of structure. While 81 percent of the total judgments of this attribute are in accordance with the intended specifications, 5 of the 18 cases failing to meet the criterion involve judgments of this attribute. All 5 of these cases

TABLE 5.1. Agreement of Students' Codings with Problem Specifications

Problem	X_a	X_b	X_d	X_e	X_f	X_g	X_h
1	100.0%	100.0%	–	94.7%	89.5%	94.7%	89.5%
2	84.2	100.0	–	73.7*	[73.7]	94.7	84.2
3	89.5	–	–	94.7	100.0	–	89.5
4	94.7	100.0	63.2%*	68.4*	[84.2]	94.7	94.7
5	94.7	–	–	84.2	89.5	–	94.7
6	84.2	100.0	68.4*	94.7	89.5	94.7	100.0
7	73.7*	100.0	94.7	89.5	78.9	94.7	100.0
8	84.2	84.2	–	89.5	84.2	73.7*	94.7
9	100.0	100.0	63.2*	94.7	[84.2]	84.2	94.7
10	94.7	100.0	94.7	94.7	94.7	100.0	84.2
11	94.7	94.7	–	100.0	94.7	100.0	84.2
12	89.5	94.7	–	73.7*	94.7	100.0	94.7
13	94.7	78.9	68.4*	84.2	84.2	84.2	94.7
14	94.7	–	–	89.5	78.9	–	78.9
15	89.5	–	–	89.5	73.7*	–	89.5
16	84.2	94.7	84.2	84.2	84.2	94.7	78.9
17	100.0	–	–	78.9	[88.9]	–	94.7
18	94.7	100.0	47.4*	84.2	94.7	94.7	68.4*
19	89.5	94.7	94.7	89.5	94.7	73.7*	84.2
20	100.0	73.7*	–	100.0	84.2	73.7*	73.7*
21	100.0	89.5	94.7	78.9	[68.4]	94.7	94.7
22	100.0	89.5	–	89.5	89.5	89.5	84.2
23	100.0	100.0	100.0	94.7	[94.7]	94.7	100.0
24	100.0	78.9	94.7	73.7*	78.9	100.0	89.5
25	89.5	94.7	–	94.7	[84.2]	100.0	89.5
26	94.7	94.7	–	84.2	[78.9]	94.7	73.7*
27	94.7	89.5	–	78.9	[78.9]	78.9	89.5
28	84.2	–	–	94.7	[84.2]	–	100.0
29	84.2	94.7	–	100.0	89.5	100.0	78.9
30	100.0	94.7	–	100.0	78.9	78.9	89.5

*Indicates that the case does not satisfy the 75% rule for this attribute.
[ ] Proportion of subjects coding prior probability as high in problems for which acceptance is irrelevant (see principle 3).
– Values not manipulated (see principles 1 and 2).

were intended to be unstructured. This finding documents a conclusion reached in chapter 3 that the question used to measure the structure attribute produces too high a level of false positive judgments and deserves reexamination.

The thirty problems for which coding data is shown in table 5.1 will be called Problem Set 1. It has been used in some of the research to be reported in this chapter. Two other problem sets

(2 and 3) based on the same experimental design shown in figure 5.1 have also been developed. Problem Set 2 was an outgrowth of an effort to remove any remaining ambiguities from Problem Set 1; Problem Set 3 evolved in a similar fashion from Problem Set 2. In both revisions some of the original cases were retained, some were rewritten, and some new cases were added.

DATA COLLECTION

As in the studies reported in chapter 4, the data were collected as a part of management development programs. Results will be reported here for eight distinct populations that have responded to one of the three versions of the problem set. Table 5.2 lists these populations, describes their salient characteristics, and indicates the version of the problem set used.

Each manager received a copy of the booklet containing the thirty cases and was asked to indicate which of the five decision processes (AI, AII, . . . , GII) was closest to the one he would employ if he were the manager confronted with that problem. They were assured of the confidentiality of their responses and promised that an individualized report on their leadership styles would be furnished to them during the training session. (A sample computer printout may be found in chapter 8 along with excerpts from the manual that accompanies it.) For four of the eight populations (P_1, P_2, P_4, and P_8) the problem booklet was mailed to the managers about three weeks in advance of the program. In two other cases (P_6 and P_7), it was distributed during the program itself after participants had been exposed to a number of course sessions, including lectures and exercises relevant to the issue of participation in decision-making but not including the normative model presented earlier in the book. Finally, in two populations (P_3 and P_5) the administration of the problem set occurred after both extensive training in participative management and exposure to the normative model. Thus, the eight populations chosen here for analysis represent wide variation in the version of the problem set used and in the timing of its administration.

INDIVIDUAL AND SITUATIONAL MAIN EFFECTS

In chapter 4, it was not possible to compare the relative importance of individual and situational differences as determinants of

TABLE 5.2. Populations Studied

Problem Set	Population Designation	General Characteristics	N	Timing of Administration
1	P_1	Middle-level managers from a large industrial corporation manufacturing electrical products	92	prior to course
	P_2	Middle-level managers from a large commercial bank	73	prior to course
	P_3	Executives from a wide range of industries attending a nine-week residential senior executive program	32	subsequent to training and model
2	P_4	Middle-level managers from the same large industrial corporation as population P_1	153	prior to course
	P_5	Middle-level managers from the research center of a large corporation in telecommunication	27	subsequent to training and model
	P_6	Middle-level managers from a variety of firms	64	subsequent to training
3	P_7	Executives from a wide range of industries attending a nine-week residential senior executive program	35	subsequent to training
	P_8	Middle-level managers from the same industrial corporation as populations P_1 and P_4	75	prior to course

a manager's choice among alternate decision-making methods. Without attempting to specify what these factors might be, it is possible to test the hypothesis that the level of subordinates' participation is a function of both individual differences and situational characteristics and to estimate the variance accounted for by each of these factors. Writing y_{ij} as the ith manager's style on the jth case study in the problem set, we have

$$(5.1) \qquad Y_{ij} = \mu + \tau_j + \gamma_i + \epsilon_{ij}$$

where μ is the expected behavior for any manager on any problem and τ_j and γ_i are the deviations from μ resulting from problem and individual differences, respectively. Then the null hypotheses, $H_0(S)$ and $H_0(I)$, that the variations in the level of subordinate participation are invariant with situational or individual differences, can be written $\tau_j = 0$ and $\gamma_i = 0$, respectively.

The data to test the two null hypotheses are most simply presented in an analysis-of-variance table. Table 5.3 presents such

TABLE 5.3. Analysis-of-Variance Table for a Two-Way Classification Model to Test for the Existence of Individual and Problem Main Effects in Population P_8's Response to the Case Studies

Source of Variance	Degrees of Freedom	Sums of Squares	Mean Squares	F
Total	2,249	32,952		
Due to γ_j (problem)	29	8,978	309.6	30.8*
Due to λ_i (individual)	74	2,384	32.2	3.2[†]
Error	2,146	21,590	10.1	

*$F_{0.01}(29, \infty) = 1.79$.
[†]$F_{0.01}(74, \infty) = 1.47$.

data for population P_8. The large F values lead us to reject both the null hypotheses, $H_0(S)$ and $H_0(I)$, and to conclude that both situational and individual differences do influence managers' choices among alternative decision processes and, hence, the level of their subordinates' opportunity to participate in decision-making.

The existence of significant individual and problem main effects is not in itself a surprising finding. Of more interest is their relative size. Table 5.3 shows that the situation accounts for 27.2 percent of the variance whereas individual differences account for only 7.2 percent. Thus, for that population the amount of influence of situational factors in determining choice of leadership method is roughly four times the influence of individual differences in mean level of participation. The literature is replete with references to autocratic leaders and democratic leaders but contains almost no mention of autocratic or democratic situations. The relatively large differences among situations suggests the importance of developing some understanding of the properties of such situations, which induce different levels of participation.

It is conceivable that the results shown in table 5.3 reflect a high degree of homogeneity in the population studied or peculiarities of the particular problem set used. Table 5.4 presents the magnitude of situational and problem main effects for each of the eight samples discussed above. Across the three problem sets and the diverse samples of managers, the problem main effect accounts for more than three times the variance attributed to individual differences. Furthermore, combining all eight data sets, individual differences account for 8.5 percent of the total variance, situational differences for 29.2 percent, and interpopulation differences for only 0.9 percent.

The remainder of the variance can be explained by neither a person's mean score nor the nature of the problem he faces. Since this portion represents more than half of the total variance, it is necessary to speculate concerning its sources. Undoubtedly some of it can be accounted for by uncontrolled factors, such as a telephone interruption, fatigue, or what the manager ate for breakfast, which are independent of the problem itself and transient in nature. Some further part of the unexplained variance can be attributed to the use of a discrete rather than continuous scale for the measurement of subordinates' participation in decision-making.

The remainder of the variance to be explained may result from an interaction between person and problem. People may vary in the decision rules they employ in determining how much power to share with their subordinates. Imagine two leaders who show identical distributions of usage of the five decision processes in the thirty cases. By definition their mean scores are identical, but the

TABLE 5.4. The Proportion of the Variance in Behavior Which Is Accounted for by Individual and Situational Differences

	P_1 N = 92	P_2 N = 73	P_3 N = 32	P_4 N = 153	P_5 N = 27	P_6 N = 64	P_7 N = 35	P_8 N = 75
Individual main effect	10.0%	9.4%	7.9%	7.8%	3.8%	11.6%	8.1%	7.2%
Problem main effect	30.1%	26.8%	35.8%	31.0%	33.4%	27.1%	26.9%	27.2%
Mean	4.5	4.6	5.1	4.4	5.1	4.9	5.8	4.5
Multiple r for equation 5.1	.63	.60	.66	.62	.61	.62	.59	.59

situations in which they make use of each process may be very different. One may be more autocratic in situations in which his subordinates are likely to be in conflict than in cases in which they are likely to be in agreement, while the other may show the reverse relationship. Later in this chapter we will examine this possibility in more detail.

It would seem reasonable to conclude that situational variables as determinants of the level of participation warrant more attention than has been given to them in the literature. The relatively large differences among situations suggests the importance of developing an understanding of the properties of such situations that induce different levels of participation.

The relatively small proportion of the total variance accounted for by differences among persons in their mean level of participation is also worthy of some examination. We have become accustomed to conceiving of autocratic or authoritarian behavior as a general trait that determines behavior independent of the situation. This conception has been reflected in our methods of measurement of this trait, all of which have involved either the assessment of attitudes or opinions or the measurement of behavior by aggregating across situations. Neither method is likely to yield the identification of situational effects.

An analogy can be drawn between our research and the pioneering work of Hartshorne and May (1928) on the trait of honesty. Prior to their work it had been generally assumed that honesty was a general trait. The measures of this trait were of a pencil-and-paper variety and, to be sure, did yield differences among persons. But Hartshorne and May developed standardized situations in which the degree of honesty exhibited by the subject could be measured without his knowledge. While these tests had a high test-retest reliability, the correlations between tests involving cheating in different situations were too low (.00 and .40) to warrant the conclusion that the various tests measured the same trait.

An analysis has been made of the correlations between participativeness in the thirty different situations, and the conclusion is similar to that of Hartshorne and May. The 435 correlations ranged from +.34 to - .08 with a median of .10 (N = 551). Apparently neither honesty nor participativeness is usefully regarded as a general trait. While the trait concept is appealing in its simplicity, it leaves no room for the influence of situational variables or for interactions between them and personal characteristics.

PROBLEM ATTRIBUTES AS DETERMINANTS OF BEHAVIOR

The preceding analyses have shown that some properties on which the thirty cases varied influenced the managers' choice of a decision process. But which properties produced these effects? By design, these case studies varied with respect to seven problem attributes used in the normative model. In fact, no two problems contained identical combinations of the seven problem characteristics. In the following analysis, we will explore the extent to which variations in the level of participation are a function of differences among these characteristics.

As in the previous chapter, we will employ the method of multiple regression in exploring this question. A linear model will be fitted to the results of population P_8. This population used Problem Set 3 which, it is believed, represents the best manipulation of the seven independent variables. The level of the subordinates' participation was the dependent variable and the main effects and interactions among the seven situational attributes were the independent variables. Only a subset of the situational attributes and their interactions could be investigated within the experimental design employed here.[2] The following is a list of all the effects represented in the initial exploratory regression equation.

Main effects. Quality, Leader's Information, Structure, Acceptance, Trust, Conflict.

First order interactions. Leader's Information $\times$ Acceptance, Leader's Information $\times$ Prior Probability, Leader's Information $\times$ Trust, Leader's Information $\times$ Conflict, Structure $\times$ Acceptance, Structure $\times$ Prior Probability, Structure $\times$ Trust, Structure $\times$ Conflict, Acceptance $\times$ Prior Probability, Acceptance $\times$ Trust, Acceptance $\times$ Conflict, Prior Probability $\times$ Trust, Prior Probability $\times$ Conflict, Trust $\times$ Conflict.

2. In developing the regression model, it was necessary to assign values to each of the seven variables for each of the thirty cases. Where one variable (e.g., b) was nested within another variable (e.g., a), some assumptions were necessary to permit a specification of the value of the nested variable for those cases in which it was not (or could not be) varied. The assumptions used for this purpose are as follows: (1) $X_a = 0 \Rightarrow X_b = 1$, $X_d = 1$, $X_g = 1$; (2) $X_b = 1 \Rightarrow X_d = 1$ and (3) $X_e = 1 \Rightarrow X_f = 1$. The reader interested in the justification for these assumptions is referred to the discussion of the three nesting principles presented earlier in this chapter. The numbers 1, 2, and 3 above refer to principles 1, 2, and 3, respectively, stated earlier in this chapter.

Second order interactions. Leader's Information × Trust × Conflict, Acceptance × Trust × Conflict

Variables were retained and included in the final model if their marginal contribution to the proportion of the variance accounted for by the model was significantly greater than zero, all other variables being held constant. The resultant empirically derived model can be written:

$$Y_{ij} = 4.1 + 0.7X_{aj} - 0.8X_{bj} - 0.9X_{dj} + 1.7X_{ej}(1 - X_{fj})$$
(5.2)
$$+ 2.7X_{ej}X_{gj}(1 - X_{hj}) + \epsilon_{ij},$$

where Y_{ij} is the level of participation used by the ith manager on the jth problem and $X_{aj}, X_{bj}, \ldots, X_{hj}$ are dummy variables. Specifically, X_{aj} refers to the importance of quality; X_{bj}, to the adequacy of the leader's information; X_{dj}, to the degree of structure in the problem; X_{ej}, to the importance of acceptance; X_{fj}, to the prior probability of acceptance of an autocratic decision; X_{gj}, to the level of the subordinates' trustworthiness; X_{hj}, to the presence or absence of conflict.

Equation 5.2 contains a number of specific findings that relate the situational variables to differences in managerial behavior. These findings can be summarized as follows:

1. Managers use decision processes providing greater opportunities for participation when the quality of the decision is important than when the quality of the decision is irrelevant.

2. Managers use decision processes providing less opportunity for participation when they possess all the necessary information to generate a high quality decision than when they lack some of the needed information.

3. Managers use decision processes providing less opportunity for participation when the problem they face is well structured than when it is unstructured.

4. Managers use decision processes providing more opportunity for participation when both the subordinates' acceptance of the decision is critical for its effective implementation and the prior probability of this acceptance existing of an autocratic decision is low than when either or both of these conditions are not satisfied.

5. Managers use decision processes providing a greater opportunity for participation when the subordinates' acceptance of the decision is critical for its effective implementation, the manager trusts his subordinates to pay attention to organizational rather than personal goals, and conflict among subordinates is absent, than when one or more of these conditions are not satisfied.

We observed previously that the eight populations were very similar in the proportion of variance that could be attributed to problem (treated as a nominal variable) and to individual differences in mean level of participation. But, how similar are these populations in the specific nature of the effects of situational variables? Table 5.5 presents the coefficients obtained by fitting an equation similar to equation 5.2 to the responses made by the eight groups of managers to the cases in the three problem sets. With the exception of the response to the presence or absence of a quality requirement, the findings reported above are replicated across the different groups of managers and the three versions of the problem set. Even the magnitudes of the responses to the presence or absence of the problem attributes are approximately equal across the eight populations. With the possible exception of response to differences among the cases in the importance of the quality of the decision, it would appear reasonable to conclude that the findings presented above are common to a wide range of managers.

Miles (1965) has distinguished between two "theories" of participative management corresponding to different goals managers expect to achieve through encouraging subordinate participation. Under the human relations model, the manager used participation to "buy" cooperation from subordinates in implementing the decision. Under the human resources model, he uses participation to increase the quality of his decisions by tapping the full range of experience, insight, and creative ability in his unit. These two models are expressed by Miles in terms of alternative goals to be achieved or purposes to be served by participation. They correspond roughly to the concepts of decision quality and decision acceptance that we (following Maier 1963) have treated as outcomes in terms of which alternative decision processes can be assessed.

Let us examine the findings in table 5.5 to see if the conditions under which the typical manager in the eight populations decides

TABLE 5.5. Coefficients for Terms in the Descriptive Model for the Eight Populations

	P_1 N = 92	P_2 N = 73	P_3 N = 32	P_4 N = 153	P_5 N = 27	P_6 N = 64	P_7 N = 35	P_8 N = 75
Quality	.2*	-.3*	.2*	.4	.0*	.5	.8	.7
Information	-.5	-.8	-.6	-.8	-1.0	-.5	-.2*	-.8
Structure	-1.6	-1.3	-1.6	-1.3	-1.5	-1.3	-1.6	-.8
Acceptance × prior probability	2.0	1.7	2.3	1.9	2.3	1.7	2.1	1.7
Acceptance × trust × conflict[c]	2.6	2.6	2.2	2.7	3.1	2.5	1.9	2.7
Multiple r	.44	.41	.44	.44	.49	.39	.40	.42

*Not significantly different from zero at .05 level of significance.

to retain or share power correspond to a human relations or a human resources model. Of the seven variables, quality (X_a), leader's information (X_b), structure (X_d), and trust (X_g) are variables relevant to the quality of the decision. In the construction of the normative model these variables provided the basis for three rules designed to protect decision quality. Strong effects of these variables on participation indicate that managers' decisions to share or retain their power are influenced by considerations of decision quality. The extent to which the behavior of managers in these eight populations corresponds with Miles's human resources model will be indicated not only by the strength of these effects but also by their direction.

Three findings in table 5.5 deal exclusively with what we have termed "quality" variables. All are simple main effects. The first of these effects deals with differences in behavior on problems with and without a quality requirement. Managers in four of these populations behave more participatively when there is a quality requirement than when such a requirement is lacking. Essentially, the typical manager in each of these four populations is acting in accordance with the human resources model of which Miles states, "The more important a decision is to the manager's department, the greater should be his effort to tap the department's resources" (1965, p. 151). The four populations not showing a significant effect of this variable include two in which the effect is similar in direction and one (P_2) in which the direction is reversed.

The second main effect, that of leader's information, observed in seven of the eight populations, shows that the typical manager is more participative when he does not have the information necessary to make a high quality decision than when he does. The managers acted in a manner consistent with the human resources model by using participative decision styles as a mechanism for expanding the information base on which the decision is made.

The third main effect observable in table 5.5 concerns the consequences of problem structure. The typical manager in each of the eight populations is more participative on unstructured than on well structured but otherwise similar problems. The use of participative decision processes to deal with complex ill-structured decisions was not mentioned by Miles in connection with his description of the human resources model but appears generally consistent with his position. A similar effect was incorporated into the normative model presented in chapter 3. If the problem was unstructured and the leader lacked the necessary information, a process of information collection that involved interaction among those with information, including the leader (like CII and GII), was deemed more effective and efficient than a process (like AII and CI) which does not permit such interaction.

The remaining three variables, importance of acceptance (X_e), prior probability of acceptance (X_f), and conflict (X_h), all deal with considerations that are much more related to Miles's human relations model. They were used in the formulation of the four rules designed to protect the acceptance of the decision in the normative model. There is one effect shown in table 5.5 involving these variables, and it occurs in all eight of the populations. This effect is examined in table 5.6. The mean of 5.95 on problems

TABLE 5.6. Interaction Between Acceptance and Its Prior Probability
in Population P_8

		Importance of Acceptance	
		High	Low
Prior probability	High	3.87	3.76
of acceptance	Low	5.95	Not observed*

*See principle 2, p. 96

with a high acceptance requirement and low prior probability is significantly higher than the mean on problems with a low acceptance requirement or a high prior probability of acceptance of an autocratic solution. The reader will note that the cell corresponding to "low" on both variables is empty due to the nesting of prior probability under high acceptance. As a result, the interpretation of the effect as an interaction or as a main effect of prior probability is, statistically speaking, inconclusive. Our decision to treat it as an interaction is based on the assumption that the mean level of participation in the empty cell would be of the same order of magnitude as 3.76. This assumption, while not empirically verified, reflects a belief in the essential rationality of the managers studied. If acceptance of the decision on the part of subordinates is truly irrelevant, why would their behavior be affected in any way by the degree to which they could "sell" their solution to their subordinates?

Clearly, the managers in each of the eight populations were also using participation in a manner consistent with Miles's human relations model. In the situations contained in the lower left-hand cell of table 5.6, the typical manager recognized the need to gain commitment from his subordinates and the inadequacy of an autocratic process to secure that commitment.

Finally, let us consider the most complex term in the equation, which shows an interaction between acceptance, trust, and conflict. This term includes variables relevant to both the quality and the acceptance of the decision. The beta weights for this effect are significant and similar in magnitude for all eight populations. Table 5.7 illustrates the nature of the interaction using data from

TABLE 5.7. Interaction Between Acceptance, Trust, and Conflict in Population P_8

	Importance of Acceptance	
	High	Low
Trust high, conflict low	6.82	3.67
Trust high, conflict high	3.97	2.99
Trust low, conflict low	3.78	4.80
Trust low, conflict high	4.56	4.02

population P_8. In this term, the effects of an increase in the importance of securing acceptance or commitment to the solution by subordinates appear to be limited to those situations in which the managers can trust them and the level of conflict among them is low. The three low values in the left-hand column suggest that the managers limited their subordinates' participation either to protect the quality of the solution from being adversely affected by subordinates' pursuing different goals, or to avoid having to deal with conflict in a group setting. It appears that avoiding a risk to the quality of the decision dominates the need to develop commitment to the solution and that managers believe that decision processes such as CII and GII are less effective when there is conflict present among the subordinates.

In summary, evidence concerning the conditions under which managers employed different decision processes in dealing with the standardized problems is partially consistent with both of Miles's alternative models. The circumstances under which managers utilize participative decision processes is consistent with the view that they are attempting to improve the quality of decisions by tapping the resources in their operating units. But these circumstances also show a marked concern on the part of a typical manager with securing the commitment or acceptance of decisions by subordinates where necessary. Neither the human resources nor human relations model, by itself, is adequate to explain the complete pattern of findings presented here.

The reader may have noted a general correspondence between the factors that managers consider in choosing the decision process and those incorporated into the normative model. For example, on a problem for which both the quality and the acceptance of the solution are irrelevant, equation 5.2 predicts that the manager would use 2.4 units of participation. From chapter 3, we can determine that such a problem is of type 1, all styles are within the feasible set, and the minimum man-hours solution is AI. In contrast, on a problem for which quality is important, the manager does not have sufficient information to make a high quality decision, the problem is unstructured, acceptance of the solution by the subordinates is critical for its effective implementation and unlikely to exist for an autocratically made decision, the subordinates can be trusted, and there is no conflict present among the subordinates, equation 5.2 predicts 9.2 units of participation. Such a problem is of type 12 for which the feasible set is GII. A more detailed discussion of the correspondence between the normative and descriptive models is presented in chapter 7.

INDIVIDUAL DIFFERENCES IN EFFECTS OF PROBLEM ATTRIBUTES

The findings concerning situational effects in table 5.5 refer to how a typical manager in any of the eight populations responds to different features of the problems he faces. There may be wide variations in the nature of these effects for different individuals within the same population. Thus, in P_8, a typical manager is 0.7 units higher on the scale of participation for problems on which there is a quality requirement than on problems without such a quality requirement. But there is considerable variance in both the magnitude and direction of this difference for managers within the same population. In fact, one manager in that population was 4.0 units *less* participative on problems with a quality requirement than on problems without such a requirement, while another was 6.5 units *more* participative on problems with than without such a quality requirement. The former was more inclined to use participative methods on such decisions as when the departmental picnic should be held or that the walls should be painted. The pattern of his behavior suggests what Miles has called the human relations model of participation. On the other hand, the latter was more participative on decisions that had a clear and demonstrable impact on the goals of the organization. His behavior fits Miles's description of the human resources model.

Statistically, these differences among managers could correspond to interactions between individual differences and problem attributes. Conceptually, they can be thought of as differences among managers in the decision rules they employ in deciding when to use each of the decision processes. It is likely that a large proportion of the variance that is unexplained by main effects of situational variables or mean level of participation is due to the influence of these interactions.

There is a problem, however, in separating true interactions from errors of measurement. Some differences in the observed effects of a situational variable would be expected to result from random errors of measurement. The experimental design used here does not permit a direct test of the magnitude of the variance that is directly attributable to such interactions. In the standard two-way analysis of variance model used to investigate the individual and problem main effects, there is only one observation in each cell, and therefore the interaction effect and the error terms are confounded.

Yetton (1972) suggested a method to test for the existence of certain of these interaction effects. He used a clustering technique to partition individuals into homogeneous groups. In terms of the analysis of the variance model described above, this effectively collapses across certain cells giving multiple observations in each of the remaining cells, and makes it possible to estimate the interaction effects and error term independently.

The procedure first entails fitting the descriptive model presented earlier in this chapter to each manager's set of responses to the standardized cases. The individual's beta weights are then used to define his position in a six-dimensional space (where the six dimensions correspond to the five terms in equation 5.2 and the

individual's intercept). Similar managers, or those who at least respond similarly to the situational variables contained in the model,
would be located near each other in this space. To identify which
of the managers are similar to which others, a clustering technique
modeled after ISODATA (Ball and Hall 1967) is used to partition
the space.

The above procedure was applied to the data from P_8. As there
is no reason to believe that managers do in fact form clusters, the
number of clusters could be arbitrarily specified. The clustering
procedure was used essentially to partition the space in such a way
that similar managers were grouped together, rather than to investigate the structure of the space. Twenty was chosen as the
number of clusters to be used, as it was conjectured that this number would result in sufficient observations per cell to make possible an investigation of the interaction effects.

The interaction effects between the five situational variables in
equation 5.2 and typical managers from each of the clusters account for 4.8 percent of the total variance. This is significant at
the .05 level. Yetton (1972) reports that there is also a significant
conflict interaction effect. Managers differ in their response to
conflict as represented in the cases. The lack of evidence concerning a conflict main effect in equation 5.2 is attributable in part to
the fact that some managers respond to conflict by becoming
more participative, whereas others respond by becoming more
autocratic.

It should be emphasized that the procedure used here is crude;
it is likely to have seriously underestimated the magnitude of the
variance attributable to interactions between individual difference
variables and problem attributes. The investigation was restricted
to only five of the terms on which individual differences might
exist, and the method of clustering that treated managers within
the same cluster as the same person is far from precise. The analysis does demonstrate, however, the existence of individual differences both in effects of conflict and in effects of the five terms
contained in equation 5.2.

TESTING THE GENERALITY OF THE DESCRIPTIVE MODEL

The conclusions drawn so far in this chapter are based solely on
people's reports of what they would do if faced with standardized

hypothetical problems. While the conclusions are relatively interpretable and consistent over the various populations studied,
they could be greatly strengthened by evidence that they are not
"method-bound." If similar conclusions result from the application of different research methods, even though each has possible
biases or defects, confidence in the validity of these conclusions is
increased.

So far in this book, two very different methods have been used
to study situational effects on a manager's choice of a decision
process. In Study 4, reported in detail in the previous chapter, 268
managers were asked to recall a problem that they had recently
solved, to indicate which of the five decision processes (AI–GII)
was closest to the one they had used, and to code each problem's
status on the eight problem attributes presented in chapter 2.
Hereafter, we will refer to this method as "recalled problems" and
to the method on which this chapter is based as "standardized
problems."

One way of determining the generality of the results reported in
this chapter is to measure the degree to which a descriptive model
developed from findings obtained with one method can account
for data collected with a different method. Let us take equation
5.2, which was empirically developed to fit the responses of P_8
and based on their responses to the thirty standardized cases. The
reader will recall that the multiple correlation for that equation
used to account for behavior of that population was .42. Now let
us use that equation to predict the results for the population of
268 managers who furnished "recalled problems." This analysis
constitutes not only a cross-validation of the results using a different population but a cross-method validation. The recalled problems were not standardized but self-selected, and the coding used
was the manager's own perception of the properties of the case
rather than that of independent coders.

When equation 5.2 is used to predict the behavior of the 268
managers on problems they had had to solve, the multiple correlation between predicted and reported behavior is .22. Although
there is substantial shrinkage, as is normally found in cross-validation studies, the correlation does show evidence that the descriptive model in equation 5.2 is not limited to explaining behavior on
hypothetical or standardized problems.

As well as investigating the gross similarities between the findings from the two methods, let us consider them in detail. Do both sets of data support the same relationships between specific situational variables and the decision processes used by a typical manager? Table 5.8 contrasts the managers' reactions in recalled

TABLE 5.8. Comparison of Managers' Responses to Standardized and Recalled
Problems

	Standardized Problems (P_8)	Recalled Problems
Quality	.7	.3*
Information	−.8	−2.3
Structure	−.9	−.7
Acceptance X prior probability[c]	1.7	1.7
Acceptance X trust X conflict[c]	2.7	.5*

*Not significantly different from zero at the .05 level.

and standardized problems to the presence or absence of the variables contained in equation 5.2. It depicts the beta weights obtained by fitting an equation similar to equation 5.2 to both data sets. Table 5.8 reveals that both research methods provide a rather similar picture of the effects of situational variables on decision-making behavior. By construction, the beta weights estimated from P_8's responses are significantly different from zero at the 0.05 level. The beta weights estimated from the managers' behavior on the recalled problems have the same sign as those estimated from P_8's responses to the standardized cases, and, with the exceptions of the quality main effect and the acceptance-trust-conflict interaction term they are all significantly different from zero at the .05 level.

On both standardized and recalled problems, leaders tend to use participative processes when they lack the necessary information to solve the problem by themselves and when their subordinates have a high probability of possessing that information. This use of participation is a means of protecting the quality of the decision by ensuring that the decision-making system contains the information needed to generate and evaluate the alternatives. The results from both methods also indicate that acceptance considerations enter into the choice of decision process. Managers tend to employ more participative styles when it is critical for their subordinates to accept the decision in order to get it effectively implemented and when the likelihood of selling an autocratic decision is low.

While the similarity between the two sets of findings is apparent, the two differences shown in table 5.8 are worthy of note. A quality main effect was observed for P_8 on standardized problems but not replicated on recalled problems. It should be remembered that the beta weight for the effect of quality showed greatest variability across populations (table 5.5), and this difference is most easily attributable to a population rather than a method difference.

The findings on the effect of congruence between subordinates' goals and those of the organization are also different for the two studies. For the standardized problems, the effect of this variable is found in situations in which the acceptance of the decision by subordinates is critical and the potential conflict among subordinates is low. This finding is not replicated on the recalled problems, perhaps because of the small variance in the acceptance variable (see table 4.3). Although not shown in table 5.8, the behavior on the recalled problems supports the existence of a trust main effect.

In chapter 4, the regression equation developed for recalled problems also contained a significant effect of subordinates' information. Managers were significantly more participative when they perceived that their subordinates had additional information that could contribute to the solution of the problem they faced than when this was not the case. This result could not be replicated for standardized problems since this variable was not manipulated in the experimental design.

The similarity in findings obtained using the two very different data collection techniques provides strong evidence for the existence of the situational effects discussed above. It should be noted that these findings describe the typical leader but not necessarily all leaders. As shown earlier in this chapter, individual differences exist not only in average score but also in the factors that induce participative or autocratic behavior.

SUMMARY

The language traditionally used for the description and analysis of leadership styles has been based largely on differences in aggregate behavior among leaders. In the literature on participation, the domain of leadership behavior to which this work is addressed, leaders have been typed as autocratic, consultative, or participative, or as varying in a trait anchored at the extremes by the concepts autocratic and participative. The findings contained in this chapter—based on managers' statements of the decision processes they would use in sets of thirty standardized cases—seriously question the explanatory power of either the type or the trait concepts.

There were, to be sure, overall differences among the managers studied, in the extent to which they said that they would permit the participation of their subordinates in the concrete situations. A manager whose behavior on the thirty problems generated a mean participation score of 2.2 can certainly be said to be more autocratic than one with a mean of 8.6. But such differences in mean behavior fall far short of accounting for all the variance in behavior that was observed. In fact, only about 10 percent of the variance in behavior could be attributed to mean score. Each manager studied indicated that he would use at least four of the five leadership methods. There was variance both within and between managers.

Some of the variance in behavior within managers can be attributed to common tendencies to respond to particular situations by sharing power and to others by withholding it. By treating problem as a nominal variable, we have been able to account for an additional 30 percent of the total variance in behavior. The manager's choice of a decision process was influenced much more by the properties of the situation depicted than it was by his average style.

While we believe that the results clearly establish the importance of the situation as a determinant of autocratic or participative leadership behavior, the reader should be cautioned against generalizing directly from our estimates of the relative importance of situational and individual differences to the real world. There are a number of features of the methodology employed that may have inflated the estimate of variance attributable to the situation relative to the individual.

First, we should consider the heterogeneity of the problem set itself. The thirty cases covered, by design, a range of leadership situations that probably exceeds the variety encompassed in any one leadership role. A problem set made up of more homogenous problems, for example all of type 6b, might have been expected to decrease markedly the amount of variance in behavior within persons without altering the variance between persons.

Second, the use of a standardized problem set means that all persons are exposed to the same case regardless of their behavior on prior cases. In a typical leadership role a leader's response to one situation may have a marked influence on the nature of subsequent problems. The leader's behavior on one problem may effect the extent to which subordinates are likely to be in conflict or can be trusted or have the necessary information on subsequent problems. One can conjecture that in a real leadership role a leader uniformly pursuing an AI decision style and one uniformly pursuing a GII style might start off being exposed to the same problems but, in the long term, the kinds of problems and situations that they were required to confront would be very different. This feedback mechanism in which behavior on "case n" influences the nature of "case $n + 1$" was not built into the case studies, which were constant for all subjects. If our conjecture here and elsewhere in this book about possible long-term effects of leadership styles is correct, some of the variance which is represented here as an effect of a situational variable (like trust) is actually traceable, at least in part, to individual differences.

Nonetheless, the findings indicate that the situation does play an important role in determining the nature of the leader's decision process. Clearly, it makes at least as much sense to talk about autocratic and participative situations as it does to talk about autocratic and participative managers. Some of the properties that determine whether a situation is participative or autocratic are contained in equation 5.2.

Behavior in leadership positions is influenced not only by the situation, and by the average tendency of the leader to behave participatively or autocratically, but also by the interaction of situational variables and individual differences. Only 40 percent of the total variance observed can be attributed to the independent effects of situations and average behavioral tendencies of persons. Some proportion of the remainder of the variance (unestimable by the methods used here) is due to differences among persons in their response to problem characteristics either singly or in combination. For example, two managers may display identical distributions of use of each of the five decision processes, but one may be more autocratic on problems involving a high level of conflict among subordinates while the other may be more autocratic on problems in which conflict was absent.

The possibility that the findings concerning the influence of situational factors might be an artifact of the method was tested by using the descriptive model developed in this chapter to predict the behavior of managers on recalled problems. Some shrinkage in the multiple correlation was observed (.42 to .22), but the similarity in the pattern of findings supports the conclusion that the results are not restricted to the particular method used.

The major implication of the research utilizing behavior on standardized cases is that the conception of leadership style as a fixed method of behavior deserves to be reexamined. The degree to which a manager shares his power with his subordinates is a function of situational factors, individual differences, and interactions between them. The use of standardized cases as the basis for a multidimensional representation of leader behavior is examined in the next chapter.

CHAPTER 6

A Multidimensional Measure
of Leader Behavior

The sets of problems developed for the research in chapter 5 could be potential tests of leadership behavior. While they were not developed for that purpose, it is conceivable that they might provide a useful means of measuring leadership style. In this chapter we will examine this possibility and will compare the problem sets with other kinds of tests that have been developed for predicting how leaders would behave in carrying out their leadership roles.

Let us begin by examining the meaning of the term "test" as it relates to the measurement of leader behavior. Such measures can be divided into two distinct categories: (1) those examining how the leader behaves in an actual leadership role embedded within a formal organization, and (2) those measuring the behavior of individuals in standardized situations. The former category includes the Leader Behavior Description Questionnaire (Stogdill and Coons 1957), developed at Ohio State University, utilizing subordinates' descriptions of their superiors' behavior. It also includes the use of time sampling and trained observers such as have been employed by Wirdenius (1958) in his study of the behavior of industrial supervisors in Sweden. Scores on such measures can be obtained only for persons who are presently occupying leadership roles, a fact which limits their potential use in selection.

The value of measures of the first type for assessing individual differences is also limited by the fact that scores are influenced by differences in the situations that leaders encounter. Consider for example two leaders who differ in the amounts of consideration and initiating structure they exhibit in their relations with their subordinates. Can one conclude that the same differences would exist if they exchanged roles or if each was moved to a third role. To do so would require the assumptions (1) that there were no differences in the situations the two leaders faced or (2) that the behaviors in question were unaffected by the situation. The first assumption is, at best, highly questionable; the second is patently false, as Lowin and Craig (1968) have demonstrated. The importance of controlling for situational factors in the measurement of individual differences led Cronbach (1960) to define as psychological tests only those measures in which the situation to which people were asked to respond was held constant. By this definition measures of the first type do not qualify as tests.

If one desires a measure that can be applied economically to large numbers of persons, some of whom are not presently occupants of leadership positions, or one that will yield differences among people which are not confounded by situational factors, the measures in the second category are indicated. The defining property of this category is that of a psychological test, in other words, a relatively standard set of stimuli to which each of the persons is asked to respond. To be useful, such stimuli must generate reliable differences in behavior across persons. The scores obtained must predict behavior in the situation to which one wishes to generalize, that is, behavior in actual leadership situations.

An examination of the measures that fit this definition of a test reveals two distinct subcategories, differing primarily in the kinds of stimuli to which responses are elicited. One subcategory consists of measures such as How Supervise? (File and Remmers 1948), the Leadership Opinion Questionnaire (Fleishman 1957), and the Attitudes Toward Management Practices (Haire, Ghiselli, and Porter 1966). The stimuli are verbal statements with which the respondent is requested to express his degree of concurrence on a predetermined scale. For example, the scale developed by Haire et al. for measuring attitudes toward participation asks subjects to rank, on a seven-point scale ranging from strongly agree to strongly disagree, their response to the following statement: "A good leader should give detailed and complete instructions to his subordinates rather than giving them merely general directions and depending upon their initiative to work out the details."

In the second subcategory of test, the stimuli are not attitude statements but standardized replicas of the situations to which one wishes to generalize. Examples include observations of participants' behavior in leaderless group discussions (Bass and Coates

1952), in-basket tests (Frederiksen 1962), or the leadership tests used by the Office of Strategic Services during World War II (OSS Assessment Staff 1948).

In each of the above, the stimuli are complex, multidimensional simulations of situations presumably representative of those likely to occur in the roles about which one wishes to make predictions, and the responses are not limited to predetermined alternatives. The first example is clearly an interactive situation in which the behavior exhibited by one subject may be influenced by the behavior of other subjects who are being assessed simultaneously. In the latter two, an attempt is made to program all elements of the environment to which the person is responding. Typically, the range of possible behaviors is sufficiently large that judgments by trained observers or assessors are required to obtain quantitative measures. Situational tests of this type are typically costly to administer and subject to unreliability due to inadequate sampling of situations, but they have potentially higher validity than those of the first type.

In the light of this discussion, let us consider the properties of the measure utilized in the previous chapter. Each manager was given a set of thirty standardized cases representative of the kinds of problems that leaders encounter in organizations and was asked which of the five decision processes he would have employed in each. Since the set of cases was held constant across persons, the measure falls clearly into the second type and is appropriately termed a test. It is not confounded by natural differences in the kinds of problems leaders encounter, and its application is not limited to persons presently occupying leadership positions.

To which of the two subcategories of this type of test does our measure most closely correspond? This question is not so easy to answer. If one considers the set of stimuli that comprise the test, there is an obvious identity with the second category. The stimuli are situations in which the person is asked to place himself rather than statements about attitudes or typical behavior. To be sure, the stimuli are expressed in written form as cases rather than in terms of cues by which situations are normally revealed to leaders. This eliminates from the measurement process any individual differences in the search for information, but it has the virtue of simple administration and a much larger sampling of situations than would be possible by other means.

However, if one examines the nature of an individual's response to each of the situations, this measure displays some similarity to those in the first category. One observes not how a person actually reacts to each situation, as is generally true of the second type, but rather his verbal report of how he would react. Furthermore, the respondent is given a choice among five possible responses corresponding to the levels of participation employed in the normative model shown in chapter 3. If there are any differences between subjects in other aspects of their behavior in such situations, for example, indecisiveness, anxiety, or even lack of skill in implementing the alternative selected, they cannot be directly revealed by this measuring instrument. This latter property eliminates the necessity for observers and greatly simplifies the task of quantifying behavior but limits the kinds of behaviors that can be observed with the instrument.

In the previous chapter, it was noted that on any one of the three problem sets the proportion of variance in a leader's behavior attributable to his mean score was relatively small, accounting for approximately 10 percent of the total variance. While mean score on level of participation is certainly one of the descriptive statistics that can be generated from observations, it is by no means sufficient to account for all of the subject's behavior. Fortunately, the selection of the problems in accordance with an experimental design makes it possible to identify other determinants of the subject's behavior. The cases varied in seven attributes, and the nature of this variation was such that the covariance among attributes was either logically necessary or nonexistent. Consequently, a person's behavior on the set of case studies could be examined to determine the main effects and interactions among the attributes. While the attributes were taken from the normative model, their usefulness as predictors of behavior is not dependent in any way on the validity of the normative model.

The following are nine of the principal scores that one can obtain from a person's behavior on any of the problem sets used in chapter 5.

1. Mean level of participation (MLP). This score indicates the average level of participation employed by the person across the thirty problems. It is simply his reported number of decision processes of each type (AI, AII, CI, CII, GII) multiplied by its appropriate scale value (0, .625, 5.0, 8.125, 10.0) and divided by

30. Its theoretical range is 10 for a person utilizing GII on all thirty situations to 0 for a person utilizing AI on all thirty situations. The actual range is 8.6 to 1.7.

2. *Variance in level of participation (Var-P).* This score indicates the variance in the level of participation chosen in the thirty case studies. It is a measure of the extent to which the person varies his behavior with the situation.

3. *Main effect of importance of acceptance (ME-Acc).* As can be seen from the experimental design presented in the previous chapter, the problem set included twenty problems with high requirements for acceptance on the part of subordinates and ten problems with low or zero requirements for acceptance. This score represents the difference (high minus low) between the mean values of the decision processes chosen by the person for these two types of problems. The larger the positive value of the difference, the greater the tendency for the person to accord his subordinates more opportunity to participate in making deicisons requiring their acceptance.

4. *Main effect of prior probability (ME-PP).* This score represents the difference (high minus low) between the mean values of the decision processes chosen by the person for problems in which the leader possessed and those in which he lacked the expert, referent, or legitimate power (French and Raven 1959) necessary to ensure a high probability that his decision would be accepted. The more negative the difference, the greater the tendency for the leader to discriminate between these two types of situations by capitalizing on the time saved by autocratic decisions where it is safe to do so without sacrificing decision acceptance.

5. *Main effect of conflict (ME-Conf).* This score represents the difference (high minus low) between the mean values of the decision processes for problems in which subordinates are likely and unlikely to disagree in the course of solving the problem. A negative value indicates a tendency to respond autocratically to conflict while a positive value indicates a more participative response.

6. *Main effect of quality requirement (ME-QR).* This score represents the difference (high minus low) between the mean values of the decision processes chosen by the person for problems with and those without a quality requirement. The more positive the difference the greater the tendency to encourage more participation on decisions with quality requirements than on those without.

7. Main effect of trust (ME-Tr). This score represents the difference (high minus low) between the mean values of the decision processes chosen for problems in which the goals of subordinates are depicted as congruent with those of the organization and those in which their goals are depicted as incongruent. The more positive the difference, the greater the tendency to respond to situations of low trust by using a lesser degree of participation.

8. Main effect of leader's information (ME-LI). This score represents the difference (high minus low) between the decision processes used on problems in which the leader has and does not have the necessary information to solve the problem by himself. The more negative the difference, the greater the extent to which the person utilizes participation on the part of his subordinates to augment the information brought to bear on the decision.

9. Main effect of structure (ME-St). This score represents the difference (high minus low) between the mean scores of the decision processes used on structured and unstructured problems. The more negative the difference, the greater the extent to which the person employs a higher degree of participation in the solution of unstructured problems than on those that are structured.

It should be clear that these nine scores do not exhaust the possible measures of a person's behavior on the thirty cases. They do not include any indications of the strength of interaction among the problem attributes in determining an individual's behavior, and they do not include any comparison of the subject's behavior with the normative model. In chapter 7, we will consider the similarity between the model's behavior and that of the typical manager, as well as additional measures of individual differences, which involve the degree and nature of the correspondence between a person's behavior on a set of hypothetical problems and the behavior of the model on the same problems.

Table 6.1 reports the correlations between the nine scores obtained from administering Problem Set 2 to 201 managers from a large number of different firms. Of the thirty-six correlations only three are significant at the .01 level. These three significant correlations are between variance in behavior and main effects of acceptance, prior probability, and structure. Since variance in behavior is a necessary condition for covariance between an attribute and behavior, all three significant correlations are easily interpret-

TABLE 6.1. Correlations Among the Nine Descriptive Measures of Leader Behavior

	1	2	3	4	5	6	7	8	9
1. MLP	—								
2. Var-P	−.03	—							
3. ME-Acc	.03	.28*	—						
4. ME-PP	.12	−.26*	−.11	—					
5. ME-Conf	.01	−.04	−.00	−.04	—				
6. ME-QR	.13	.01	−.08	−.15	−.07	—			
7. ME-Tr	−.04	.16	.13	−.03	−.00	.07	—		
8. ME-LI	.16	−.17	−.06	.22	−.03	.10	.06	—	
9. ME-St	.08	−.23*	−.19	.18	−.04	.15	−.10	.15	—

*P < .01.

able. It is interesting to note that mean level of participation is relatively independent of all of the main effects and is not correlated in a linear manner with variance. Further examination of the relationship between an individual's mean and variance revealed that the relationship is curvilinear. (A second-order polynomial equation accounts for 22 percent of the variance in Var-P using MLP as a predictor.) Managers who have either very high or very low mean scores tend to have low variance, while those whose scores are closer to the middle of the distribution have relatively high variance.

RELIABILITY OF THE MEASURES

We can conclude from table 6.1 that the nine descriptive measures are quite independent of one another. But how reliable are they? To what extent are the differences which are observed among people a function of real differences as opposed to measurement errors?

The reliability of each of the nine scores was determined by subdividing the thirty cases into two sets, one consisting of odd and the other of even items. For the last seven measures, which use difference scores, a slightly more complex procedure was used. The cases that have a high level of the attribute were divided into two equal sets (A and A^1). In making this division, we tried to equate the odd and even subsets more clearly by using the mean behavior on a case as the basis for matching items. Similarly, cases involving a low level were divided into two sets (B and B^1) with a comparable effort at matching. The two scores $A - B$ and $A^1 - B^1$ were then treated as separate tests and correlated with one another.

This procedure was carried out using data from 306 persons, each of whom had indicated how he would behave if he were the leader in each of the cases in Problem Set 2. Estimates of reliability were corrected by the Spearman-Brown formula and are shown in table 6.2.

TABLE 6.2. Reliability of the Nine Descriptive Measures and Comparison of Students' and Managers' Scores

Measure	Split-half Reliability (N = 306)	Students' Mean (N = 105)	Managers' Mean (N = 201)
1. MLP	.81	5.61*	4.68*
2. Var-P	.64	13.75*	14.41*
3. ME-Acc	.17	1.53*	1.32*
4. ME-PP	.30	−2.67*	−2.15*
5. ME-Conf	.11	−.63*	−.97*
6. ME-QR	.14	.01*	.73*
7. ME-Tr	.00	1.16	.95
8. ME-LI	.16	−1.38	−1.38
9. ME-St	.01	−.97	−1.24

*Mean difference significant at .01 or better.

The reliabilities of the first two scores, mean and variance, are reasonably high, but the difference scores are highly unreliable. There are at least three reasons for the low reliability of the difference scores. First, the subtests (A and A^1, B and B^1) are made up of many fewer cases than the fifteen on which subtest scores on mean and variance were based. For example, there were only six cases in which structure was high and six in which it was low. Dividing these up in the manner indicated above generates four scores, each based on behavior on only three cases! Second, the scores which are thought to affect the main effects of attributes are difference scores computed by subtracting one score (on a test or subtest) from another. If errors of measurement in both scores are independent, the amount of variance in the difference score that is attributable to measurement error is greater than the error variance in each of the components. Hence the reliability of $A - B$

is less than the reliability of either *A* or *B* alone. Finally, the complex experimental design in which seven variables were manipulated simultaneously undoubtedly contributes to variance within a given subtest, and hence the unreliability of the differences between them. The reliability of the difference scores could presumably be improved by an increase in the number of cases or a decrease in the number of attributes in which they vary. However, given the length and method of construction of the present test, it is clear that they are not useful for purposes of individual prediction.

Even though a measure may lack the reliability necessary for individual prediction, it may still be useful in predicting differences among groups. The group of 306 persons on whom the estimates of reliability were based can be broken down into two subgroups: (1) students working for their master's degrees in industrial administration (105); (2) middle-level managers employed in large firms (201). The latter were older by about fifteen years and all had had considerable experience working in managerial capacities.

The right-hand side of table 6.2 shows substantial evidence of differences in mean scores between these two populations. Not only were the students more participative in their reports of how they would deal with the thirty cases, but they also showed more substantial differences in effects of the problem attributes. Most of these differences occurred on attributes relevant to the acceptance of decisions. Students were more likely to respond to the existence of a requirement for acceptance of the decision by subordinates than were the managers. Both groups tended to be more participative when acceptance was critical, but the students responded more strongly to this requirement. Similarly, the behavior of the students was influenced more heavily by prior probability of acceptance. Like the managers, they were more participative when they lacked the ability to sell their solutions, but they were more affected by this attribute. The managers showed a relatively strong tendency to employ a more autocratic decision process when the subordinates in the case were depicted as likely to disagree. The difference for the students is in the same direction but much smaller in magnitude.

The differences on problem attributes relevant to the quality of the decision are far less marked. On three of these attributes—

leader's information, structure, and trust—there were no significant differences between the two groups. However, on the remaining quality attribute there was a very large difference. Managers showed a greater tendency than did the students to use more participative decision processes on problems with a quality requirement than on those without such a requirement.

In summary, choices of decision processes by students were more influenced by considerations relevant to the acceptance of decisions by subordinates, whereas the choices of managers tended to be more influenced by considerations relevant to the quality or rationality of the decision. At the risk of oversimplifying, the students may be said to be acting more in accordance with what Miles (1965) has called the human relations model of participative management, whereas the managers are acting more in accordance with his human resources model.

RELATIONSHIPS BETWEEN THESE
AND OTHER TESTS OF LEADER BEHAVIOR

We turn from a consideration of differences between managers and students of management to examine relationships between the nine measures and other tests of leader behavior. Several populations of managers and a group of ninety master's students in industrial administration completed both Problem Set 2 and one or more standard pencil-and-paper tests of leadership behavior such as were described at the beginning of this chapter. Several tests were used, but all were not administered to all populations. The tests employed were (1) LPC (Fiedler 1967), (2) the Leadership Opinion Questionnaire (Fleishman 1957), (3) Attitudes Toward Management Practices (Haire, Ghiselli, and Porter 1966), and (4) the Orientation Inventory (Bass 1962). Rather than describe all of the findings, we will restrict ourselves to summarizing the major conclusions from this research.

First, the correlations between other tests and the nine scores presented above are extremely low. One might expect low correlations with the unreliable difference-score measures, but even mean participativeness and variance are not highly correlated to any of the existing measures. The largest correlation in the entire set is .26 between LPC and the main effect of conflict (ME-Conf).

While small in magnitude and generally insignificant, the correlations are typically in a direction indicated by the constructs which the tests are supposed to measure. For example, the Haire, Ghiselli, and Porter measure, which purports to assess the degree to which a leader's attitudes are consistent with McGregor's Theory Y, is positively correlated with manager's mean level of participativeness (MLP) (r = .21, N = 126). Similarly, the task orientation score on Bass's Orientation Inventory shows a small nonsignificant negative correlation (-.10) with that same variable.

One of the surprising findings concerned the correlation between mean level of participativeness and Fiedler's LPC measure. This measure requires the subject to think of the person with whom he can work least well and to describe him by placing a check mark on eight-point scales separating pairs of bipolar adjectives. Examples include: pleasant-unpleasant; friendly-unfriendly; and open-guarded.[1] A person with a high LPC score describes his least preferred coworker in relatively favorable terms, whereas one with a low score describes his least preferred worker in negative terms.

The behavioral correlates of LPC have always been matters of considerable uncertainty. Fiedler assumes that a person with a high LPC score "derives his major satisfaction from successful interpersonal relationships" whereas one with a low LPC score is depicted as "deriving his major satisfaction from task performance." The interpretation of LPC as a motivational predisposition rather than as a behavioral pattern makes it difficult to make precise predictions concerning the correlations that should be obtained if Fiedler's conception were correct. Nonetheless, it was of considerable surprise to find that the correlations between LPC and Mean Level of Participation (MLP) was -.12 for managers (N = 126) and -.08 for students (N = 90). Neither of these correlations is statistically significant, but it is of interest to note that the direction is opposite to that which might be expected.

SUMMARY

In this chapter we have treated the procedure for studying situational determinants of leader behavior as a potential test of individual differences in leadership style. This "test" is different

1. The particular version of the LPC score used here is contained in Fiedler 1967, p. 41.

from all existing measures, combining the ease of scoring and administration of existing attitude and opinion questionnaires and the face validity of situational tests. Furthermore, the test produces a large number of scores, each potentially relevant to the way leaders respond to elements of their jobs. We restricted our interest here to scores that were potentially descriptive of the way in which leaders would behave on their jobs. Another set of scores, which evaluate the consistency between the leader's behavior and the normative model, will be examined in the next chapter.

The results indicate that the reliability of the measures of situational effects described in this chapter fall far short of that needed for accurate individual prediction. Mean participativeness (MLP) is reasonably reliable and variance (Var-P) slightly less so, but the reliabilities of the main effects of situational variables are exceedingly low. Presumably, estimates of interaction terms would be even less reliable. The potential advantage of the large number of scores could only be realized if a test of substantially greater length were constructed.

These considerations strongly argue against the possible use of the difference measures in their present form for predicting how leaders would behave on their jobs. While the critical consideration for this purpose is the construct validity of the measures, the unreliability of the difference scores will place an upper bound on their validity. Studies are now underway to determine the construct validity of the two "reliable" descriptive scores. These studies are concerned with answering such questions as the following: Do persons who indicate that they would use a preponderance of autocratic methods on the standardized problems also behave more autocratically in carrying out their jobs? Do those who display the greatest variance in the decision processes they employ on the problem set also display greatest variance in the opportunity that they provide their subordinates on the job?

While the unreliability of the scores for the measurement of the main effects of situational variables argues against their successful use for purposes of individual prediction, they can be used for aggregate prediction in answering questions of a research nature. The fact that these measures did reflect differences between students of administration and practicing managers that were quite large and easily interpretable suggests their possible value in answering other questions of interest to scholars in the area of management and organizational behavior. How do leadership styles vary among cultures and subcultures? In what kinds of organizations does one find the most participative leadership styles? What factors influence the leadership styles that people acquire? How easily and in what ways can they be most easily altered?

For purposes such as those outlined above, the low reliability of the measures is compensated for by comparing groups of people exposed to the same treatment or working in the same culture or organization. The errors of measurement, which pose a significant problem for individual prediction from behavior based on small numbers of items or cases, are effectively canceled out by averaging across persons, assuming such errors to be independent. Of course, even for research applications, the effective use of the measures described here is contingent on their construct validity. If the differences in scores among groups, organizations, or treatments do not correspond to real differences in the underlying property, then the measure is invalidated even as a research tool. It was reported in the previous chapter, however, that an aggregate regression model based on behavior on the problem set was able to predict the behavior that other managers reported they had used in carrying out their jobs. This is one indication that the behavior on the problem set is not unique to that situation, but more such evidence is needed.

CHAPTER 7

A Comparison of Normative
with Actual Behavior

In the first three chapters of this book, a normative model was presented in which a problem's status on each of seven attributes was used to define a feasible set of decision processes from which the manager should select his management style. Chapters 4 to 6 reported empirical investigations of the decision processes that managers actually use in various administrative problems. Two methods, one involving recalled problems and the other using standardized cases, were employed for this purpose. Since the empirical investigations utilized the same problem attributes as the normative model and employed the same decision processes as the dependent variable, it is possible to use the same empirical data to determine how managerial behavior is similar to or different from that prescribed by the normative model.

This chapter will attempt to answer such questions as the following: How often is the decision process used by a manager identical to that prescribed by the normative model? In what kinds of problems do the model and managers most often agree or disagree? What rules underlying the model are most frequently violated by managers? What differences exist among managers in their tendency to behave in a manner similar to the model?

In seeking answers to such questions we are not trying to validate the normative model. This model was intended to specify how managers should behave, not how they do behave; there is little reason for believing that managers always select the most effective method of making decisions. On the other hand, one should be cautious about assuming that the model is valid and that all instances in which managers deviate from it reflect some deficiency on their part. The kinds of questions posed above can best be regarded not as a basis for evaluating either the model or the managers studied, but rather as a basis for predicting the changes in leader behavior that would take place if the normative model became the basis for selecting leadership styles.

IS THE MODEL MORE PARTICIPATIVE?

The most general comparative question that we can ask is whether a typical manager's average behavior is more or less participative than the behavior of the normative model when applied to similar sets of problems. In chapter 4, we described an investigation in which 268 managers were asked to recall a problem they had recently solved, to code it on the problem attributes used in the normative model, and to indicate which of the five processes (AI, AII, CI, CII, GII) was closest to the one they used. Table 7.1 presents the average normative and reported behavior on

TABLE 7.1. Level of Participation for Normative Versus Actual Behavior

	Recalled Problems N = 268		Standardized Problems N = 16,530	
	Mean	Variance	Mean	Variance
Managers' behavior	6.4	12.5	4.7	15.3
Normative behavior	5.8	19.5	4.1	19.1

these recalled problems.[1] The normative behavior was determined by the manager's coding of his problem and the decision tree presented in figure 3.2, that is, the minimum man-hours (or short-term) model in which the process furthest to the left within the feasible set is always chosen. Table 7.1 also reports the average scale value of the decision processes used by the 551 managers (included in P_1 to P_8) in the standardized cases developed in chapter 5 along with the average scale value of the decision processes prescribed by the normative model for the same problems. The normative decision process in a standardized case was derived from the model presented in figure 3.2. The coding was that of

1. As in previous analyses, the scale values used for AI, AII, CI, CII, GII are those developed in chapter 4.

experts verified by managers in accordance with the procedures described in chapter 5.

On average, the normative model generated slightly more autocratic behavior than was reported by managers on either recalled (5.8 versus 6.4) or standardized problems (4.1 versus 4.7). The latter difference is highly significant due to the large number of observations; the former difference just fails to reach significance at the .05 level. Thus, if the managers had acted in a manner consistent with the normative model, they would, on average, have behaved in a manner that was slightly more autocratic. Unlike Likert's System 4 (Likert 1967) and other human relations models, the adoption of the normative model developed in this work is not synonymous with an increase in participation.

The difference in managers' behavior on recalled and standardized problems (6.4 versus 4.7) is likely to be an artifact of the problem mix included in each data set. There were substantial differences in the proportional representation of several problem types between the recalled and the standardized problems. Problem types such as 6a, 6b, and 12, for which the normative model prescribes GII, were drastically underrepresented in the standardized problem sets when compared with their incidence in recalled problems. Managers acted more participatively on the recalled compared with the standardized problems and, according to the normative model, they should have responded that way.

The most obvious difference between managers' behavior and that of the normative model reported in table 7.1 is not between mean behavior but between the variances in behavior. On both standardized and recalled problems, the normatively prescribed behavior exhibits substantially greater variance in decision processes than does the managers' recalled (19.5 versus 12.5) and hypothetical behavior (19.1 versus 15.3). Both differences are significant at the .01 level. The normative model varies the decision process from one problem to another to a greater extent than do the managers.

AGREEMENT WITH THE NORMATIVE MODEL

The differences between the behavior of the model and that of the typical manager can also be illustrated without reference to the values of the five decision processes on the scale of participation.

The frequency with which the behavior reported by managers agreed with that of the normative model can be shown. Table 7.2 compares model and managerial behavior on the set of 268 recalled problems.

TABLE 7.2. Comparison of Model Behavior with Managerial Behavior on Recalled Problems (N = 268)

| | | Managerial Behavior | | | | | | |
		AI	AII	CI	CII	GII	N	Percentage of Total
	AI	26.8%	12.7%	26.8%	18.3%	15.5%	71	26.5%
Model	AII	–	26.9%	23.1%	34.6%	15.4%	26	9.7%
Behavior	CI	–	21.4%	42.9%	21.4%	14.3%	14	5.2%
	CII	7.7%	3.8%	23.1%	48.1%	17.3%	52	19.4%
	GII	5.7%	3.8%	15.2%	27.6%	47.6%	105	39.2%
	N	29	25	59	79	76	268	
Percentage of total		10.8%	9.3%	22.0%	29.5%	28.4%		

A comparison of the marginal percentages for rows and columns indicates the basis for the previous observation that the model varied its behavior more with the situation than the managers did. The model makes more extensive use of the two extreme decision processes than do the managers. AI is prescribed for 26.5 percent of the recalled problems, whereas it is used in only about 10.8 percent of those instances. GII is prescribed for 39.2 percent of the problems but is employed only 28.4 percent of the time. Managers, on the other hand, make more extensive use of the consultative methods, CI and CII. In a sense, we can regard the model as both more autocratic and more participative than the typical manager.

The main part of table 7.2 shows the degree of correspondence between managers and the model. The top row of that table shows the percentage of times that managers reported using each of the five decision processes for problems in which the normative method was AI. Rows 2 through 5 present similar data for problems in which the normative model used AII, CI, CII, and GII respectively. The main diagonal in that table shows the proportion of cases in which the managers' behavior and the behavior of the model were in perfect agreement. Considering all 268 problems, agreement was perfect in 107 or 39.9 percent of the cases. If the managers had randomly selected from the set of five decision processes in accordance with the same marginal distribution as that shown for the normative model, perfect agreement would be expected in only 21.7 percent of the cases. Thus, while there is less than perfect correspondence between managers' behavior and that of the model, the frequency of agreement is almost double that which would be expected by chance. Furthermore, in 68.3 percent of these problems the managers' behavior was within the feasible set; that is, it did not violate any of the rules designed to protect decision quality or acceptance.

The possibility that these conclusions are dependent on the particular distribution of problems reported by the 268 managers or on the methods employed can be checked by a similar analysis of the results obtained with standardized problems. Table 7.3 presents such an analysis.

TABLE 7.3. Comparison of Model Behavior with Managerial Behavior on Standardized Problems (N = 551 managers, 16,530 observations)

		Managerial Behavior					
		AI	AII	CI	CII	GII	Percentage of Total
	AI	46.2%	11.2%	14.2%	18.7%	9.7%	40.0%
	AII	16.5	39.7	16.6	23.5	3.7	13.4%
Model	CI	10.5	4.9	21.8	43.4	19.4	3.3%
Behavior	CII	7.0	16.3	27.5	32.2	17.0	23.3%
	GII	9.6	9.0	19.0	32.0	30.3	20.0%
	Total	24.6%	15.5%	18.8%	26.0%	15.1%	

From a comparison of the marginal percentages for rows in tables 7.2 and 7.3, we can see that the distribution of problems is quite different. The standardized set contains a much larger proportion of problems in which the model prescribes AI (40 percent as compared with 26.5 percent) and a substantially smaller proportion of problems in which the model prescribes GII (20 percent as compared with 39.2 percent). Despite these differences in problem mix and the large differences between the research methods used, the conclusions are remarkably similar.

By comparing the marginal percentages for rows and columns in table 7.3, we can obtain support for the previous conclusion that the model makes greater use of the extreme styles (AI and GII) and less use of the consultative styles (CI and CII). The incidence of perfect agreement is 37.1 percent, compared with 39.9 percent for recalled problems and an expected agreement due to chance of only 21.6 percent. The incidence of agreement with the feasible set is 69.7 percent, a figure comparable in magnitude to that (68.3 percent) for the recalled problems.

Tables 7.2 and 7.3 also show that the rate of agreement between the behavior of the model and that of managers varies somewhat with the decision process prescribed by the normative model. These rates of agreement between actual and normative behavior shown along the main diagonal of both tables were obtained by aggregating across very different problem types. For example, the agreement rate for problems in which the normative model prescribes GII is a composite of the agreement rates for problems of type 3, 6*a*, 6*b*, and 12. An investigation of the rate of agreement by problem type rather than by normative style reveals that the tendency to act in a manner identical to the normative model varies markedly from one problem type to another. The findings for problems of type 3 and 6*b* are not atypical. On problems of type 6*b*, the rates at which managers used the GII method prescribed by the model are 73 percent and 57 percent for the recalled and standardized problems respectively. In contrast, on problems of type 3, for which the model also prescribes GII, the agreement rates for recalled and standardized problems are only 22 and 24 percent.

The most obvious reason for differences between the model and managers in behavior is that they use different decision rules. There is good reason to believe, from the results presented in chapters 4 and 5, that the factors that influence the typical manager to share or retain his decision-making power include many of the attributes contained in the normative model, but the agreement was far from perfect. It is also possible for deviations from model behavior to result from differences in perception of the situation. A given manager's behavior may be different from that of the model even though his decision rules were identical, if he failed to perceive accurately all of the features of the situation.

An analogy may prove helpful. Let us assume that there are two computer programs designed for the same purpose and it has been observed that they generate different output. The variation in output could be due to differences in the structure of the programs (the decision rules employed by the manager and of the model) or differences in the input data (the perceived properties of the situation).

In the analogy, the resolution of the question is simple. Control for the input by insuring that the same sets of data are provided in identical form to both programs. If the variance in output remains, then one can conclude that it is due to the structure of the programs; if it is eliminated, it was due to variance in input.

To a degree, the comparison between the results for recalled and hypothetical problems accomplishes this goal. In the recalled problems, the model's behavior was determined by using the managers' coding of the problems. Hence, the input to the model and to the managers was identical since the behavior of both was based on the mangers' view of the situation. The slightly greater rate of agreement with the normative model using this method than using standardized problems (39.9 percent as compared to 37.1 percent) could be taken as evidence that perceptual factors are relatively unimportant. However, there are many other differences between these two studies—in the kinds of managers studied and in problem mix—that render this evidence somewhat questionable.

To investigate this question more directly, it would be necessary to compare the incidence of perceptual errors in standardized problems when behavior was consistent and inconsistent with the model. If the incidence of perceptual errors was approximately equal in cases of agreement and disagreement, then one could conclude that idiosyncracies in how managers perceive and interpret situations have little to do with agreement with the model. Lack of agreement with the model could be attributed solely to differences in decision rules. On the other hand, if perceptual errors are far more frequent when the subjects disagree with the model, we could conclude that idiosyncracies in perception of the relevant features of the situation play an important role in determining whether a person's behavior will agree with the model.

Since information on how each of the 551 managers coded the thirty problems in their version of the problem set was not collected, we designed another investigation to shed some light on this question. This study utilized as subjects 18 managers who were not included in the previous analysis. They had received, in the course of a management development program, a brief exposure to the model but were inexperienced in its use or application. Each was given the set of thirty cases and was asked to indicate the decision process he would employ on each case. He was promised a detailed analysis of his leadership style on the basis of his responses and was asked to ignore the model in making his choices as this would interfere with the meaningfulness of the feedback he would receive. After each manager had specified what he would do in each of the cases, he was asked to use the flow chart shown in figure 3.1 to determine problem type.

There is some evidence that the management development program may have influenced the managers in their choice of the decision-making styles. Their choices agreed with the normative model in 50.5 percent of the cases, whereas the comparable figure for the 551 managers shown in table 7.3 was only 37.1 percent. In addition, these managers were substantially more participative in their behavior in the problem set than was true of the larger group. Their mean level of participation was 5.1 compared with 4.6 for the larger group.

To carry out the analysis of the relationship between agreement with the model and misperceptions of the situation, it is necessary to determine how accurately each of the eighteen managers coded each problem. Coding of a problem by a manager was deemed accurate if (1) his specification of a problem type was identical to that of both experts and the modal judgment of managers trained in applying the model, or (2) his coding of problem type deviated from expert and modal judgments in only one attribute and that error made no difference in the decision process specified. Of 540 judgments of problem type, over two-thirds were accurate by this definition.

Agreement with the model was determined by the same procedures as that employed in table 7.3, that is, by comparing the managers' choices of a decision process on a problem with the model's behavior employing expert coding.

The relationship between coding accuracy and agreement with the model is shown in table 7.4.

It can be easily seen that the two variables are highly related. If a subject's behavior agrees with the model, the odds are about nine out of ten that he will subsequently code the problem correctly.

TABLE 7.4. Relationship Between Coding Accuracy and Agreement with the Model

	Accurate	Inaccurate	Total
Agreement with model	243	30	273
Nonagreement with model	119	148	267
Total	362	178	540

NOTE: X^2 = 179.6; $p < .01$.

On the other hand, if his behavior disagrees with the model, the odds are better than 50 percent that in his subsequent coding of the problem he will "miss" some significant and relevant feature of the situation. For example, he may believe that he has the necessary information when the facts indicate that he does not or that acceptance of the decision by his subordinates is unimportant when, in fact, they are going to have to carry out the decision under conditions of great autonomy. Differences between the subject's behavior and that of the model tend to be accompanied by perceptual "errors" reflected in miscoding of the problem. Similarly, accurate problem coding is accompanied by agreement with the model about two thirds of the time, whereas inaccurate problem coding is associated with agreement with the model only 17 percent of the time, which is less than would be expected if the manager were selecting his method of making decisions by chance.

Problem differences could account for the relationship between accuracy and agreement. Conceivably problems vary in a property, such as ambiguity, that could be negatively correlated with both agreement and accuracy. To eliminate the possibility that the relationship is spurious, the analysis shown in table 7.4 was replicated for each of the thirty problems. Twenty-seven problems exhibit the same relationship; in the remaining three problems the relationship was indeterminate due to lack of variance in either accuracy or agreement.

On standardized problems, we conclude that inaccurate perception of the situation is an important cause of behavior which is inconsistent with the model. In those instances when subjects' responses are different from the model, it is frequently true that their judgments about the nature of the situation would also be at variance with those of experts and of most managers.

While perceptual errors appear to be responsible for many more of the instances of disagreement with the model than had been thought from the previous comparison of agreement rates for recalled and standardized problems, they are by no means the only factors. When the individual manager's coding of a problem is used as the basis for determining how the normative model would have behaved, the rate of agreement goes up from 50.5 percent to 61.9 percent. The increase in agreement rate of about 11 percent provides a crude estimate of deviations from the model on standardized problems resulting from idiosyncratic interpretations of the situation. If there were no differences in the decision rules used by the model and by managers, the agreement rate using the manager's own coding of the problem would, of course, be 100 percent. Differences in decision rules still appear to be a major factor in producing behavior different from that of the model.

RULE VIOLATIONS BY MANAGERS

In chapter 3, seven rules were presented which determine the feasible set of decision processes applicable to a given problem and which are the basis for defining problem type. Three rules serve to protect the quality of the decision and four to protect its acceptance. Each rule defines a set of conditions, specified in terms of the problem's status on seven problem attributes, which contraindicate one or more of the five decision processes. From the previous analysis, we know that the behavior of managers was not always consistent with these rules. Rates of agreement with the feasible set of 68.3 percent and 69.7 percent, for recalled and standardized problems, indicate that, on slightly under a third of the problems, one or more rules underlying the behavior of the model was violated. But we have not yet stated which rules were violated and with what frequency. For the reader's convenience, the seven rules are condensed here.

1. The information rule. If the quality of the decision is important and the leader does not possess enough information or expertise to solve the problem by himself, AI is eliminated from the feasible set.

2. The trust rule. If the quality of the decision is important and subordinates cannot be trusted to base their efforts to solve the problem on organizational goals, GII is eliminated from the feasible set.

3. The unstructured problem rule. When the quality of the decision is important, if the leader lacks the necessary information or the expertise to solve the problem by himself, and if the problem is unstructured, AI, AII, and CI all are eliminated from the feasible set.

4. The acceptance rule. If the acceptance of the decision by the subordinates is critical to its effective implementation, and if it is not certain that an autocratic decision made by the leader would receive that acceptance, AI and AII are eliminated from the feasible set.

5. The conflict rule. If the acceptance of the decision is critical, and an autocratic decision is not certain to be accepted, and if subordinates are likely to be in conflict or disagreement over the appropriate solution, AI, AII, and CI are eliminated from the feasible set.

6. The fairness rule. If the quality of the decision is unimportant and if acceptance is critical and not certain to result from an autocratic decision, AI, AII, CI, and CII are eliminated from the feasible set.

7. The acceptance priority rule. If acceptance is critical, not assured by an autocratic decision, and if subordinates can be trusted, AI, AII, CI, and CII are eliminated from the feasible set.

The two sets of data we have used to determine the frequency of agreement between actual and normatively prescribed behavior can also be used to determine the frequency with which each of the above seven rules is violated. As before, the use of these two different types of data guards against the possibility that conclusions are method specific.

Before the results of this analysis can be presented, three basic terms must be defined:

Frequency of applicability (f_a). This term refers to the frequency with which a rule is applicable to the problems from each data set. Each rule is only applicable to certain combinations of problem characteristics. Such combinations may occur in more than one problem type. Thus, the acceptance rule (rule 4) is applicable to problem types 3, 6, 7, 8, 12, and 13. In contrast, the fairness rule (rule 6) is only applicable to problems of type 3.

Frequency of Violation (f_v). This term refers to the frequency with which a rule is violated in a given set of data. Each rule contraindicates one or more of the five decision processes. The rule is violated if any one of the contraindicated processes is used by a manager. Of course, a rule can only be violated if it is applicable. Thus, by definition, f_v is always less than or equal to f_a.

Probability of Violation (p_v). This term refers to the probability of a rule being violated given that it is applicable. Thus $p_v = f_v/f_a$. This measure is of greatest interest in understanding the differences between managers' behavior and that of the model. Unlike f_v it permits comparisons of behavior among different populations with very different problem distributions. Whereas no simple direct comparison can be made between the frequency of violation of a particular rule for the recalled and standardized problems because of the different incidence of problem types in the two data sets, such comparisons can be made for the probability that a given rule is violated.

TABLE 7.5. Rule Violations by Managers

Rule	Recalled Problems (N = 268)			Standardized Problems (N = 16,530)		
	f_a	f_v	p_v	f_a	f_v	p_v
1	122	2	.02	6,612	463	.07
2	80	9	.11	6,612	595	.09
3	40	4	.10	3.306	1,587	.48
4	157	19	.12	5,510	1,212	.22
5	66	20	.30	2,755	1,397	.51
6	9	7	.78	1,102	835	.76
7	96	48	.50	2,204	1,477	.67

Table 7.5 reports the magnitudes of each of the above statistics for all seven rules applied to both the recalled and the standardized problems. As noted above, of the three statistics only p_v, the probability of violating a rule, is independent of the distribution of problem types and directly comparable for the two methods.

Of the seven rules, the fairness rule has the highest probability of being violated, with p_v of .78 and .76 for the recalled and standardized problems, respectively. In descending order of their probability of being violated, we have the acceptance priority rule (.50 and .67), the conflict rule (.30 and .51), the unstructured problem rule (.10 and .48), the acceptance rule (.12 and .22), the trust rule (.11 and .09), and the information rule (.02 and .07).

In chapter 3, we separated the rules into two classes in accordance with the outcome of decision-making that they were designed to protect. Thus, rules 1, 2, and 3 were termed "quality rules" since they were intended to guard against low quality or irrational solutions, and rules 4, 5, 6, and 7 were termed "acceptance rules" since their function was to protect against inadequate acceptance of or commitment to the solution on the part of those who were to carry it out. Comparing the probability of rule violations reported in table 7.5 for these two classes reveals that acceptance rules have a much higher probability of being violated than do quality rules. The four acceptance rules are ranked 1, 2, 3, and 5 in order of frequency of violation. If the two classes of rules are equally valid, this finding means that the typical manager is much more likely to employ a decision process that risks the necessary commitment on the part of his subordinates than one that risks the quality of the decision.

The only rule for which there is a large discrepancy between the two sets of estimates is rule 3 (the unstructured problem rule). It was violated only 10 percent of the time on recalled problems but 48 percent of the time on standardized problems. Thus, managers have over four times the likelihood of using AI, AII or CI on an unstructured standardized problem as on an unstructured recalled problem. How can this discrepancy be explained?

One possibility is that the unstructured problems in the standardized problem sets were frequently perceived as structured. The reader may recall from chapter 3 that our study of coding errors indicated a large proportion of false positives on the structure attribute. (A false positive indicates that a manager coded a problem as structured when it was intended to be unstructured.) At the time, we concluded that the question used to measure structure produced a threshold for yes judgments that was much lower than intended.

If this fact is indeed the explanation of the difference in violations of rule 3 observed in recalled and standardized problems, we should observe a much lower rate of violation of this rule on standardized problems when the individual manager's coding of this attribute was used. This possibility was checked using the data from the eighteen managers who both indicated how they would behave on thirty cases and then coded the problems' attributes. Violations of the unstructured problem rule were calculated for this group in two ways: (1) by the procedure in table 7.5 for standardized problems—expert coding verified by managers—and (2) by using their own coding of the problem. For the first of these methods, the violation rate is .31. This figure, compared directly with the .48 for 551 managers, probably indicates the effects of the leadership training that the eighteen managers had received.

When the managers' own coding was used (the second method above), the violation rate was found to be only .12. This figure is close to the value shown for recalled problems (.10), confirming the fact that the discrepancy for rule 3 was an artifact of the research methods used.

INDIVIDUAL DIFFERENCES IN AGREEMENT
WITH THE NORMATIVE MODEL

So far in this chapter we have considered the "typical manager" in our examination of similarities and differences with the normative model. The results presented on agreement rates and probabilities of rule violations are statistical averages based on observations of large numbers of managers.

The use of standardized problems, in which multiple observations are made for a single manager, permits one to examine the variance around these averages. For example, while the average manager violated rule 4 (the acceptance rule) 2.2 times ($p_v = .22$), there were some who did not violate it at all and others who violated it as many as 7 times ($p_v = .70$).

It is conceivable that such rule violations are really random events brought about by momentary "lapses" on the part of the individual manager. The probability of violating a given rule on one problem to which that rule is applicable could be independent of the probability of violating the same rule on a second problem to which it is equally applicable. Alternatively, it is possible that managers vary in their predisposition to violate each rule. If that were the case, it might be possible to measure the strength of that predisposition using a version of the problem set as a measuring instrument.

There are eleven different measures that could be useful in reflecting differences among managers in their agreement with the normative model; seven of these correspond to the probabilities with which the individual violates the rules defining the feasible set of decision processes. These eleven measures can be termed "evaluative measures" to distinguish them from the nine descriptive measures considered in chapter 6. They are:

1. *Agreement with the normative model (AgNM).* This score represents the number of problems in which the person's behavior agrees exactly with the solution of the short-term normative model for that problem type.

2. *Absolute distance from the normative model (ADNM).* This score is related to #1 (above), but cases of disagreement with the model are weighted by the amount of disagreement. It is given by the formula $\Sigma D/30$ where D is the absolute value of the distance between the scale value of the decision process used by the person and the scale value of the decision process prescribed by the normative model. Thus, if the person used CII and the model prescribed GII, the distance is $|8.125-10|$ or 1.875.

3. *Agreement with the feasible set (AgFS).* The score shows the number of problems in which the person's behavior falls within the feasible set of methods for that problem type. By definition this constitutes the number of problems in which no rule violations occurred.

4. *Absolute distance from the feasible set (ADFS).* This score indicates the average absolute distance between the decision process selected by the person and the closest decision process within the feasible set. It is related conceptually to #3 (above). The method of computation is analogous to that employed for measure 2.

5. *Probability of violating rule 1.* This score is the proportion of the instances when the individual violates rule 1 given that it is applicable to the problem. As previously noted $p_v = f_v/f_a$ (f_a is a constant for a given problem set).

6 *through 11. Probability of violating rules 2 through 7.* These scores are computed as above, using observations relevant to rules 2 through 7.

Table 7.6 shows mean scores on these eleven evaluative measures for the two populations—students of administration and practicing managers—examined in chapter 6. Both groups responded to the same version of the problem set (2), so direct comparison of their results is possible. The results round out our picture of the differences between these two populations presented in the previous chapter. The students have significantly fewer violations of all of the rules except one. The differences in favor of the students are greater in magnitude on the four acceptance rules, supporting the observation made in the previous chapter that acceptance considerations play a more important role in governing the decision processes employed by the students than by practicing managers. The one rule on which students show greater violations is rule 2. This rule prohibits the use of GII when the decision has a quality requirement and the goals of subordinates are in conflict with those of the organization. It is interesting to note that several of the students, after receiving feedback based on their results, questioned the moral values implicit in this rule. They reasoned that the leader's job should be to represent the interests of his "constituency" even though he might jeopardize the goals of the organization in so doing.

Table 7.6 also shows reliability coefficients for each of the

TABLE 7.6. **Reliabilities of the Eleven Evaluative Measures and Comparison of Students' and Managers' Scores**

		Mean Scores	
Measure	Split-half Reliability (N = 306)	Students (N = 105)	Managers (N = 201)
1. AgNM	.46	10.47	11.45
2. ADNM	.46	1.23	1.19
3. AgFS	.46	22.64	21.11
4. ADFS	.59	0.35*	0.50*
5. Rule 1	.50	0.03*	0.07*
6. Rule 2	.57	0.15*	0.10*
7. Rule 3	.50	0.40*	0.48*
8. Rule 4	.47	0.11*	0.22*
9. Rule 5	.50	0.33*	0.50*
10. Rule 6	.14	0.50*	0.76*
11. Rule 7	.39	0.56*	0.68*

*Mean difference significant at .01 level or better.

eleven measures, which were obtained by subdividing the problem set into two halves, correlating the scores on each half, and applying the Spearman-Brown correction. These reliability coefficients provide a simple test of the hypothesis that deviations from the normative model are due to the operation of random events rather than real individual differences. Were that the case, the reliability coefficients would have an expected value of zero. In fact, they range from .59 to .14 with a median of .47.

The reliability coefficients for the rule violations vary predictably with the frequency with which the rules are applicable in the problem set (f_a). The latter statistic gives the number of cases in the problem set that are used in the calculation of rule violations. It ranges from a high of twelve for rules 1 and 2 (reliability coefficients of .50 and .57 respectively) to a low of two for rule 6 (reliability of .14).

While the magnitude of the reliability coefficients clearly substantiates the existence of individual differences, they are too small to support the use of the present form of the problem set as a predictive instrument. The number of cases would have to be increased substantially for use in individual prediction. For example, to achieve a reliability of .80 for a measure of a person's predisposition to violate rule 6 would require approximately forty-eight cases in which this rule could be violated rather than the two in the present version. A problem set of greater length could be constructed for purposes of leader selection, but there are many questions that would have to be resolved before such an undertaking could be useful. The predictive validity of such a measuring instrument would be limited by the validity of the normative model. In addition, if such a test were used for selection, the motivation of people taking it would be substantially different from that of the managers studied here. One might expect a candidate for a leadership position to respond as he thought he should act rather than as he would act. Whether such responses would increase or decrease his agreement with the model is unclear, provided, of course, that he did not know the model. It would, however, most certainly reduce the construct validity of the measures. On the basis of such considerations we believe that the transformation of the problem set into a test for effective use in leader selection and evaluation is a highly remote possibility.

SUMMARY

Let us now return to the issue with which we began this chapter. From the evidence presented, what conclusions can we draw concerning the changes in leader behavior that would occur if managers voluntarily used the normative model as the basis for choosing their decision process?

Probably the most striking change would be the increase in the extent to which managers varied their method with the situation. They would become both more autocratic and more participative. Autocratic methods would be used more frequently in situations in which their subordinates were unaffected by the decision, and participative methods would be used more frequently when subordinates' cooperation and support was critical and/or their information and expertise required.

Acceptance considerations would play an even greater role in determining the decision-making process used. Subordinates would experience greater involvement in decisions that they had to execute, and, if rules underlying this part of our model are valid, they would respond with much greater commitment to these decisions. Managers would show much greater reluctance to attempt to influence decisions that were essentially matters of equity and fairness (such as type 3 problems) and would encourage their subordinates to resolve such matters among themselves.

The extent to which leader behavior would change in the directions indicated above through use of the model may be limited by managers' ability to make accurate judgments of problem attributes. We have seen that managers are presently more likely to agree with the model when their own coding of the problem is used than when the problem is coded by experts and verified by managers. We have also shown both here and in chapter 3 that there are substantial errors in these judgments, particularly on the part of untrained managers. Training is likely to increase the accuracy of these judgments and also the extent to which changes in behavior would result from use of the model.

Finally, we should note that the amount and nature of the changes in behavior from use of the model would vary markedly from one manager to another. As evidenced by their behavior on the standardized problems, some managers are already behaving in a manner highly consistent with the model, while others' behavior is clearly at variance with it. Eleven "evaluative" measures were developed to reflect the degree of agreement with various parts of the normative model. While the reliabilities of these measures are presently too low for accurate individual prediction, they are high enough to confirm the existence of variance among managers in their tendencies to behave in accordance with the model.

The possibility of developing a test for use in leader selection and evaluation based on the concept of the problem set was rejected. In the next chapter we will consider the use of the problem set in leadership development.

CHAPTER 8

A Technology for
Leadership Development

The investigations we reported in preceding chapters were conducted for the purpose of research on the determinants of power-sharing. Over a thousand managers have given up to twenty hours of their time as subjects in the research. The reader may have wondered how we were so successful in gaining the cooperation of subjects. We did not have a close friend who was a corporation president. It is rather that being a subject in the research was perceived by these people as valuable in its own right and as contributing to their own learning and development. The fortunate coincidence of interest between the personal goals of subjects and our own research goals certainly made the task easier; but subsequently we realized that the data collection procedures, with appropriate additions and modifications, might also serve as a valuable approach to leadership development. The central issue in this chapter is these by-products of the research program. We will be concerned with how the model and data collection activities can be adapted to serve the functions of leadership development.

AN OUTLINE OF A PROGRAM OF LEADERSHIP DEVELOPMENT

Let us assume that one of the critical skills required of all leaders is the ability to adapt their behavior to the demands of the situation. One component of this skill involves the ability to select the appropriate decision-making process for each problem. The following program is directed toward developing that skill. Like the model on which it is based, it is still experimental and is continuously being updated and improved.

At the present time the program consists of seven phases. The

155

amount of time devoted to each phase is highly variable as is the total amount of time devoted to the program. The first six of the phases have been covered in as little as fifteen hours or as long as thirty-two hours. Following is a brief description of each phase:

Phase I. Training in recognizing differences in own and others' decision processes. The object of this phase is to familiarize the participants with the taxonomy of decision processes defined in chapter 2 and to provide them with sufficient practice in using that taxonomy to describe the behavior of themselves and others so that it becomes a part of their vocabulary. Films illustrating different leaders handling identical situations have been useful in this phase.

Phase II. Diagnosis of one's own leadership style. Every participant is given the same set of standardized cases, each depicting a leader faced with an administrative problem. (See chapter 5 for a guide to the construction of a problem set.) Using the taxonomy developed in Phase I, they are asked to indicate how they would handle each problem. Responses are recorded on a standard answer sheet and turned in for processing. The participant keeps the cases along with a copy of his responses. Each participant "discovers" that his method varies across the problems and he is encouraged to think about the circumstances under which he uses each method.

Phase III. Practice in using decision processes. Each decision process requires certain skills for its effective execution. Being an effective leader requires not only knowing what to do but also how to do it. In this phase, participants are provided with practice in carrying out certain of the methods, particularly GII with which they typically have the least familiarity. This is accomplished through the use of films depicting leaders utilizing this process[1] or through practice (followed by a critique) in a leadership role with fellow participants in simulated situations.

Phase IV. Understanding the consequences of different decision processes. This phase is preparatory to Phase V in which the normative model is presented. It is intended to provide an experiential base for the concepts in the model and to enable participants to judge the effects of participation on decision quality, acceptance,

---

1. The films are stopped at preselected points and each participant is asked what he would do next if he were leader.

and man hours in controlled situations. Standard human-relations training exercises have been selected or adapted for use in this phase.

Phase V. Training in the normative model. In this phase, participants are shown the normative model, which is depicted as another means of deciding which decision process to use in different situations. The logic underlying the model is explained thoroughly. Emphasis is placed upon the concept of the feasible set, and one's choice among alternatives within the feasible set is based on such considerations as time pressure and one's interest in the development of subordinates. After each participant thoroughly understands the model he receives practice (with feedback) in applying it to another set of cases, so that he can see if it behaves in a way that makes sense to him.

Phase VI. Feedback based on behavior on the standardized problems. Each participant receives a detailed analysis of his own leadership style based on his report of how he would have handled each of the standardized situations. This analysis is accompanied by a manual that helps him to interpret it.

Phase VII. Follow-up. This phase is intended to facilitate transfer of developed skills back to the leadership role and to deal with any idiosyncratic problems that have not been provided for adequately in Phases I through VI. It begins with an offer to provide help in enabling each participant to make maximal use of what he has learned. The form this help takes is highly variable and depends on the unique needs and circumstances of the participant. It has included such activities as providing a comparable problem set so that he can see how his leadership style has been affected by the program; providing comparable feedback to his subordinates or his superiors; arranging for a program of organization development based on the model (see discussion later in this chapter); providing feedback based on performance on a set of real-life problems; providing additional reading; counseling on both personal and job-related problems.

Instead of elaborating on all of these phases, we will focus here on only two of them, Phases II and VI. These are the most unusual and probably the most critical to the effectiveness of the program.

During Phase II, each participant is given a set of standardized problems or cases. He is asked to select the decision process that most closely approximates the one he would employ were he the leader faced with the problem. Each person is told that he will receive a complete analysis of his responses and that the results will not be furnished to anyone else. He has the option of using a code number instead of his name to further protect his anonymity. These precautions are taken to reduce the possibility that subjects might attempt to fake their responses, indicating behavior that they think they *should* employ or that they believe would be "expected of them" rather than what they *would* employ.

There are a number of options available in the make-up of this problem set. One of these involves the number of problems. In most instances, we have found it convenient to use thirty cases, but there is nothing critical about the number thirty. Apart from the time and ingenuity in writing, selecting, and adapting cases, the relevant considerations are the time investment by participants in reading the cases and deciding how they would deal with them, and the amount they learn from the feedback. Thirty cases require roughly two and one-half hours and can be completed within a single evening. The reliability of the scores provided in the feedback can be increased by an increase in the number of problems, but it is not clear that reliability is critical for purposes of development though it obviously is for assessment.

A second option concerns the nature of the institutional setting depicted in the cases. The sets used most frequently are heterogeneous in institutional setting. The leaders depicted include directors of research laboratories, company presidents, university deans, and manufacturing foremen. Such a large variance in setting can, independent of the feedback, be an educational experience as one attempts to project oneself into the role of leader in a wide number of different situations. It can also be used with almost any managerial population with the assurance that at least some situations will closely match those that they have previously encountered.

The alternative to a standardized heterogeneous problem set is one specifically tailored to the population being trained, with the institutional setting being held constant. It is a relatively simple matter to develop problem sets with these characteristics if one has a detailed knowledge of the institutional environment. Similarly, one can translate cases originally based in one institutional environment into another. Limited problem sets have been developed for such diverse populations as school principals and military officers.

The three cases below show the same problem (of type 3) cast into different institutional settings.

Industrial version. The company for which you work has been taken over and the new parent company has replaced your boss. The parent company has moved in a manager to whom you now report, a man with little management experience and for whom you have little respect.

He has sent you, as head of the applied research department, a directive to the effect that some changes must be made in general work habits—primarily in the area of dress and office etiquette. You have argued in defense of the present practices and have informed him that the nature of the changes he is requesting is likely to cause a lot of resentment, a fall in morale, and may even result in some of your best junior staff leaving.

He is willing to concede the fact that your department has an excellent performance record and that these changes are not likely to result in any improved performance, but he says that he will not reconsider his decision, whatever the outcome. He has given you a month, after which he expects to see some results. In the event you do not introduce the necessary changes, he will issue a detailed set of rules and regulations to cover all personnel in your department. The problem you have to resolve is to see what rules to adopt to bring behavior into line with his general directives.

Nearly all the personnel in your department are under thirty and have graduate degrees in mathematics or the physical sciences. These common factors of age and training, plus the department's success, have resulted in a highly cohesive group with some strongly held group norms. These norms sanction the dress and office etiquette behavior that is now under review. For instance, while not permitting the extremes seen on a campus, your personnel believe that the length of a person's hair or sideburns and the width of his tie are questions of the individual's personal taste. You believe that any movement in the direction your superior has indicated will obviously receive universal opposition.

Military version. You are head of a task group on leadership. A reorganization has replaced your superior. You now report to his executive officer who has been moved in from another assignment, and he has had no experience in this type of assignment.

He has sent you a note that some changes must be made in

general appearance—primarily in the area of hair length. You have argued in defense of the present practices and have informed him that the nature of the changes he is requesting is likely to cause a lot of resentment, a fall in morale, and may even result in some of your best staff's resigning.

He is willing to concede that your staff has excellent performance records and that these changes are not likely to result in any improved performance, but he says that he will not reconsider his decision, whatever the outcome. He has given you a month, after which he expects to see some results. In the event you do not introduce the necessary changes, he will issue a detailed set of rules and regulations to cover all personnel on your staff. It is difficult to see what rules to adopt in order to bring appearance into line with his requirements, but this is the problem you must resolve.

Nearly all the personnel on your staff are under thirty and have graduate degrees in the social sciences. These common factors of age and training, plus the success of the project, have resulted in a highly cohesive group with some strongly held group norms. These norms sanction the general appearance that is now under review. For instance, it is clear that, while not permitting the extremes seen on civilians, your personnel believe that the length of a person's hair or sideburns is a question of the individual's personal taste. You believe that any movement in the direction your superior has indicated will obviously receive universal opposition.

School principal version. The enrichment school of which you are principal has been consolidated into a new system, which has replaced your superintendent. You now report to an assistant superintendent who has been moved in from the larger school area, and he has had no experience in an enrichment school.

He has sent you, as principal, a directive to the effect that some changes must be made in general work habits—primarily in the area of dress and classroom etiquette. You have argued in defense of the present practices and have informed him that the nature of the changes he is requesting is likely to cause a lot of resentment, a fall in morale, and may even result in some of your best staff's leaving.

He is willing to concede the fact that your school has an excellent performance record and that these changes are not likely to result in any improved performance, but he says that he will not reconsider his decision, whatever the outcome. He has given you a month, after which he expects to see some results. In the event you do not introduce the necessary changes, he will issue a detailed set of rules and regulations to cover all personnel in your school. It is difficult to see what rules to adopt in order to bring behavior into line with his general directives, but this is the problem you have to resolve.

Nearly all the personnel in your school are under thirty and have graduate degrees in mathematics or the physical sciences. These common factors of age and training, plus the school's many outstanding National Merit Scholars, have resulted in a highly cohesive group with some strongly held group norms. These norms sanction the dress and classroom behavior that is now under review. For instance, it is clear that, while not permitting the extremes seen on a campus, your personnel believe that the length of a person's hair or sideburns and the width of his tie are questions of the individual's personal taste. You believe that any movement in the direction your superior has indicated will obviously receive universal opposition.

The advantages of tailoring the problem set to the population are, at this point, purely matters of speculation. It seems likely that cases with which the subject is able to identify, due to their similarity to those he has experienced, are more likely to produce habitual responses or recall of how he has acted in such situations in the past. On the other hand, cases that are outside the realm of experience of the subject deprive him of cues from his past behavior and encourage him to examine more closely the attributes of the situation and their relevance to the leadership style to be employed.

A third option involves the considerations used in the selection of cases. The cases contained in the problem sets most frequently used were selected in accordance with the specifications of the experimental design depicted in chapter 5. This fact makes it possible for the subject to compare his behavior with the behavior of the normative model and to determine the main effects of each of seven variables. Many other designs would provide this opportunity of comparison with the model. As long as a problem can be coded in relatively reliable fashion by trained observers, it can be included in the problem set. If the problem attributes are also uncorrelated with one another, the main effects of problem attributes can be simply determined. Within these constraints, there are many problem-set configurations that could be constructed.

We have experimented with the use of the problem set at several different points during a course. In some applications a problem set was mailed to participants in advance of the training program, along with detailed instructions and examples, for completion before the program began. Typically, the answer sheets are mailed to a central source, where the data is processed and then distributed to participants at some point during the training program. This method provides maximum time for processing and insures that the results are not influenced by any content of the training program. It is possible, however, that the written instructions, which include definitions of the five decision processes, are not totally successful in creating a uniform conception of the meaning of each of these alternatives. It seems preferable to incorporate the problem set into the training program itself and precede it with instruction in the meaning of the five decision processes (phase I).

We have also tried using a problem set at the conclusion of a leadership training course that included instruction in the model. The results, clearly showing the influence of training, reveal greater use of participative methods and substantially fewer rule violations. Many participants found it difficult to avoid using the model in making their decisions. It is our judgment that the use of a problem set after training in the model is less helpful than its use prior to such training. If it is to be employed after training, this use should be supplemental to that at the start of the course. The comparison between performance at the two points in time then constitutes additional feedback to the participant and to those conducting the program.

PROCESSING OF DATA

The large number of measures that can be generated from responses to a standardized set of problems makes processing of results by computer highly desirable. Use of the computer makes it possible to report calculations such as differences between the subject and others in his training group which would be prohibited by a manual scoring system.

In our use of a problem set for purposes of leadership development, each subject has been furnished with a computer printout containing an individualized analysis of his leadership style as it is reflected in his reports of how he would behave on the standardized cases. The data for all participants in the training program are typically processed simultaneously, permitting the economical representation of differences between each person and others participating in the same training program. An option has also been developed that permits the comparison of a given person with any one of a large number of comparison groups for whom results on the same problem set have been collected.

Many different printout formats have been employed. In early work, the format consisted of a written report in narrative form presenting both the trainees' results and their possible interpretation. More recently, we have found it more economical to cover matters of explanation and interpretation in a manual that accompanies the report and to confine the printout to a presentation of the results in both numeric and graphic form.

A SAMPLE PRINTOUT

We will illustrate such a printout by showing the results received by one of the several hundred managers who have participated in the leadership development programs. It might be helpful for the reader to put himself in the recipient's role and try to work through the example. During the first week of a four-week management development course you and twenty-six other managers from your firm would have completed phases I through V as outlined earlier in this chapter. You have in your possession a copy of the problem set (containing a record of your responses), and a number of handouts describing the normative model (presenting the content of chapters 2 and 3 in highly condensed form). In addition you have just received three pages of computer output based on your responses to the problem set, and a fourteen-page manual to help you to understand the printout. You are now ready to begin an examination of your own leadership behavior. On the following pages, the figures and tables are excerpts from the computer printout,[2] while the quotations are excerpts from the accompanying manual.

> The data that you have received is based on your responses to the thirty case studies contained in your problem booklet. The degree to which what people say they would do in hypothetical situations matches what they would in fact do were they confronted with that situation is certainly open to question. However, if we assume that your responses were similar to

2. The authors are indebted to John Scherzi for developing the computer program used in generating this version of the printout.

what you would actually do then this data can potentially say a lot about your leadership style.

It is suggested that you first examine the content of the printout thoroughly using the guidelines presented here. Make notes to yourself either on the printout or on a separate sheet of paper about what this may mean about you or even about the feelings which it creates in you. Later it may prove useful for you to compare your observations with one or more other members of the group. . . .

Begin by considering the frequencies with which you, your group, and the normative model use each of the five decision processes. This is reported in Table I. Look first at how your responses to the thirty problems distribute themselves across the five leadership methods as represented in the row marked *individual frequency*. What was your most frequent method in these problems? Your next most frequent method? Your least frequent method? . . .

TABLE I. Proportion of Cases in Which Each Decision Process Is Used

	AI	AI	CI	CII	GII
Individual frequency	20%	23%	23%	20%	13%
Group frequency	25%	14%	11%	29%	21%
Model (A) minimize participation	40%	13%	3%	23%	20%
Model (B) maximize participation	0%	0%	0%	40%	60%

Now compare your distribution with that of other members of the group shown in the column marked *group frequency*. Which methods do you employ more frequently than average? Which methods do you employ less frequently than average?

Now look at the third row showing how the model presented on the flow chart (Model A)[3] distributes itself across the five methods when applied by the authors to the thirty problems. You will recall that this model was termed a short term model because it placed substantial weight on the number of man-hours required as the basis for choosing among alternative methods and no weight on the development of subordinates or the building of a work team that might represent, in the longer term, benefits of greater participation. What methods does Model A use more frequently? use less frequently?

The last line shows a similar analysis for Model B, a model that places no

3. Model A was the term used in phase V to refer to the normative model shown in figure 3.2. Model B was a term used to refer to a normative model which selected the most participative decision process within the feasible set.

weight whatsoever on time and maximum weight on development and team building. . . .

To get an overall picture of how participative your responses to the thirty problems are in relation to other members of the class, it is necessary to assign numbers to the five processes: AI, AII, CI, CII, GII. The numbers 1, 2, 3, 4, 5 would be mathematically simple but would inadequately represent a belief shared by most managers that the distances between the five alternatives are not equal.

The numbers for the five processes that are used are based on a research program the methods of which are complex and need not be described here. The critical things are the numbers themselves which are shown on the following scale.[4]

AI	AII	CI	CII	GII
0	.625	5.0	8.125	10.0

One thing to note about this scale is that the higher numbers represent more participation (GII = 10) and lower numbers less participation (AI = 0). You might also note that AI and AII are very close together in terms of the amount of participation they provide; then there is a very large distance to CI, a moderately large distance to CII and a smaller distance to GII.

A mean score representing the extent to which you would have provided your subordinates with an opportunity to participate in the thirty problems can be obtained by multiplying the percentage of times you used each decision process by its scale value and dividing by 100. Your average level of participativeness (individual mean) and the average for your group are reported below the frequency distribution of the individual means for all members of your group. In the frequency distribution presented in Figure I, the symbol G shows the location of the group mean and I indicates the position of your own mean behavior. . . .

FIGURE I. Frequency Distribution of Individual Mean Levels of Participation

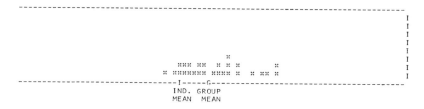

GROUP MEAN=   5.1
INDIVIDUAL MEAN= 4.3

4. The research on which these numerical assignments are based is reported in chapter 4.

The data considered so far are aggregated across different situations. The evidence presented in Table II is intended to permit you to compare your behavior in each case study with that of the normative model. If either Model A or Model B makes sense to you as a rational model of behavior then these comparisons should be of interest to you; if not, this part of the feedback should prove to be of little importance.

The normative model identifies 14 different problem types corresponding to the terminal nodes on the decision tree shown in your handout [the reader should see figure 3.2].

For problems of type 6, 7, and 8, there are in fact two alternative paths to the same node depending on your response to question 2 (dealing with whether you have enough information on which to base a decision). Thus, each of these problem types can be further subdivided. Those case studies in which you do have enough information are designated by the label A (6A, 7A, 8A) and those in which you do not have enough information are designated by the label B (6B, 7B, 8B).

There are case studies in the problem booklet which have been designated by the authors and most managers as representative of each type (except 8B). Their numbers are shown in the two left-hand columns of Table II. In the third column you will see the prescription of Model A for each problem type. . . .

TABLE II. Behavior by Problem Type

PROBLEM TYPE	PROBLEM NUMBERS	MODEL A BEHAVIOR	FEASIBLE SET	YOUR BEHAVIOR
1	28,17	AI	AI,AII,CI,CII,GII	AII AI
2	15,14	AI	AI,AII,CI,CII,GII	AI GII
3	5,3	GII	GII	CI GII
4	2,26,27,25	AI	AI,AII,CI,CII,GII*	CII AI CI CI
5	22,29,30,12	AI	AI,AII,CI,CII,GII*	CII AI CiI AI
6A	8,20	GII	GII	CI GII
6B	7	GII	GII	GII
7A	1	CII	CII	CI
7B	10	CII	CII	CI
8A	11	CI	CI,CII	CII
8B	P R O B L E M T Y P E N O T I N C L U D E D			
9	19,24	AII	AII,CI,CII,GII*	AII AI
10	21,23	AII	AII,CI,CII,GII*	AII AII
11	16,6	CII	CII,GII*	AII CII
12	13	GII	GII	AII
13	18	CII	CII	CI
14	9,4	CII	CII,GII*	CII AII

*GII NOT IN THE FEASIBLE SET (TRUST-NO. SEE RULE 2) FOR PROBLEMS 1,4, 10,11,12,16,18,21,24,25,26,29.

To the immediate right is a column designating the feasible set for each problem type. The method preferred by Model A is always the furthest to the left in the feasible set. You can easily determine for yourself the method preferred by Model B by looking at the extreme right of the feasible set. *Caution:* GII is shown as within the feasible set for problem types

4, 5, 9, 10, 11, and 14 but is, in fact, excluded for half of the examples of these problems [see footnote to Table II for the relevant problem numbers].

The last column marked *Your Behavior* indicates your response to each of the cases of the indicated problem type. If there is more than one case of that type, the methods you used are shown in the same order as the problem numbers at the left-hand side.

The data in Columns 3, 4, and 5 in Table II are summarized in Table III which reports the frequency with which your behavior agreed with the normative model. For comparison purposes the average rates of agreement for members of your group are also presented. The rates of agreement with the models vary quite markedly from one person to another. For example, in one group of managers the lowest rate of agreement with the feasible set was 14 while the highest was 26. If your score is substantially different from that of the group, you may wish to look for the rules which account for this difference. The data for such an analysis are reported later in Table IV.

TABLE III. Frequency of Agreement with the Normative Model

	Individual Frequency	Group Mean
Agreement with feasible set	21	22.1
Agreement with Model A	13	14.1
Agreement with Model B	5	9.0

Finally, look at the difference between your agreement with Model A and Model B. This may reflect the relative priorities which your leadership style places on short-term considerations such as time as opposed to longer-term considerations such as development of subordinates. Thus, a person whose behavior agrees with Model A twenty times and Model B only twice usually chooses a method which, other things being equal, minimizes the number of man-hours which goes into the decision. A person who agrees with Model B fifteen times and Model A five times has a style which takes up more time in meetings and discussions with subordinates but probably does so with an expectation of longer-term payoffs in the development of his subordinates. Which description comes closest to fitting you? Does it match your image of yourself? Which comes closest to fitting the average group member? Does it match your conception of them? (For comparison purposes, in one large group of managers from several different firms, agreement with Model A ranged from a high of 20 to a low of 2 whereas agreement with Model B ranged from 17 to 0.)

Each time your behavior was outside the feasible set you violated at least one of the seven rules underlying the normative model [for a detailed exposition of the rules the reader should see chapter 3]. Table IV reports the frequencies with which you and the members of your group violated each rule. See how many times you violated rules designed to protect the quality of the decision (rules 1, 2, and 3) and rules designed to protect the acceptance of the decision (rules 4, 5, 6, and 7). Which set do you violate more frequently? How does your behavior compare with that of the average member of your group.

TABLE IV. Frequency of Rule Violations

| Rule Numbers | Rule Violations | | Problem Numbers | | | | | |
	Individual	Group						
1	1.0	0.4	24	0	0	0	0	0
			0	0	0	0	0	0
2	0.0	1.5	0	0	0	0	0	0
			0	0	0	0	0	0
3	4.0	2.1	4	13	16	18	0	0
4	1.0	1.6	13	0	0	0	0	0
			0	0	0	0		
5	5.0	1.9	1	5	8	10	13	
6	1.0	1.4	5	0				
7	2.0	2.2	8	13	0	0		

Now determine the rule you violated most often and reread the definition of that rule. Does it make sense to you? If it does *not*, try and see what it is that you object to or how your own position would differ. If it does make sense to you, it would be in order to reexamine the problems in which you violated the rule and see if you think it is applicable. The problem numbers are printed at the right-hand side of the table. A "0" indicates that the rule could have been violated but was not. You may find it worth while to repeat this activity for every rule.

The rules underlying the normative model prescribe different behaviors in different situations. You undoubtedly found, when responding to the case studies, that your decision process also varied from one situation to another. The data in Table V examine some of the factors that might influence your choice of decision process—to put it succinctly, that might influence you to share power or retain it.

The case studies in the problem booklet vary in a number of respects. While all of them are real (or based on real situations) the cases were selected in such a way as to make it possible to assess the effects of seven factors on your leadership style. These seven factors are identical to those

TABLE V. Main Effects of Problem Attributes

ATTRIBUTE		PROBLEM NUMBERS
IMPORTANCE OF ACCEPTANCE (ATTRIBUTE E)	HIGH I=4.97 G=5.79 ----------------------I--A--G-----------------B-----	(1,3,5,6,7,8,10,11,12,13,14, 15,16,18,19,20,22,24,29,30)
	LOW I=2.88 G=3.71 ------------A--------G-----------------------B-----	(2,4,9,17,21,23,25,26,27,28)
PRIOR PROBABILITY OF ACCEPTANCE (ATTRIBUTE F)	HIGH I=3.56 G=4.66 --------A--------I---G---------------------B-----	(6,12,14,15,16,19,22,24,29,30)
	LOW I=6.38 G=6.93 ----------------------------I--G----------A-B-----	(1,3,5,7,8,10,11,13,18,20)
CONFLICT AMONG SUBORDINATES (ATTRIBUTE H)	HIGH I=3.17 G=4.66 ----------I---------A-G-------------------B-----	(1,2,5,8,9,10,13,15,16,19, 21,22,26,28,29)
	LOW I=5.38 G=5.54 ----------------A--------IG---------------B-----	(3,4,6,7,11,12,14,17,18, 20,23,24,25,27,30)
TRUSTWORTHINESS OF SUBORDINATES (ATTRIBUTE G)	HIGH I=6.04 G=5.63 ------------------------A---G---I--------------B	(2,6,7,8,9,13,19,20,22, 23,27,30)
	LOW I=2.50 G=4.71 ----------I-----A----G------------B-----	(1,4,10,11,12,16,18,21,24, 25,26,29)
LEADER'S INFORMATION (ATTRIBUTE B)	HIGH I=5.21 G=4.30 --------------A---------G-----I----------B-----	(1,2,8,11,12,20,22,25,26, 27,29,30)
	LOW I=3.33 G=6.04 -----------------I-------------AG---------B-----	(4,6,7,9,10,13,16,18,19, 21,23,24)
IMPORTANCE OF QUALITY OF DECISION (ATTRIBUTE A)	HIGH I=4.27 G=5.17 --------------------IA---G---------------B-----	(1,2,4,6,7,8,9,10,11,12,13, 16,18,19,20,21,22,23,24,25,26, 27,29,30)
	LOW I=4.27 G=4.82 -----------A-----I---G-------------------B	(3,5,14,15,17,28)
DEGREE OF STRUCTURE IN PROBLEM (ATTRIBUTE D)	HIGH I=2.81 G=5.28 ----------I---A--------G---------------B-----	(7,10,19,21,23,24)
	LOW I=3.85 G=6.81 -----------I----------------G--------A---B-----	(4,6,9,13,16,18)

used in the normative model. Table V indicates the extent to which each of these factors influenced your behavior on the case studies.

Importance of acceptance. Included in the set of 30 cases, there are 20 in which the authors and most managers feel that it is critical to get acceptance or commitment to the decision if the decision is to be effective. The numbers are shown at the right-hand side under problem numbers and opposite *high* importance of acceptance. There are also ten cases in which acceptance of the decision by subordinates is much less critical (see problem numbers opposite *low* importance of acceptance).

Now let us see whether your leadership behavior is different for these two sets of cases. Examine your score opposite *high* under individual mean and compare it with your score opposite *low*. These scores are specified at the left-hand side of each row and are designated by the symbol I (for individual). They are also designated by the symbol I on each of the scales and the slope of the line given by connecting the two letters (I) will give you a visual representation of the difference. If the score opposite *high* is greater (i.e., more toward the right side of the scale) it means that you permit more participation on the part of your subordinates when it is necessary to get their acceptance or commitment. This is the pattern found for most managers. The larger the difference the more influence this factor has on your behavior. If there is no difference or a very small difference between these two numbers (i.e., +.5 to −.5),[5] it may signify that you do not use participation as a means of enhancing the acceptance of decisions. About 5% of managers studied so far show a substantial difference (i.e., greater than .5) in the opposite direction. If this is the case for you, it means that you use a higher degree of participation on those problems for which acceptance is unimportant.

Prior probability of acceptance. There are ten cases in which the manager depicted in the situation has a low probability of getting an autocratic solution accepted by his subordinates. Typically, the subordinates feel strongly about the decision and the manager is seen by them as having neither the legitimate right nor any superior expertise which would warrant his making the decision by himself. There are also ten cases in which the manager has a high probability of getting an autocratic solution accepted by his subordinates. Typically, the subordinates do not feel strongly about the decision and the manager enjoys their respect.

All twenty of these cases are those in which acceptance of the decision is critical to its effective implementation. Model A, which you will recall is "stingy" with regard to time, responds overwhelmingly to this difference. The mean score for the cases in which there is low likelihood of the leader "selling" the solution is much higher than the mean score for those in

5. This is +.5 and −.5 units of participation on the ten-point scale presented near the beginning of this excerpt.

which the likelihood is high. In effect this model is based on the premise "if you can sell it, do so, you save time that way!" Most managers also respond to this factor in the same way but to a lesser degree. About 8% of managers show no real difference on this factor (between +.5 and −.5) and an even smaller percentage show a difference in the reverse direction ("high" is greater than "low").

On the other hand, Model B which places no weight on time in selecting decision methods shows no influence of this factor. It is uniformly and highly participative in both types of situations. It acts on the premise that if the leader sells the solution, subordinates will learn appreciably less than if they are forced to wrestle with the problem themselves.

Conflict among subordinates. This is one of the most interesting factors in reflecting differences among managers. About 75% of the managers studied are more participative for the low conflict cases than for the cases in which conflict among subordinates is high. (The score opposite low is higher than the score opposite high.) This suggests that they are more autocratic when conflict is likely. Their rationale may be that conflict is unpleasant or destructive and increases the time required to make decisions and this mitigates against the use of CII or GII when conflict is present. Another 20% show no effect of this factor. The high and low scores do not differ by more than .5. The remainder of the managers show the reverse effect. They are more participative in the face of conflict among their subordinates than when conflict is not present. You will note that Model A behaves in a similar fashion. If you reexamine the decision-flow chart for this model you will see the reason. Conflict only enters into the choice of decision process when acceptance of the decision is critical and when it is not likely that the leader can sell his solution. In the face of situations like this—in which there is a real need for commitment from subordinates—Model A uses participative methods which not only bring the conflict out into the open but also have some prospect of resolving it.

Trustworthiness of subordinates. Among the twenty-four cases in which there is some quality requirement to the decision, there are twelve in which the subordinates can be trusted and twelve in which they probably cannot. The former may be loosely described as "win-win" situations in which there is clearly a mutual interest between the leader and his subordinates. The latter are "win-lose" situations in which the personal goals of subordinates are opposed to those of the organization. In representing these two types of problems in equal number, it is not suggested that they are equally represented in actual managerial situations. Other research suggests that situations in which subordinates cannot be trusted are distinctly in the minority.

Both Model A and Model B are more participative in problems in which trust is high than in those in which it is low. This results from application of a rule which eliminates GII from the feasible set when trust is low.

Most managers exhibit the same tendency varying only in degree. About 30% show no influence or a slight reverse influence of this factor on participation.

Leader's information. The twenty-four cases possessing a quality requirement can also be divided into two equal-size groups on the basis of whether the manager has the necessary information to solve the problem by himself. As might be expected, Model A and more than 70% of managers share a tendency to be more autocratic when the leader has the necessary information than when he does not, i.e., higher participation scores opposite low than opposite high. Model B does not possess this tendency and is equally participative in both types of problems.

Importance of the quality of the decision. The thirty cases include twenty-four with a "quality requirement" and six without such a requirement. In a technical or rational sense, the former are "important decisions" because they can have potentially large effects on the attainment by the organization of its external goals. It clearly makes a difference which course of action is adopted even though one may not know what the right course of action is. From the same point of view, the latter are trivial decisions. It really makes no difference which alternative is chosen provided people accept it.

Like conflict among subordinates, this factor is quite revealing of differences among managers not only in the amount of difference in behavior on these two types of problems but also in the direction of the difference. About 60% of managers show the same effect as Model A. Their mean score opposite *high* is greater than the mean score opposite *low*. This means, in effect, that they are more likely to encourage participation of subordinates on important decisions than the so-called "trivial" ones. Another 20% exhibit no difference (+.5 to −.5). The remainder show the opposite effect. They are willing to use participative methods on problems for which it makes no difference which course of action is adopted but are more autocratic on "important" decisions. Model B shows a slight effect of this kind. Since it places no weight on time in selection of decision process, it uses GII on all problems without a quality requirement but uses CII on problems with a quality requirement in which subordinates cannot be trusted.

Degree of structure in problem. Highly structured problems are those in which the alternatives and the parameters for evaluating them are known. In effect the leader has a formula for making the decision and all he needs in order to make a high quality decision is to obtain certain specifiable information. Unstructured problems are those for which these conditions do not hold. Typically, the leader has little knowledge of what the alternatives are and how to go about evaluating them. There are six problems of each type in the case booklet, all of them problems with a quality requirement and in which the leader lacks the necessary information to solve the problem by himself.

Model A and about 65% of managers show a marked tendency to employ a higher degree of participation in unstructured problems than in highly structured ones. (The mean score opposite "low" is higher, by more than .5, than the mean score opposite "high.") The underlying premise is that free-wheeling group discussions of the CII or GII variety are more efficient and effective in dealing with unstructured problems, than AII or CI. Only 5% show a tendency that is in the opposite direction.

The exercise described above is intended to start the participants thinking consciously about behavior which for most managers has become a matter of habit and custom. It is not intended to "program" a person with a particular way of making decisions but rather to help him reappraise his own style and ask himself whether he believes that his present behavior is optimal; it should be emphasized that this has been an analysis of one manager's behavior and of course, the reader's own behavior may in no way correspond to that of the individual discussed above. Different managers act very differently in the same set of cases, and hence the behavior discussed above may not have been comparable with that exhibited by another manager. However, we believe each manager should ask himself the questions used in the analysis; since they are expressed in very general terms, they are applicable to most people.

THE EFFECTS OF COMPUTER-GENERATED FEEDBACK

In the previous section, a method of providing individuals with feedback concerning their leadership style was described. On the basis of previous research showing the value of highly specific feedback or knowledge of results in learning, we can conjecture that the method has the necessary ingredients for an effective learning experience for the feedback recipients. However, it would be useful to determine the specific effects of the particular kind of feedback that has been described.

To date, no systematic evaluation of the effects of feedback on behavior in leadership roles has been undertaken. There are, however, two sources of data that, while admittedly falling far short of the previous criterion, seem worth reporting. The first source is the observations of the senior author, who has provided feedback of the type described to several hundred managers under conditions in which he could casually observe their behavior for a period of approximately twenty-four hours following receipt of the computer printout. He could observe the kinds of questions, comments, and reactions the managers directed to him and frequently to one another. The impressions generated by these observations are vivid although undoubtedly subject to biases generated at least in part by the author's participation in the development of the system. Furthermore, they are short-term and at best can provide insight into only the immediate effects of the feedback.

The second source of data took the form of written descriptions by one group of feedback recipients of their reactions to the feedback, its meaning to them, and its likely effects on their behavior. These descriptions, ranging in length from two to twenty pages, were solicited by the senior author for the purpose of finding out how people react to the feedback in order to improve its usefulness. The decision to provide such a description was voluntary, and 40 percent of those of whom the request was made wrote up their views.

The clinical or anthropological nature of both sources of data contrast sharply with the methods used elsewhere in this book and are subject to the typical limitation of such an approach. But it is the authors' shared conviction that the results are interesting and worth reporting even though the skeptical reader might prefer to treat them as hypotheses for a more conclusive test.

Since the results of the two data sources both reinforce and complement one another, we will discuss them together, using selected comments from the written descriptions to illustrate many of the general points being made. Generally speaking, people show interest in feedback that can potentially reveal something about themselves and their differences with others. When the feedback is evaluative (as in some parts of the printout), this interest is accompanied by some degree of apprehension that the results may reflect unfavorably on their leadership ability.

When a typical manager receives his printout, he immediately goes to work trying to understand what it tells him about himself. Frequently, there are marked signs of relief for those who expected that the results might have shown them to be markedly different from others (on descriptive measures) or markedly inferior (on more evaluative criteria). The examination of results typically begins with the aggregated measures, such as mean participativeness and agreement with feasible set, and then extends to those that are more specific, such as rule violations and main effects of attributes. Only after all of the results of the printout have been understood does the recipient go back to the problem set to reread cases for the purpose of understanding his rule violations or to further his understanding of a problem attribute that had little or no effect on his behavior.

Sometimes the person develops hypotheses about the factors influencing his leadership style that are not directly inferable from the scores reported. Using the raw observations of behavior on the thirty cases, he makes additional calculations of such things as interactions among problem attributes. The written descriptions include several accounts of detailed reanalysis of the data, often resulting in significant discoveries not apparent from the original printout.

After a manager has put in the time necessary to understand the major features of his results, he typically shows an interest in discussing them with others, particularly with those who he believes will be supportive. Gatherings of four to six people comparing results and conclusions, often for several evening hours, were such a common feature that they have recently been institutionalized as part of the procedure.

Most managers accept the descriptive characterization of their leadership style as indicated by the printout. The following comments are representative of those obtained:

> I have found that the results do tend to correlate highly with the actual decision style which I employ in my position and actually help to explain much of my behavior in terms that seem applicable.

> I think the results of this test give a good picture of my leadership style—at least they fit my own perception of it.

> I think that the results reflect very well my own sensitivity toward conflict. While my own individual degree of participation was higher than that of the group for both conflict likely and conflict unlikely situations, it was markedly higher for the latter case. . . . I know I tend to behave warily when I am the one who actually has to lift the lid on such conflict.

> My first observation was that my most frequently used style, CI, was used only moderately by the group and almost never by the normative models. I may have a tendency to "use" my subordinates, that is, extract opinions and information from them while reserving decision-making power for myself! It also indicates a "divide and conquer" strategy on my part in which I neutralize any group power or influence by dealing with subordi-

nates individually. In reflecting on my past experiences and behavior, I can recall numerous incidents in which I displayed this pattern.

The results came out, in general, as I had predicted, in that I generally favor high participation from subordinates and your information displayed this fact on all counts. The two most notable aspects were that 1) when conflict is high among subordinates I choose to permit more participation than when conflict is low; 2) when the importance of the quality of the final decision is high, I permit my subordinates a lower degree of participation than when the importance of the quality of the final decision is low. On the first point, this is extremely accurate and I am surprised that your facts were able to show this aspect of my leadership style. . . . The second aspect correctly indicates that I allow more participation when the quality of the decision is unimportant. I do this to allow subordinates as much participation in "perception-forming decisions" as possible.

It is tempting to see agreement with the description as evidence for the validity of the scores contained in the printout. However, a measure of caution should be exercised. Clinical psychologists have long recognized the tendency of people to see themselves in case studies they have read, and Stagner (1958) has provided a striking illustration of a similar phenomenon using a standardized personality test. He provided a fake personality analysis to sixty-eight personnel managers who had all responded to a published personality inventory. Each manager received the same "analysis" and consequently it was based in no way on his responses to the inventory. Despite this fact, 50 percent of the managers rated the analysis as amazingly accurate and another 40 percent rated it as "rather good." Clearly, endorsement of the accuracy of results by their recipients should not be interpreted as unequivocal evidence of their validity.

Agreement with the descriptive characterization provided in the printout does not, however, necessarily imply agreement with the evaluative parts of the feedback. Argyris (1962) has pointed out the tendency of evaluative feedback that is negative in character to produce defensiveness. It is possible that recipients of the feedback might accept the description of their behavior but deny the validity of the model or the rules underlying it.

The feedback process has been designed to minimize such defensiveness by stressing the concept of the feasible set rather than the short-term normative model (model A) shown in figure 3.2. The latter is depicted as just one example of a method of choosing within that set—a method that places a high premium on time. Furthermore, the conceptual system surrounding the normative model is cast as "an attempt to formulate your thinking" rather than as an effort to "program you with a particular leadership style."

Most reactions to the evaluative feedback, particularly the rule violations, show high flexibility and a willingness on the part of recipients to consider and explore alternatives to their own behavior. Following are some typical responses.

> After considering my answers and tracing each case in question through the model, I had to admit (to myself) every time that my solution was less desirable and even less logical. This came as a bit of a revelation to me.

> I checked the rule violations I made and in all but one case I agree with the model.

> There were only five instances in the thirty cases that my chosen management styles were outside the feasible set. The printout showed that I violated two rules, the Trust rule and the Acceptance Priority rule. My response in these five cases indicate that I find it extremely difficult to assess whether subordinates can be trusted. . . . This is probably the most valuable piece of information I received.

> In terms of rule violations . . . , I can rationalize these discrepancies by saying that I perceive my role as leader as being one in which I have the respect and confidence of my subordinates when I make a decision and, therefore, acceptance poses a small problem. These arguments have some merit and agree with my conception that a leader should lead with positive action on his own part. I do, however, recognize from the outcome of the model that, at times, I may be too quick to rely on my own perceptions of the problem and not those of my subordinates and to be too confident in my ability to manipulate them. Clearly, this last point is not an attribute that I would like to place much emphasis on, for in the long run it does not pay off.

> I found the rule violations chart very useful. In most cases I was forced to admit that I was guilty of a violation where I was so cited.

Whatever defensiveness the feedback creates appears to be short-lived as indicated in the following comment.

> When I got the feedback, my first reaction was shock and anger. I didn't feel that authoritarian and I did not expect the degree to which the results would depict me in that way. Out of my 30 responses, 11 were outside of

the feasible set and 10 of these cases were instances of too authoritarian behavior. . . . My initial reaction to this as a crock of bullshit no longer exists. After careful study of the model, rules, cases and my answers, I understand and accept my errors. This whole process has been very helpful.

One of the consequences of the feedback appears to be to make one conscious of the choices that are implicitly reflected in one's leadership style. Much of the post-feedback behavior that has been observed can be described as rethinking questions that have become matters of habit. A number of written comments reflect this theme.

> Having given it this much thought I am already conscious of efforts to consider the elements of the conceptual framework in decision situations.

> Of equal, if not more importance to me is the realization that group decision making is a very good way to achieve a high level of commitment to a decision. I am not sure why this had never occurred to me before but it is probably because I have never taken an objective look at the decision-making process. This to me is the true value of this program.

> I would venture to say that not many managers ever get a chance to confront their leadership style and scrutinize it. . . . It will indeed be unfortunate if we never re-think the implications of how we treat our subordinates in the business world for the remainder of our careers.

It should be noted that these comments were written about two weeks after receipt of the feedback, and it is not clear how successful the recipients were in translating their new insights into changed behavior. The following comment typifies a difficulty visualized by several managers in putting these insights to work.

> So where does one go from here? On the face of it, I can say that I should be more careful about the assumptions I make about subordinates' commitment to organizational goals, become less concerned with my own lack of knowledge, and look for ways to either bring structure to decision problems or recognize those that are unstructured and better suited to group discussion than individual action. What concerns me, of course, is that it is easy to say and write this, but much more difficult to implement an action program for even one year, let alone thirty or forty. Perhaps there is hope. I am at least considering problem features never before articulated and that at least feels in my gut like a step in the right direction.

Considering all sources of data available, the feedback from performance on standardized cases appears to be almost uniformly regarded as helpful and valuable to recipients, as implied in the following comments.

> The feedback I received has provided more information about my management style and how my personality affects my working behavior than I have ever had.

> This output was perhaps the most informative, personalized and comprehensive piece of relatively immediate feedback which I have ever received.

> The feedback was very helpful. Overall, it has made me feel less insecure about trying to be participative, and if anything has reinforced my desire to be participative as opposed to an authoritarian manager.

Only one comment raised a question about the value of the experience, and its writer proposes that the critical element is not the feedback but the practice in the cases.

> I feel that the problem set was valuable in that one had an opportunity to think about his leadership style instead of just doing it while solving each case. But I think the output is an attempt to place numerical values on certain qualities that are difficult to define let alone quantify. Thus, I feel that the analysis of the output is a less rewarding experience than the creation of the input.

It appears possible that the research method developed for the purpose of investigating situational and individual factors in leadership style has considerable promise as a method of leadership development. The observations that have been made to date, while admittedly subject to many sources of bias, suggest that it causes people to examine their leadership behavior. They show evidence of considering alternative decision processes that they had not thought of before and attending to properties of the situation that they had previously ignored. There is no evidence that they automatically embrace the normative model as the guide for their actions by working through the decision tree whenever faced with a problem to solve. Rather, the basic framework of concepts and processes that underlies the model is incorporated into the managers' ways of thinking about situations. For the managerial populations that have been studied the net effect of these changes is most likely to be greater use of participative decision processes, although different effects could be anticipated for some other populations.

How long-lived these changes are is still a matter of considerable uncertainty. The main objective of the follow-up phase (VII) is to provide mechanisms necessary to reinforce new behavior patterns in the work situation. One promising approach has involved the use of organizational families consisting of a manager and his immediate subordinates. A manager who has been through the program of leadership development outlined in this chapter provides copies of the problem set to each of his subordinates. They are instructed to answer in two modes, (1) how they would deal with the case if they were the leader and (2) how they believe their own superior would deal with the case. Both sets of responses are sent to a central source and processed by computer. At present, two forms of output are generated. One is furnished to the manager and consists of a comparison of his own view of his leadership style (as represented in his statements of how he would behave in each situation) with the aggregate view of his subordinates. The format follows the general outline described, with group data replaced by subordinate perceptions of their superior. While this feedback is furnished to the manager alone, he is encouraged to share it with his subordinates and, in fact, to involve them in a collective effort to work through its implications for their relationship.

The second form of output is furnished to each of the subordinates and is identical in structure to that previously received by their manager during training but utilizes their own statements of how they would deal with each case. Each subordinate has the option of discussing or not discussing the results with his superior.

The procedure described is too new and our experience with it too limited to make any definite statements about its consequences. It does appear to be a promising method of extending the effects of training beyond those who have received the training and of encouraging open discussion of the leadership process between the leader and his followers.

The reader should be reminded that the conclusions concerning the possible efficacy of the approach to leadership development described in this chapter are tentative and, at present, rest on a weaker empirical foundation than conclusions reported elsewhere in this book. It is conceivable that the authors' identification with and enthusiasm for the development program caused them to select evidence to support their convictions and encouraged only those who felt the program was valuable to voice their opinion. Despite the difficulty of precisely determining the effectiveness of educational and development programs, we believe that the highly promising results reported here warrant attempts to assess the long-term effects of this approach on the effectiveness with which leaders carry out their assigned roles.

CHAPTER 9

Revising the Normative Model

In chapters 2 and 3, a normative model was developed to show which of the five decision processes (AI, AII, CI, CII, and GII) should be employed in different situations. It was pointed out that the model was not fixed but evolving. Evidence presented at several points in this book suggests ways in which the normative model could be strengthened and improved. In this chapter we will utilize this evidence to revise the model and to discuss the directions which might be taken in future revisions.

The most clear-cut evidence on which to base a revision would be data concerning the validity of the model itself. It would be useful to know whether decisions that were consistent with the model turned out "better" than those which were not. Even more useful in pointing the way to revisions would be evidence concerning the validity of specific components of the model. To what extent and in what ways would the outcomes of decisions be different if each of the seven underlying rules were violated? While the various assumptions and rules that are integral to the model seem to most managers to have a "ring of truth" and are consistent (even if not uniquely consistent) with existing empirical evidence, it would be desirable to determine their validity empirically.

The principal effort toward validating the model has involved asking managers who did not know of the model to describe a problem they had recently had to solve and to specify the decision process they had used in solving it. The consistency between the process a manager indicated and the model was determined with the aid of the manager's assessment of the status of the problem attributes for his problem. The success of the decision was measured by having each manager rate the quality and acceptance of the decision on a seven-point scale ranging from extremely high to extremely low.

Presumably, the validity of the rules underlying the model would be indicated by the degree to which employment of methods used that were outside the feasible set result in decisions of lower quality or lower acceptance than those within. The validity of the acceptance rules would be reflected in the degree to which ratings of acceptance were greater for decisions which did and did not violate these rules and the validity of the quality rules would be reflected in the degree to which ratings of quality were greater for decisions which did than for those which did not violate quality rules.

Data were collected from 136 managers, each of whom described one problem. The analysis along the lines indicated above was handicapped by the fact that the problems chosen by the managers were almost invariably ones in which the outcomes, in terms of both acceptance and quality, were judged to be favorable. Only one of the decisions was judged to have less than adequate acceptance, and only three were judged to have less than adequate quality. The modal response on the seven-point scale for both ratings was "6," corresponding to "very high" quality or acceptance.

In thirty-nine of the problems the manager's behavior was outside the feasible set. The mean ratings of quality and acceptance for these thirty-nine problems were 5.32 and 5.35 respectively, as compared with 5.42 and 5.48 for problems in which the manager's behavior was within the feasible set. The differences are both in the right direction but neither is statistically significant.

There were only six problems in which the manager's behavior violated one or more of the quality rules. The mean rating of decision quality for those cases is 4.16 compared with 5.40 for those in which behavior did not violate a quality rule. Again the difference is in the right direction but is not significant due to the small number of quality violations. Similarly, for the thirty-four instances in which behavior violated an acceptance rule, the mean rating of acceptance was 5.32 compared with 5.49 for all other cases. These results are all in a direction consistent with the hypothesis that the model has a higher "probability" of generating decisions of high quality and acceptance, but none reach conventional levels of statistical significance.

The small number of rule violations in the problems selected and the tendency for managers to select problems in which the results had been favorable made it difficult to carry out an adequate test of the hypothesis. In retrospect, it appears that it would have been better to ask each manager to report two problems or decisions—one in which the outcome was in his judgment highly successful and the other in which it was unsuccessful. This method would guarantee variance in the dependent variable and would control for possible differences among managers in their ability to code problems accurately using the problem attributes. Future research will attempt to assess the validity of the model using this method.

The principal data on which the normative model as a framework for making decisions presently rests is not evidence of its overall validity but rather the empirical evidence supporting the underlying rules (presented in chapter 3) and its face validity, that is, the plausibility of the various assumptions that have been used to generate prescriptions for action. Furthermore, and perhaps even more critical at this stage, the attempts to validate the model have not pointed the way to improving it.

However, other evidence presented at various places throughout the book as well as our experiences with managers who have attempted to use the model do indicate some possible improvements. Most of these improvements pertain to the wording of questions intended to measure the problem attributes. The reader will recall that these questions were intended as surrogates for much more detailed definitions of the attributes. Each question was merely intended to be a reminder of the actual definition. However, in chapter 3 when various kinds of coding errors were examined, it was noted that certain of the questions produced high error rates, particularly among managers untrained in the use of the model. It is possible that by clarifying the wording used in the questions the error rates and/or the required training time would be reduced. The wording of the questions pertaining to four of the problem attributes has been altered. The attributes are shown below, along with both old and new wordings and the rationale for the change:

A. Quality requirement
   Old question: Given acceptance, does it make a difference which course of action is adopted?
   New question: Is there a quality requirement such that one solution is likely to be more rational than another?

Rationale: The previous question was intended to define the concept of quality requirement without using the term. It was based on the assumption that the concept was a difficult one to understand. Subsequent experience has shown that the concept is found by leaders to be quite simple and most, when using the model, have found it less confusing to ask themselves the simple question, "Is there a quality requirement?" than the more complex question that appeared in the original wording.

D. Problem structure

Old question: Do I know exactly what information is needed, who possesses it, and how to collect it?

New question: Is the problem structured?

Rationale: The difficulty with the old question was similar to that noted in connection with the quality requirement. To eliminate the necessity of defining the concept of structure, a question was asked which it was assumed would correlate highly with the degree to which the problem was structured. The high error rate obtained with this question (see chapter 3) and the fact that managers were quickly able to learn the underlying concept strongly suggested the wording employed in the new question.

F. Prior probability

Old question: If I were to make the decision myself, is it certain to be accepted by my subordinates?

New question: If I were to make the decision by myself, is it reasonably certain that it would be accepted by my subordinates?

Rationale: The changes in the wording of this question are small but significant. In chapter 3, evidence was presented to indicate that most of the errors made in answering this question were false negatives, or persons answering no

when the answer to the question was intended
to be yes. It was apparent that some managers
were taking the word "certain" too literally.
The change to "reasonably certain" was intended to alter the threshold for the yes-no
judgments to that intended.

G. Goal congruence (trust)
    Old question: Can subordinates be trusted to base solutions
                  on organizational considerations?
    New question: Do subordinates share the organizational goals
                  to be attained in solving this problem?
    Rationale: From chapter 3, it may be recalled that this
                  attribute had one of the highest error rates,
                  with false negatives dominating by a very
                  large margin. In discussions with managers, it
                  became apparent that the word "trust" had a
                  great deal of surplus meaning which had an
                  unintended influence on the judgments made.
                  Responses tended to be influenced by general
                  beliefs about whether people could or could
                  not be trusted rather than by an analysis of
                  the motives or goals of the participants in the
                  situation. The substitution of the term "goal
                  congruence" for "trust" was intended to
                  minimize this tendency.

In addition to these changes in the wording of questions, there
is one change in the structure of the model that has been indicated
by subjecting it to "the scenario test," that is, observing its behavior in a large number of situations. If the reader examines the
decision tree shown in figure 3.2, he can see that on problems on
which the leader lacks information, he asks himself whether subordinates have the necessary additional information. If he judges
that they do not, he is directed to collect the additional information, or augment the group and go back to start. If the information
cannot be collected, he is instructed to redefine the problem.
These predecisional routines deserve reconsideration for two
reasons. First, there is considerable uncertainty in the minds of
many managers about whether their subordinates possess the nec-

essary information. If they judge no, they are led into a set of activities (augmenting group or collecting additional information) which would be unnecessary if subordinates possessed the information. Furthermore, the burden is placed on the leader for collecting the needed information. There is no reason why the outcome of any one of the other decision processes (AII, CI, CII, or GII) might not be a decision to collect additional information, or augment the group, or redefine the problem. In fact, they could well be more effective processes by which to select the most effective predecisonal mechanism.

Second, and even more compelling, was the observation that managers almost never used the predecisional routines. They invariably assumed that their subordinates might possess the necessary information and proceeded through the decision tree with a yes answer to that question.

The structural change suggested by these considerations simplifies the model. It eliminates attribute C and the two questions regulating the predecisional mechanisms. The new model, incorporating this change along with the revised wording of questions, is shown in figure 9.1.

LEADERSHIP METHODS AND LEADERSHIP SKILLS

In the form shown in figure 9.1, the model prescribes a leadership method that will protect both the quality and the acceptance of the solution and, at the same time, minimize the man-hours consumed by the process of decision-making. It does not, however, subsume all of the skills of leadership. Even within the framework of the model there are important skills involved in the implementation of a decision process once it is selected. Maier (1963) has emphasized the distinction between leadership methods and leadership skills. Two leaders may employ the same autocratic (AI) approach to a particular problem but might achieve very different degrees of success due to differences in their ability to make high quality decisions or to persuade and inspire subordinates. Similarly, two leaders might both employ the method of group decision (GII), but one might be much more successful than the other due to differences in their skills in discussion leadership.

Effective use of the model is contingent on the degree to which the user has the skill required to carry out successfully each of the

A. Is there a quality requirement such that one solution is likely to be more rational than another?
B. Do I have sufficient info to make a high quality decision?
D. Is the problem structured?
E. Is acceptance of decision by subordinates critical to effective implementation?
F. If I were to make the decision by myself, is it reasonably certain that it would be accepted by my subordinates?
G. Do subordinates share the organizational goals to be attained in solving this problem?
H. Is conflict among subordinates likely in preferred solutions?

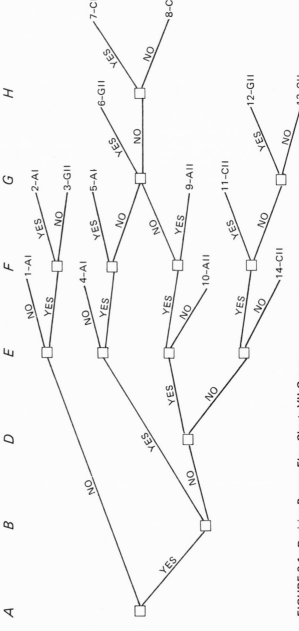

FIGURE 9.1. Decision-Process Flow Chart: VII-Group

five decision processes. As was pointed out in chapter 8, the training efforts have been concerned with not only when to use each decision process but how to use it effectively.

The distinction between methods and skills stems from the fact that a method such as AI or GII does not represent a complete specification of the leader's behavior. AI can subsume a variety of decision processes ranging from flipping a coin to linear programming. Similarly, GII can include a leader simply stating the problem and then letting the group do the work or someone playing a very active role in guiding and controlling the discussion. The greater the variance in alternatives which are consistent with a given method, the greater the need for skill on the part of the person who is using it.

It should be possible to be as analytical about leadership skills as we have attempted to be concerning leadership methods. Wherever alternatives exist, one can do research on their consequences under different conditions and build a prescriptive framework based on this research. For example, Maier (1963) describes a number of different discussion methods that are consistent with our general specification of GII and discusses the circumstances under which each is applicable. In a different context, Wagner (1969) describes the methods that have been developed for solving problems in operations research and gives extensive examples of the kinds of problems on which each has been used. At the present time both of these fall short of being exhaustive prescriptive frameworks, but such a list does represent a feasible goal for the future.

While the present problem attributes and problem types were not selected for the purpose of specifying the precise form of each decision process, they could provide a start in that direction. For example, in problem types 1 and 2 (quality of decision irrelevant, acceptance either irrelevant or automatic) the prescribed method AI could well take the form of flipping a coin. On the other hand, linear programming would be the optimal method in some of the highly structured problems of types 4 and 5. Similarly, Maier's description of free discussion appears applicable to problems of type 3 (in which there is no quality requirement but a strong need for acceptance). However, his concept of developmental discussion seems more suited to the structured problems of type 6.

It is our objective here not to attempt to build a model of

leadership skills, but rather to indicate a possible direction for future elaboration of the model. Wherever there are alternative methods of solving problems that are consistent with the general specification of the five decision processes, the objective would be to try to develop a prescriptive framework to guide choices among them.

A ROUTINE FOR PROBLEM DEFINITION

In reading the several hundred recalled cases that were obtained from managers, we came to one very compelling conclusion that was not reported in chapter 4. The manner in which a manager defines his problem has considerable bearing both on his answers to the questions concerning problem attributes and on the method he uses in solving it. Let us consider one example. One manager wrote up a case involving his subordinates typically abusing their coffee-break privileges. Their fifteen-minute coffee break had turned into twenty minutes and more recently into twenty-five minutes. His problem as stated was how to get his subordinates back from their coffee break on time. His coding of the problem appeared quite appropriate to his conception of it (Quality requirement—yes; Leader's information—yes; Acceptance—no; Trust—no; Conflict—no); and his behavior, AI, was appropriate to that coding. But there are several other ways of conceiving of the same problem, most of which would generate different specifications of problem type. Was his problem really that his subordinates were coming back late from their coffee break, or was it that production schedules were not being met or even that his subordinates were losing interest in their work? These two alternative specifications of the problem not only provide for a greater breadth of solutions but also are more likely to generate a "no" answer to the question concerning leader's information and "yes" answers to the questions concerning acceptance and trust.

Similar conclusions were reached from managers' behavior on the standardized problems. One of the cases in Problem Set 2 depicted an office supervisor, faced with the necessity of cutting costs, trying to decide whether to replace the present office copying machine with a cheaper but less efficient model. The case was intended to be of Type 9 and, in fact, was coded in that way by most managers (Quality—yes, Information—no, Acceptance—yes,

Prior probability—yes, Trust—no) with a prescription of AII. The authors were surprised to find a small number of managers who used GII, which is outside the feasible set for this problem. In discussions with managers who used this decision process, we invariably found that they had not accepted the problem as stated but, in fact, had broadened it from "whether or not to replace the present office copier" to "how to cut costs by the needed 10 percent." The latter conception of the problem is most frequently coded as type 12, for which the prescribed decision process is GII. One of these managers described the logic underlying his problem redefinition as follows: "Whenever I find a problem in which the organizational objectives are in conflict with the interests of my subordinates, I try to broaden my conception of the problem until the two sets of objectives are brought into agreement and a mutual interest is established. Of course, I am not always able to do that since there are occasions under which unpopular decisions are 'handed me' from above."

The process employed by that manager can be thought of as routine for problem definition. He starts with a given conception of the problem and applies certain tests to it before accepting it as the most appropriate definition. His process is diagrammed in figure 9.2.

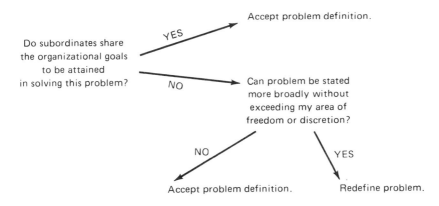

FIGURE 9.2. Partial Model for Problem Definition

The model shown in figure 9.2 is at best a partial diagram of the considerations which might be employed in determining the acceptability of a given definition of a problem. Maier (1963, chapter 4) has presented a set of six principles for stating problems that could be incorporated into a more complete routine elaborating the box at the extreme left-hand side of figure 9.1.

A COMBINED MODEL FOR INDIVIDUAL AND GROUP PROBLEMS

In chapter 2, a distinction was made between two broad categories of problems. Those involving only one of the leader's subordinates were designated as individual, while those concerning more than one subordinate were called group problems. Different sets of decision processes were assumed to be potentially applicable to these two broad categories. The feasible set of decision processes for group problems could include AI, AII, CI, CII, and GII, while that for individual problems could include AI, AII, CI, GI, and DI.

The reader should be familiar by now with the meaning of AI, AII, and CI, the three processes common to both problem categories. The other two processes assumed to be of possible value for solving individual problems, GI and DI, are undoubtedly less familiar. GI is a process of group decision (cf. GII) modified for a single subordinate. Thus, the leader and the subordinate discuss the problem until they reach agreement on its solution. In DI, the leader delegates the problem to the subordinate for solution. (For a complete definition of each of these processes, or examples of individual and group problems, the reader is referred to chapter 2, pages 13–16.)

In this book, we have focused primarily on group problems, but a similar logic could have been taken to the normative and descriptive analysis of individual problems. In fact, there are some leadership roles in which the subordinates have such limited interdependence that most of the problems confronting the leader would be of the individual type.

In developing a model for individual problems an attempt was made to preserve as closely as possible the format, structure, and logic used in the model for group problems. There were, of course, some problems involved in making this transfer. For example, one of the attributes used in the group model—conflict among subordinates—is meaningless in the context of an individual problem. Conversely the attribute, subordinate's information, should on strictly rational grounds play a much more significant role in the individual model (particularly in the choice between AI and DI) than it did in the group model.

There was one other consideration that required different treatment in the two models. For group problems, evidence was presented to indicate that the number of man-hours required by a decision process was a monotonically increasing function of the amount of participation it required. Thus, in man-hours, GII > CII > CI > AII > AI. But for individual problems, this is clearly not the case. The decision process that provides maximal opportunity for the subordinate to participate in (that is, influence) the decision is DI, and this certainly is more economical in use of time than most if not all of the intermediate styles. To order the alternatives in terms of expected man-hours, it was assumed that GI would require the greatest amount of time followed by CI, AII, DI, and AI, respectively.

All of the other considerations employed in formulating the model for group problems lent themselves neatly to the individual model. In fact, the transfer was sufficiently complete so that it was possible to depict the individual model and the group model on the same flow diagram, as shown in figure 9.3.

In this diagram, there are eighteen terminal nodes, each specifying a distinct type of problem. The feasible set for both group and individual problems is specified opposite each terminal node. The order of listing of processes within the feasible set corresponds to the estimate of number of man-hours required, with the short-term solution always furthest to the left.

The combined model shown in figure 9.3 provides prescriptions for group problems identical to those in figure 9.1. It is slightly more cumbersome to use since it contains a larger number of branches and one additional attribute. Even for group problems, however, it does have one property which could be useful. It identifies the feasible set as well as the minimum man-hours solution, something that was not included in figure 9.1.

Of course, the principal advantage of figure 9.3 is that it generates the feasible set for individual as well as group problems. Thus, if one has a problem of either group or individual nature, the same flow chart can be used to identify the feasible set of alternatives.

As was the case for the previous model, the feasible set is generated by consistent application of rules that eliminate alternatives

A. Is there a quality requirement such that one solution is likely to be more rational than another?

B. Do I have sufficient info to make a high quality decision?

C. Is the problem structured?

D. Is acceptance of decision by subordinates critical to effective implementation?

E. If I were to make the decision by myself, is it reasonably certain that it would be accepted by my subordinates?

F. Do subordinates share the organizational goals to be attained in solving this problem?

G. Is conflict among subordinates likely in preferred solutions? (This question is irrelevant to individual problems.)

H. Do subordinates have sufficient info to make a high quality decision?

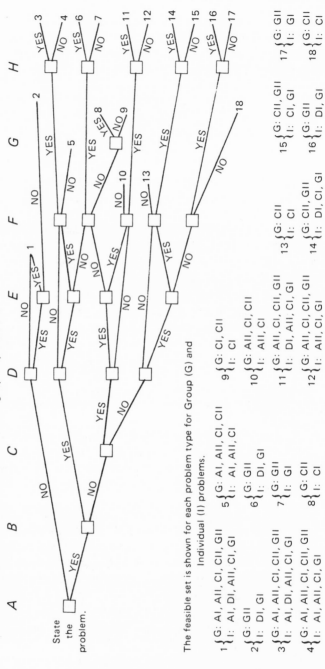

The feasible set is shown for each problem type for Group (G) and Individual (I) problems.

1 {G: AI, AII, CI, CII, GII
   I: AI, DI, AII, CI, GI

2 {G: GII
   I: DI, GI

3 {G: AI, AII, CI, CII, GII
   I: AI, DI, AII, CI, GI

4 {G: AI, AII, CI, CII, GII
   I: AI, AII, CI, GI

5 {G: AI, AII, CI, CII
   I: AI, AII, CI, CI

6 {G: GII
   I: DI, GI

7 {G: GII
   I: GI

8 {G: CII
   I: CI

9 {G: CI, CII
   I: CI

10 {G: AII, CI, CII
    I: AII, CI

11 {G: AII, CI, CII, GII
    I: DI, AII, CI, GI

12 {G: AII, CI, CII, GII
    I: AII, CI, GI

13 {G: CII
    I: CI

14 {G: CII, GII
    I: DI, CI, GI

15 {G: CII, GII
    I: CI, GI

16 {G: GII
    I: DI, GI

17 {G: GII
    I: GI

18 {G: CII
    I: CI

FIGURE 9.3. Decision-Process Flow Chart for Both Individual and Group Problems

on the basis of the attributes of the problem. The behavior of this version of the model is governed by eight rules. They encompass the previous seven rules used in the model for group problems. These seven rules have been stated more broadly to apply to individual as well as group problems, and a new rule applicable only to individual problems has been added. The rules may be found in appendix 2.

PROSPECTS FOR FUTURE MODEL DEVELOPMENT

The version of the model shown in figure 9.3 is the seventh version developed since this research program began in the fall of 1968. If the seven models were laid out side by side the reader, seeing the evolutionary process, would recognize that each model represents an improvement over those that went before. The criterion for judging the later model "better" would not be empirically demonstrated validity but rather internal consistency and plausibility, both of its assumptions and of the behaviors it prescribed in actual situations.

At this point, it seems appropriate to speculate concerning the future. What prospects exist for substantial further improvements in models of this kind? What problems will have to be solved if these improvements are to be forthcoming? Is the model shown in figure 9.3 analogous to the Wright brothers' early efforts in a bicycle shop—with the Boeing 747 only six or seven decades away?

The present forms of the model utilize rules that divide decision processes into two classes—those which risk decision quality or acceptance and those which do not. When all rules have been applied, one is left with a feasible set, defined as the methods that do not risk either decision quality or acceptance, and what might have been termed "a rejected set," those which risk either or both of these.

It is obvious that quality and acceptance are not dichotomous variables but continuous ones. A classification of decisions as "high in quality" or "low in quality" and as "high in acceptance" or "low in acceptance" is very crude. There are various amounts of both quality and acceptance, and the ultimate effectiveness of a decision is some unknown function of these magnitudes. Similarly, no decision process is certain to produce an acceptable decision or certain not to do so. For each decision process used under a given set of circumstances one could conceive of an expected level of both decision quality and acceptance. There is no reason to believe that the expected levels for all decision processes eliminated by the application of a given rule are equal or even that the expected levels are equal for all decision processes not excluded by those rules.

A model that treated quality and acceptance as continuous rather than zero/one variables would have to deal with such problems as "trade-offs" between quality and acceptance. Are five units of quality and three units of acceptance "better" than three units of quality and five units of acceptance? There is no obvious theoretical solution to such a problem, and the answer would have to be established empirically.

Constructing a model that treated quality and acceptance as continuous variables would require the formulation of attributes in continuous rather than dichotomous form. In chapter 3, we sidestepped the problem of scaling attributes by treating them as dichotomous variables potentially measured by yes-no questions. That decision made it possible to formulate the model in terms of the rules that generate the feasible set. But it is clear that there are degrees of conflict, degrees of problem structure, and so on, which would have to be incorporated in a framework permitting trade-offs among acceptance, quality, and time.

Allowing for the inclusion of additional dichotomous variables as their role in moderating the effects of participation is uncovered by research, we believe that we have gone about as far as one can go in formulating a normative model based on the treatment of both problem attributes and decision outcomes in dichotomous fashion. The next step would require a much more sophisticated model, which would impose far greater demands on empirical research for both model construction and validation and far greater need for training those who would use it.

Is it worthwhile to take this next step? The answer may depend on the purposes the model is to serve. If the principal function is a training device to make leaders more cognizant of the complexity and diversity of the situations with which they have to deal and to acquaint them with the major dimensions relevant to analyzing those situations, then the present level of model development seems sufficient. If, on the other hand, the intent is to produce a model that could be used by leaders to select the optimal decision process to solve "on-line" problems, it could be worthwhile to develop a multilevel model. The immensity of the problems, both conceptual and methodological, in such an undertaking suggests that such a development may be a long time in the making.

CHAPTER 10

A Concluding Statement

In the preceding chapters we have presented a large body of findings pertaining to the behavior of leaders in complex organizations. It is *not* our intent here to reiterate these findings but rather to attempt to put the issues that we have examined and the principal results that we have obtained in perspective. It seems appropriate at this point to look back at the terrain that we have traversed and to describe its topographical features. In so doing, we will attempt to compare our approach and conclusions with those of others who have addressed themselves to the leadership process.

We set out to examine leader behavior both normatively and descriptively. The two questions, "How should leaders behave if they are to be effective?" and "How do they behave?" have been in the background of all of the work presented in the previous nine chapters. Since one cannot effectively examine all aspects of leader behavior simultaneously, we chose one aspect that, on the basis of previous work, was likely to be of major importance. We selected the leader's role in the decision-making process, specifically the degree to which he encouraged the participation of his subordinates in solving problems or making decisions.

The conceptual framework of the research is depicted in figure 10.1. In this figure, the principal classes of variables relevant to the analysis of the leadership process are presented.

The key variable (or set of variables) in the figure is labeled #3, leader behavior—the actions or behaviors exhibited by the leader in the course of carrying out his leadership role. The decision process used by the leader (AI, AII, etc.) is one (and only one) of the variables that might be used in the analysis of such behavior.

Looking to the left of leader behavior in figure 10.1, one encounters the variables which are (on theoretical grounds) thought necessary to predict and explain it. This part of the figure has been

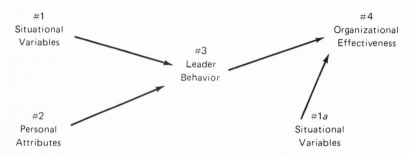

FIGURE 10.1. Relationship of Variables Used in Leadership Research

implicit in our design of investigations relevant to the descriptive
questions concerning how leaders behave and why. Such descriptive questions are conventional ones in psychological research.
Leader behavior is the dependent variable and situational factors
and individual difference are the independent variables. There is a
strong *a priori* basis for believing that the way a leader behaves in
carrying out his role (#3) is a function both of properties of the
situation with which he is confronted (#1) and of relatively stable
properties of the person including his personality characteristics,
beliefs, and attitudes (#2). Expressing leader behavior as a function of both person and situational variables is consistent with
Lewin's classic dictum that behavior is a function of the person
and the environment (Lewin 1951). Not shown in this figure are
potential interactions between person and situational variables in
determining leader behavior.

If one looks to the right of leader behavior in figure 10.1, one
encounters theoretical issues and empirical findings that are potentially normative in character. They bear on questions concerning
the conditions under which leaders *should* encourage the participation of their subordinates in decision-making.

In this case leader behavior (#3) becomes the independent rather
than the dependent variable and organizational effectiveness (#4)
becomes the dependent variable. The relevant processes are organizational as well as psychological. One is concerned here with understanding the consequences of the leader's behavior for the
effectiveness of the system in attaining its external objectives.
Organizational effectiveness (#4) is shown in figure 10.1 to be a
function not only of the leader's behavior but also of situational
variables (#1a). These effects (of #1a on #4) can be thought of as

belonging to two types. One is a simple main effect of situational properties on organizational effectiveness. The effectiveness of the organization is not solely dependent on the behavior of the leader. Despite the tendency to fire a football coach after a losing season or credit a general for winning a battle, there are many other factors, some within and others outside the organization, which can make the leader's task easy or difficult. The other role of situational variables pertains to their interaction with leader behavior. Throughout this book we have emphasized that the leader's behavior must be adapted to situational demands. The normative model is, in fact, built on interactions between leader behavior, conceived in terms of decision processes employed by the leader, and situational variables, expressed as problem attributes.

In formulating the model, we found it useful to replace the global concept of organizational effectiveness with a more specific one—the effectiveness of decisions made in the organization. This more specific concept was, in turn, broken down into components (quality, acceptance, and time).

It should be noted that situational variables enter into the schema presented in figure 10.1 in two ways. Situational variables both influence the behavior of the leader and affect the consequences of that behavior. In view of the potential differences among the specific situational variables that may be operative in these two respects, we have used the designation (#1) to represent the former and the designation (#1a) to represent the latter.

Figure 10.1 is also useful in depicting the differences between the approach to the study of leadership that has guided our work and other approaches of either historical or current interest. We will consider three of these approaches in an effort to show both their similarities and their differences from our undertaking.

LEADERSHIP AS A PERSONALITY TRAIT

Much of the early work on leadership was based on the premise that leadership is a personality trait that is distributed in varying degrees among different people. It was assumed that these differences in leadership ability are potentially measurable. This notion of leadership as a quality that individuals possess is still common in popular parlance.

If the premise were valid, it could prove highly beneficial to the functioning of organizations. Organizations are typically stratified hierarchically and are pyramidal in shape. People advance from lower-level positions to the less numerous higher ones, based on highly subjective assessments of their ability to function effectively in higher positions. If these subjective judgments could be replaced with a valid test of leadership, countless costly errors could be avoided. Such a test could also be utilized to advantage by institutions of higher learning, whose objective is to train future leaders for the public and private sector, in selecting students, and by industrial firms in screening the yearly supply of college graduates.

Research based on this premise has sought to identify the differences between the personal characteristics of leaders and nonleaders or between more effective and less effective leaders. The results (treated in detail elsewhere: Stogdill 1948, Mann 1959, Bass 1960, Gibb 1969) cast considerable doubt on the usefulness of the concept of leadership as a personality trait. They do not imply that individual differences have nothing to do with leadership but rather that their significance must be evaluated in relation to the situation.

While written more than two decades ago, Stogdill's conclusions seem equally applicable today: "The pattern of personal characteristics of the leader must bear some relevant relationship to the characteristics, activities and goals of the followers. . . . It becomes clear that an adequate analysis of leadership involves not only a study of leaders, but also of situations" (1948, pp. 64–5).

From the perspective of figure 10.1, the concept of leadership as a personality trait assumed that organizational effectiveness (#4) is affected in some simple and direct manner by the personal characteristics of the leader (#2). Implicitly, it also assumed that a leader's behavior is determined solely by his personal traits. In this respect, it ran directly counter to the findings from chapters 4 and 5, which clearly demonstrate the influence of situational factors and point to the weakness of the concept of a leadership trait (that is, autocratic or participative) in explaining leader behavior. From behavior on standardized problems, we have been able to show that about 30 percent of the variance in the decision process used by the leader is attributable to the situation, treated as a nominal variable, and only about 10 percent is attributable to individual tendencies to be participative or autocratic. A significant proportion of the remaining 60 percent has been shown to be due to interactions between personal and situational properties, which we have interpreted as differences among persons in the decision rules they use in determining when to share their power.

The concept of leadership as a personality variable also overlooked the possibility that organizational effectiveness might also be influenced by situational factors. Events not under the leader's control not only might make his task easy or difficult but might also influence the kind of leader behavior required of him.

These issues made the leadership process infinitely more complex than originally conceived in the trait concept. They also destroyed the dream of a technology by which the relative amounts of leadership possessed by different people could be measured, and the person with the largest amount of this trait selected as leader. The question, "Who would be the best leader?" became akin to asking, "What is the best medicine?" Neither question can be adequately answered.

EFFECTIVE LEADER BEHAVIOR

If there are no stable and invariant personality characteristics to distinguish effective leaders from less effective ones in all situations, it is still possible that certain behavioral patterns are more effective than others. Instead of looking at the personality of the effective leader, it is possible that a more productive approach would be to look for the behavioral correlates of effective leadership. Stable relationships between leaders' behavior and criteria of their effectiveness would have less obvious significance for leader selection but could have import for leader development and training. Knowledge of the behavior patterns that characterize effective leaders would provide a rational basis for the design of programs to instill these behavior patterns in actual or potential leaders.

The research program that provides the best example of this approach to the investigation of leadership was carried out by the Survey Research Center at the University of Michigan, although relevant research has also been done at other institutions including Ohio State University. The results from this research are exceedingly difficult to summarize due to the vast number of situations studied and differences in the methods, measures, and criteria used. Korman (1966) has reviewed the investigations utilizing measures of consideration and initiating structure, developed in the Ohio State research, as predictors of effectiveness of group performance and concludes that "very little is now known as to how these variables may predict work group performance and the conditions which affect such predictions" (1966, p. 360). Examining the relationship between criteria of effectiveness and both initiating structure and consideration (as measured by the Leader Behavior Description Questionnaire) he finds correlations ranging from .68 to –.19 for initiating structure and .84 to –.52 for consideration. He speculates that situational differences may have a great deal to do with this diversity but acknowledges that "the researchers have made little attempt to either conceptualize situational variables which might be relevant and/or to measure them" (1966, p. 359).

Similarly, Sales (1966) has reviewed both experimental and correlational findings concerning the effects of democratic and authoritarian supervision and finds the evidence conflicting. He states that "the hypothesis that democratic supervision will evoke greater effort from employees than will autocratic supervision cannot truly be either supported or rejected" (1966, p. 285). He goes on to propose an alternative hypothesis that is consistent with the position that the effects of democratic methods will vary with the conditions under which they are utilized.

Likert (1961, 1967) has provided what is probably the most optimistic picture of results to date. He concludes that there is substantial evidence that more effective leaders (1) tend to have relationships with their subordinates that are supportive and enhance the latter's sense of personal worth and importance, (2) use group rather than man-to-man methods of supervision and decision-making, and (3) tend to set high performance goals.

The contrast between Likert's conclusions and those of Sales and Korman is worthy of comment. At first glance it would appear that Likert is asserting that the situation does not have to be incorporated into the formulation of a set of leadership principles. On closer examination, there is less difference. His leadership principles and other components of what he has termed System 4 (or his participative-group system of management) are not concrete leader behaviors but rather outcomes both of the behavior of the leader and of other organizational conditions. The particular leadership acts necessary to achieve these outcomes are probably not specifiable without a detailed knowledge of the situation. His system is, in a sense, a general blueprint for action rather than a detailed blueprint, which would of necessity have to take situational factors into account. Likert recognizes the paramount role of the situation in making his principles operational in the following statement:

> Supervision is . . . always a relative process. To be effective and to communicate as intended, a leader must always adapt his behavior to take into account the expectations, values, and interpersonal skills of those with whom he is interacting. . . . There can be no specific rules of supervision which will work well in all situations. Broad principles can be applied in the process of supervision and furnish valuable guides to behavior. These principles, however, must be applied always in a manner that takes fully into account the characteristics of the specific situation and of the people involved. (1961, p. 95)

Broad principles are less vulnerable to the variability in empirical findings of which Sales and Korman write, and they are also of less prescriptive value. It is possible to state principles of leadership in such a way that they are incapable of empirical refutation and appear equally consistent with quite different forms of leader behavior. To say that a leader should manage in such a way that personnel at all levels feel real responsibility for the attainment of the organization's goals (Likert 1967) or alternatively, that he should exhibit concern for both production and people (Blake and Mouton 1964), is not saying a great deal about what he should do in the concrete situations that he faces daily.

From the perspective of figure 10.1, the search for "effective" leader behaviors assumed that organizational effectiveness (#4) was a simple function of leader behavior (#3). It represented a significant advance over the personality trait approach in the sense that it considered the actions of the leaders rather than their personal traits as influencing effectiveness of organizations. However, it failed to deal with the possibility that organizational effectiveness might reflect the joint effects of both leader behavior (#3) and situational variables (#1a) including interactions between these two sets of variables. Broad principles of leadership that allow room for the inclusion of situational variables but do not utilize them explicitly run the risk of being vacuous.

The normative model, developed in chapters 2 and 3 and subsequently revised in chapter 9, is a prescriptive framework which does *not* make the assumption that leadership methods that are effective in one situation are necessarily effective in another situation. It also avoids broad principles that leave room for the influence of the situation but do not utilize it for prescriptive purposes.

The normative model was explicitly founded on the assumption that the effectiveness of an organizational decision is a *joint* function of situational variables expressed as problem attributes and leader behavior expressed as processes for making decisions. By its very nature, it is consistent with the observations of Korman and Sales that the relationship between measures of leader behavior and effectiveness varies markedly from one situation to another. However, any normative framework which prescribes different leader behaviors in different situations could be said to be equally consistent with these observations. The principal literature on which the model is based concerns the consequences of participation on such components of decision effectiveness as quality, acceptance, and time. This literature is by no means complete and the normative model is certainly not the only one that could have been developed from it. Hopefully, the publication of the model in its present form will stimulate research to identify its weaknesses and/or resolve issues on which the literature provides only partial answers.

PERSONALITY AND SITUATION

In the previous two sections, we have asserted that an analysis of situational demands is a prerequisite to an understanding of the process of leadership. In retrospect this conclusion is not surprising. In fact, it would be surprising to find that the nature of the group or organization, its prevalent norms and values, and the critical problems it faces in its relationship with its own environment have nothing to do with the leadership process. However, it is necessary to go beyond the correct but empty conclusion that "leadership depends on the situation" to specify the nature of this relationship.

One way of attacking this problem attempts to reconcile the personal trait approach with differences in situational requirements. It assumes that persons with different characteristics or attributes are effective in different situations. Undoubtedly, the leading exponent of this approach to the study of leadership is Fiedler (1967), who with his colleagues has carried out an extensive program of research on the way in which one of the leader's personal attributes affects the performance of his group or organization. The personality variable used by Fiedler to characterize differences among leaders is called Least Preferred Co-worker (LPC). The measure of this variable was described in chapter 6. In that chapter, we also noted that the relationship between LPC and leader behavior was still a matter of considerable uncertainty.

Fiedler's research program has examined the relationship between the leader's LPC score and objective criteria of group or organizational performance. A large variety of groups has been studied, including high school basketball teams, student surveying parties, boards of directors of small corporations, army task crews, gasoline service station managers, and crews in open-hearth steel shops. In each study, coefficients of correlation were computed between the leader's LPC score and one or more measures of group effectiveness. The variation in these correlations (+.89 to −.81) was initially quite difficult to understand. It was not obvious why open-hearth crews should be more effective when their foremen had low LPC scores while boards of directors were more effective when their chairmen had high LPC scores.

Fiedler's Contingency Model (Fiedler 1967) represents an attempt to explain these diverse findings. It classifies the groups employed in his studies into eight types or octants in accordance with their status (high or low) on three dimensions: (1) the degree of structure involved in the task, (2) the amount of power given to the leader by virtue of his position, and (3) the quality of interpersonal relationships between the leader and other members.

Fiedler reasoned that these three variables have a common element. They constitute indicators of the favorableness of the situation to the leader. Thus, the most favorable situation would be one in which the task is structured, the leader has high position power, and leader-member relations are good. An additional assumption concerning the relative importance of these three dimensions in specifying "favorableness" permits a rank ordering of the octants from high to low on this dimension. When this is done it becomes apparent (see Fiedler 1967, p. 146) that the correlation between the leader's LPC score and group effectiveness is highly related to the favorableness of the situation and that the shape of that relationship approximates an inverted U. When the situation is either highly favorable or highly unfavorable, the correlations are negative. However, in situations which are only moderately favorable or moderately unfavorable for the leader, the correlations between LPC and group effectiveness are positive.

Whenever a theory or model has been arrived at by inductive means, it is critical that it be validated: it must be able to predict results other than those which entered into its formulation. Several validation studies have been conducted (Fiedler 1966, Hunt 1967, Hill 1969, Mitchell 1969). The degree to which the results are consistent with the predictions from the model is a matter of substantial disagreement. Fiedler (1967, p. 180) interprets the results as supporting the model; but Graen, Alvares, Orris, and Martella (1970) have reanalyzed the validational data and question this conclusion. Furthermore, a laboratory experiment specifically designed to test the interactions in the model (Graen, Orris, and Alvares 1971) failed to find any support for the predictions.

From the perspective of figure 10.1, Fiedler's Contingency Model treats the effectiveness of a group or organization (#4) as a joint function of situational variables (#1 or #1a) and of the LPC score of the leader (#2). The processes underlying his findings are somewhat difficult to understand, at least in part due to the difficulty in knowing precisely what aspects of leader behavior LPC measures. In chapters 4 and 5 we examined the determinants of one aspect of leader behavior—the opportunity provided to subordinates to participate in decision-making. The results, summarized earlier in this chapter, are difficult to reconcile with the view that all or even a substantial portion of the variance in how leaders behave is capable of being measured by a single score generated by a single test.

Fiedler's Contingency Model and the normative models presented in this book are similar in a number of respects. Both models attempt to come to grips with differences in the kind of leadership required in different situations. Both assume that no one style of leadership is appropriate to all conditions, and both purport to prescribe the nature of leadership required under each situation. Furthermore, Fiedler's model and the models presented here are pragmatic rather than idealistic in their conception of the leadership process. They deal with the "value issues" inextricably involved in prescriptive models by assuming that the function of leadership is to facilitate the goals of the organization, regardless of how moral or immoral those goals might be or how congruent they are with the personal wants and desires of the participants. Even though participation may be an ultimate value for some, it was not treated as such either by us or by Fiedler. For us the question "When *should* a leader encourage the participation of his subordinates in decision-making?" is synonymous with "When is participation helpful in creating decisions that are effective in achieving organizational goals?"

However, here the similarity between Fiedler's work and our own ends. There are marked differences between the two models in the kinds of variables they employ in the measurement and analysis of leadership style. In a sense Fiedler's model is a situational off shoot of the concept of leadership as a personality trait. He shares with that tradition the use of individual difference measures as independent variables but differs in his inclusion of situational moderator variables.

Similarly, our model is derived from the search for effective leader behaviors. We share with that tradition the focus on how leaders behave in carrying out their roles but differ in the explicit inclusion of differences in situational requirements. While it may be tempting to look for similarities between Fiedler's situational variables (task structure, leader's power, and quality of leader-member relations) and our problem attributes, the unit of anlaysis is quite different. For Fiedler, these variables are meant to describe relatively stable properties of the situation confronted by the leader. In our model, they are assumed to be properties of the immediate problem to be solved or decision to be made.

The way in which the two models could potentially contribute to the identification and enhancement of leadership is also different in ways that are a direct consequence of these factors. Fiedler views his model as having implications for the processes of leader recruitment and selection and also for what he terms organizational engineering. If his model is valid, it could provide a rational basis for selecting leaders with personal qualities appropriate to the roles they are expected to perform. Given a knowledge of the octant of a particular leadership position, one would know whether to seek an occupant with a high or low LPC score. Organizational engineering is predicated on the possibility of altering the situation to fit the personality characteristics of the leader. If a leader's LPC score is not suited to the demands of the position he occupies, the Contingency Model could provide an *a priori* rationale for making changes in the situation so as to improve his effectiveness.

In contrast, we have viewed leadership development as the principal application of our work. The essential purpose of the leadership development program, described in chapter 8, is to encourage people to examine critically the leadership methods they use in concrete situations in order to better fit their "style" to the situational demands. Fiedler explicitly rejects this alternative as infeasible.

> The alternative method would call for training the leader to develop a flexible leadership style and to adapt his leadership style to the particular situation. The author is highly pessimistic that this training approach would be successful. There may be some favored few who can be effective in any leadership situation and some unfortunate few who would even find it difficult to lead a troop of hungry Girl Scouts to a hot dog stand. However, our experience has not enabled us to identify these individuals. Nor have we found it possible to identify those who can switch their leadership style as the occasion demands. It would seem more promising at this time, therefore, to teach the individual to recognize the conditions in which he can perform best and then modify the situation to suit his leadership style. (1967, pp. 254–55)

LOOKING TOWARD THE FUTURE

As noted in chapter 1, the potential importance to society of an adequate understanding of the leadership process cannot be underestimated. Any knowledge that the behavioral sciences could contribute to the identification and enhancement of leadership in organized human endeavor could be of considerable value in increasing the effectiveness of organizations in society.

It is difficult to argue that research on the leadership process has contributed in an important way to the attainment of these goals. This chapter has shown one of the possible reasons for this state of affairs. Much of the research conducted appears to have been based on erroneous and oversimplified conceptions of the leadership process.

We have attempted (in figure 10.1) to provide a new framework for the investigation of leadership. This framework serves to indicate the classes of variables which we believe need to be incorporated into an adequate formulation of leadership process. It proved helpful in representing the findings reported in this book and the principal differences between our approach and those of others. While we have dealt with only one facet of leadership, the schema shown in figure 10.1 and the research methods employed in this book could prove equally relevant to an examination of other aspects of the leadership process.

As with participation in decision-making, there are many concepts and applications developed within the social sciences, the utility of which is likely to vary with the situation. Among these are decentralization, management by objectives, nondirective counseling, job enrichment, and sensitivity training. In such instances there are multiple consequences of each treatment, and estimates of their utility in a particular situation inevitably involve judgments concerning the value of each consequence and the probability of its occurring in that situation.

It is suggested that social scientists can be both more operational and potentially more useful in their prescriptive statements concerning leadership and organizational behavior if they deal with the complexities in the phenomena involved. The evidence reviewed in this chapter casts doubt on the adequacy of simple representations. The work in this book reflects our conviction that it is necessary to move beyond "broad principles" of leadership to more clearly articulated models. We are tired of debates over the relative merits of Theory X and Theory Y and of the truism that leadership depends upon the situation. It is time for the behavioral sciences to move beyond such generalities and come to grips with the complexities of the phenomena with which they intend to deal. We hope that this book represents one small step in that direction.

APPENDICES • REFERENCES • INDEX

Instructions for Coding Problems

After reading each of the cases, you should answer a set of questions concerning it. The questions are shown below and following each question is a detailed discussion of the attribute which it is expected to reflect and considerations which should bear on your answer.

1. *If decision were accepted, would it make a difference which course of action were adopted?* This attribute refers to the importance of finding a high quality solution independent of the need to satisfy any acceptance criteria. There are some problems for which the nature of the solution reached is not critical at all. Within the constraints specified in the problem you are (or should be) indifferent among the possible solutions. The number of solutions which meet the constraints is finite and the alternatives do not require substantial search. All such solutions have identical expected values, provided that those who have to carry them out are committed to them. Problems of this type should be coded *NO*. They are essentially of two kinds: (1) Neither the quality nor the acceptance of the decision is critical. You could flip a coin to decide which course of action to adopt. (2) Quality is unimportant but acceptance is critical.

All problems with any technical, rational, or analytical component should be coded *YES*. In such instances, some solutions are always better than others (less costly, more effective in attaining the objective, etc.), and you should not be indifferent as to which is chosen.

2. *Do I have sufficient information to make a high quality decision?* This attribute refers to the extent to which you have sufficient information, skill, or expertise to solve the problem by yourself without the aid of your subordinates. The information referred

to concerns the technical or rational side of the problem, i.e., you are asked if you have the information needed to achieve the external objective, not the information as to what solution would most please your subordinates. Note that what is called for is a judgment about your knowledge in relation to the demands of the problem, not a relative judgment of your knowledge versus that of your subordinates.

3. Do subordinates have sufficient additional information to result in a high quality decision? This attribute concerns the additional information, skill, or expertise possessed by your subordinates. This question is normally asked only when your answer to the previous question is *NO*, that is, when in your judgment you do not possess enough information to solve the problem adequately by yourself. However, even if your answer to the previous question were *YES*, it is possible that you might view your subordinates as having some additional valid information which would increase the quality or rationality of the solution; that is, you could make a satisfactory decision by yourself but an even better decision if you had access to their information.

4. Do I know exactly what information is needed, who possesses it, and how to collect it? This attribute refers to the location and specificity of the information. There are some problems for which missing information is highly specific. The problem is structured, the variables that enter into the final solution are known, and the task of finding what is technically the optimal solution consists of measuring these variables. You know exactly what information (levels of variables) is missing, where (in whose head or file) it is stored, and how to access it or retrieve it from storage. The task of information retrieval can be likened to that of looking up unknown facts in a reference book, even though the information here is contained in human memories rather than in printed sources. If these above conditions are satisfied, the attribute should be coded *YES*. There are other problems for which the information is missing or its location is not so easily identified, and the method of retrieving it is necessarily more cumbersome. The problem is unstructured, and the alternatives and criteria for their evaluation are unknown. If these latter criteria are satisfied, the attribute should then be coded *NO*.

5. Is acceptance of decision by subordinates critical to effective implementation? This attribute refers to the importance of getting acceptance or commitment to the solution or decision on the part of your subordinates. If none of your subordinates is involved in executing the decision or solution, your response to this question should be *NO*. If they are involved in its execution but the nature of their involvement is such that compliance rather than acceptance is sufficient for its implementation, your response should also be *NO*. Your response should be *YES* if the success or failure of the decision hinges to an important degree on enthusiastic support of the decision by your subordinates. In such instances one or more of the following conditions would be expected to be found:

1. More than compliance to specified directives is required for effective execution; that is, the task of execution requires judgment or creativity on the part of those executing it.

2. The conditions necessary for securing compliance, ability to monitor and punish deviations from directives, are not present.

3. Attempts at securing compliance are likely to have serious side effects on other decisions; for example, the subordinates might leave the organization.

6. *If I were to make the solution by myself, is it certain to be accepted by my subordinates?* This attribute refers to the extent to which you believe that your decision, made autocratically, would be likely to receive acceptance from your subordinates. There are some situations in which subordinates expect their superior to make the decision. They believe that it is his legitimate right to make the decision because he occupies the position he does, or because he is the acknowledged expert, or the only person capable of taking all the necessary factors into consideration. In such situations it is not at all difficult for the leader to "sell" his decision.

The prevalence of this condition has been shown to vary with a number of factors, including:

1. *Culture:* In some countries, particularly in those less developed, the preexisting authority and status hierarchy is preeminent, and the right of those occupying positions over you to make decisions that affect your behavior is seldom questioned.

2. *The personalities of the subordinates:* Within a given culture people vary in their desire to participate in decisions affecting them.

3. *The charisma of the leader:* Some leaders are thought by their subordinates to be imbued with almost supernatural powers, and are "unable to do any wrong."

There are some situations in which the ability of the leader to sell a solution to his subordinates, and gain acceptance, depends on the particular solution that he is trying to sell. Some solutions would be highly palatable to, and easily acceptable by, his subordinates, whereas others would be openly opposed and resisted. In such instances, consider the most rational solution and code this solution in terms of your estimate of the leader's ability to sell it to his subordinates.

7. *Can subordinates be trusted to base solutions on organizational considerations?* This attribute refers to the extent to which subordinates would be motivated to pursue a solution to the problem which is rational from the standpoint of the goals of the organization, rather than their own self-interest. As used here, the term *TRUST* deals with the motivation of subordinates rather than their information, knowledge, or expertise. (The used-car salesman might be most knowledgeable concerning the reliability of the cars on his lot, but one might be reluctant to delegate the choice of car to him due to a belief that he might be motivated to do other than choose the best value for the money.) In responding to this question, search for evidence in the problem of a common or superordinate goal, or of an area of mutual interest. When these conditions exist, you are more likely to trust your subordinates. In a sense you are all in "the same boat," having a common dilemma or objective. Respond *NO* if, in the course of trying to solve the problem, solutions suggested by, and acceptable to, the subordinates are likely to violate corporate goals. Respond *YES* if in the course of solving the problem your subordinates would attempt to promote, or at least not damage, organizational objectives.

8. *Is conflict among subordinates likely in preferred solution?* This attribute refers to the conflict or disagreement expected to exist among subordinates in their preferred solutions to the problem. There are many situations in which, at least initially, there is high variance in opinions concerning what constitutes a "good" solution to a particular problem. These may include:

1. Situations in which there is substantial commitment to the organizational goals to be pursued, but disagreement concerning

the appropriate course of action. (*TRUST* would be coded *YES*, *CONFLICT* coded *YES*.)

2. Situations in which there is no commitment to the organizational goal and disagreement concerning the most effective means of attaining it. (*TRUST* would be coded *NO*, *CONFLICT* coded *YES*.)

These are to be distinguished from:

3. Situations in which there is likely to be both substantial commitment to the organizational goal and agreement on how to attain it. (*TRUST* would be coded *YES*, *CONFLICT* coded *NO*.)

4. Situations characterized by substantial commitment to a goal other than an organizational one, and agreement on how to attain it. (*TRUST* would be coded *NO*, *CONFLICT* coded *NO*.)

Rules Underlying the Model for Both Individual and Group Problems[1]

1. The leader information rule. If the quality of the decision is important, and the leader does not possess enough information or expertise to solve the problem by himself, then AI is eliminated from the feasible set.

$$A \cap \bar{B} \Rightarrow \overline{\text{AI}}$$

2. The subordinate information rule (applicable to individual problems only). If the quality of the decision is important, and the subordinate does not possess enough information to solve the problem himself, then DI is eliminated from the feasible set.

$$I: A \cap \bar{H} \Rightarrow \overline{\text{DI}}$$

3. The goal congruence rule. If the quality of the decision is important, and the subordinate(s) is (are) not likely to pursue organization goals in his (their) efforts to solve this problem, then GII, DI, and GI are eliminated from the feasible set.

$$A \cap \bar{F} \Rightarrow \overline{\text{GII}}, \overline{\text{DI}}, \overline{\text{GI}}$$

4a. The unstructured problem rule: group. When the quality of the decision is important, if the leader lacks the necessary information or expertise to solve the problem by himself and if the problem is unstructured, the method of solving the problem should provide for interaction among subordinates likely to possess relevant

1. These rules apply to the model in figure 9.3.

information. Accordingly AI, AII, and CI are eliminated from the feasible set.

$$G: A \cap \bar{B} \cap \bar{C} \Rightarrow \overline{AI}, \overline{AII}, \overline{CI}$$

4b. The unstructured problem rule: individual. In decisions in which quality is important, if the leader lacks the necessary information to solve the problem by himself and if the problem is unstructured, the method of solving the problem should permit the subordinate to generate solutions and in so doing provide information concerning all aspects of the problem. Accordingly AI and AII are eliminated from the feasible set.

$$I: A \cap \bar{B} \cap \bar{C} \Rightarrow \overline{AI}, \overline{AII}$$

5. The acceptance rule. If the acceptance of the decision by the subordinate(s) is critical to effective implementation and if it is not certain that an autocratic decision will be accepted, AI and AII are eliminated from the feasible set.

$$D \cap \bar{E} \Rightarrow \overline{AI}, \overline{AII}$$

6. The conflict rule (applicable to group problems only). If the acceptance of the decision is critical, an autocratic decision is not certain to be accepted, and disagreement among subordinates in methods of attaining the organizational goal is likely, the methods used in solving the problem should enable those in disagreement to resolve their differences with full knowledge of the problem. Accordingly, under these conditions AI, AII, and CI, which permit no interaction among subordinates and therefore provide no opportunity for those in conflict to resolve their differences, are eliminated from the feasible set. Their use runs the risk of leaving some of the subordinates with less than the needed commitment to the final decision.

$$G: D \cap \bar{E} \cap G \Rightarrow \overline{AI}, \overline{AII}, \overline{CI}$$

7. The fairness rule. If the quality of the decision is unimportant, but acceptance of the decision is critical and not certain to result from an autocratic decision, it is important that the decision process used generate the needed acceptance. In group problems, the decision process used should permit the subordinates to interact with one another and negotiate over the fair method of resolving any differences with full responsibility on them for determining what is fair and equitable. In individual problems, the decision-making process should provide for the affected subordinate to be at least a full and equal partner. Accordingly, under these circumstances AI, AII, CI, and CII are eliminated from the feasible set.

$$\bar{A} \cap D \cap \bar{E} \Rightarrow \overline{AI}, \overline{AII}, \overline{CI}, \overline{CII}$$

8. *The acceptance priority rule.* If acceptance is critical, not certain to result from an autocratic decision, and if (the) subordinate(s) is (are) motivated to pursue the organizational goals represented in the problem, then methods which provide equal partnership in the decision-making process can provide greater acceptance without risking decision quality. Accordingly AI, AII, CI, and CII are eliminated from the feasible set.

$$D \cap \bar{E} \cap F \Rightarrow \overline{AI}, \overline{AII}, \overline{CI}, \overline{CII}$$

References

Ansoff, H. I. 1965. *Corporate strategy*. New York: McGraw-Hill.

Argyris, C. 1962. *Interpersonal competence and organizational effectiveness*. Homewood, Illinois: Irwin.

Bales, R. F. 1949. *Interaction process analysis: a method for the study of small groups*. Cambridge, Mass. Addison-Wesley.

Bales, R. F., and Slater, P. E. 1955. Role differentiation in small groups. In *Family, socialization and interaction process*, by T. Parsons, R. F. Bales et al. Glencoe, Ill.: Free Press.

Ball, G. H., and Hall, D. J. 1967. A clustering technique for summarizing multivariate data. *Behavioral Science* 12:153-55.

Bass, B. M. 1955. Authoritarianism or acquiescence? *Journal of Abnormal and Social Psychology* 51:616-23.

———. 1960. *Leadership, psychology and organizational behavior*. New York: Harper.

———. 1962. *Orientation inventory*. Palo Alto: Consulting Psychologists Press.

Bass, B. M., and Coates, C. H. 1952. Forecasting officer potential using the leaderless group discussion. *Journal of Abnormal and Social Psychology* 47:321-25.

Baumgartel, H. 1956. Leadership, motivations and attitudes in research laboratories. *Journal of Social Issues* 12:24-31.

Bennis, W. G. 1966. *Changing organizations*. New York: McGraw-Hill.

Blake, R., and Mouton, Jane. 1964. *The managerial grid*. Houston: Gulf.

Brown, R. 1965. *Social psychology*. New York: Free Press.

Coch, L., and French, J. R. P., Jr. 1948. Overcoming resistance to change. *Human Relations* 1:512-32.

Coombs, C. H. 1964. *A theory of data*. New York: Wiley.

Cronbach, L. J. 1957. The two disciplines of scientific psychology. *American Psychologist* 12:671-84.

———. 1960. *Essentials of psychological testing*. 2nd ed. New York: Harper.

Cyert, R. M., and March, J. G. 1963. *A behavioral theory of the firm*. Englewood Cliffs, N.J.: Prentice-Hall.

Fiedler, F. E. 1966. The effect of leadership and cultural heterogeneity on group performance: a test of the contingency model. *Journal of Experimental Social Psychology* 2:237-64.

_____. 1967. *A theory of leadership effectiveness.* New York: McGraw-Hill.

File, Q. W., and Remmers, H. H. 1948. *How supervise?* New York: Psychological Corporation.

Fleishman, E. A. 1957. The leadership opinion questionnaire. In *Leader behavior: its description and measurement,* edited by R. M. Stodgill and A. E. Coons, pp. 120-33. Columbus: Ohio State University, Bureau of Business Research, Res. Monogr. No. 88.

Fleishman, E. A., Harris, E. F., and Burtt, H. E. 1955. *Leadership and supervision in industry.* Columbus: Ohio State University, Bureau of Educational Research.

Frederiksen, N. 1962. Factors in in-basket performance. *Psychological Monographs* 76:1-6.

French, J. R. P., Jr. 1950. Field experiments: changing group productivity. In *Experiments in social process: a symposium on social psychology,* edited by J. G. Miller. New York: McGraw-Hill.

French, J. R. P., Jr.; Israel, J.; and Ås, D. 1960. An experiment on participation in a Norwegian factory. *Human Relations* 13:3-19.

French, J. R. P., Jr., and Raven, B. 1959. The bases of social power. In *Studies in social power,* edited by D. Cartwright. Ann Arbor, Mich.: Institute for Social Research.

Gibb, C. A. 1969. Leadership. In *Handbook of social psychology,* by G. Lindzey and E. Aronson, vol. 4, pp. 205-82. Reading, Mass.: Addison-Wesley.

Graen, G.; Alvares, K.; Orris, J. B.; and Martella, J. A. 1970. Contingency model of leadership effectiveness: antecedent and evidential results. *Psychological Bulletin* 74:285-96.

Graen, G.; Orris, J. B.; and Alvares, K. 1971. Contingency model of leadership effectiveness: some experimental results. *Journal of Applied Psychology* 55:196-201.

Haire, M.; Ghiselli, E. E.; and Porter, L. 1966. *Managerial thinking: an international study.* New York: Wiley.

Halpin, A. W., and Winer, B. J. 1957. A factorial study of the leader behavior descriptions. In *Leader behavior: its description and measurement,* edited by R. M. Stodgill and A. E. Coons, pp. 39-51. Columbus: Ohio State University, Bureau of Business Research, Res. Monogr. No. 88.

Hartshorne, H., and May, M. A. 1928. *Studies in deceit.* New York: Macmillan.

Heller, F. A. 1971. *Managerial decision making.* London: Tavistock.

Heller, F. A., and Yukl, G. 1969. Participation, managerial decision-making and situational variables. *Organizational Behavior and Human Performance* 4:227-41.

Hill, W. 1969. The validation and extension of Fiedler's theory of leadership effectiveness. *Academy of Management Journal* 12:33-47.

Hunt, J. G. 1967. A test of the leadership contingency model in three organizations. *Organizational Behavior and Human Performance* 2:290-308.

Katz, D.; Maccoby, N.; Gurin, G.; and Floor, L. 1951. *Productivity, supervision, and morale among railroad workers.* Ann Arbor: University of Michigan, Institute for Social Research.

Katz, D.; Maccoby, N.; and Morse, N. C. 1950. *Productivity, supervision, and morale in an office situation.* Ann Arbor: University of Michigan, Institute for Social Research.

Kelley, H., and Thibaut, J. 1969. Group problem solving. In *Handbook of social psychology*, edited by G. Lindzey and E. Aronson, vol. 4, pp. 1-101. Reading, Mass.: Addison-Wesley.

Korman, A. K. 1966. "Consideration," "initiating structure," and organizational criteria—a review. *Personnel Psychology* 19:349-61.

Lewin, K. 1935. *A dynamic theory of personality.* New York: McGraw-Hill.

———. 1951. *Field theory in social science*, edited by D. Cartwright. New York: Harper.

Lewin, K.; Lippitt, R.; and White, R. K. 1939. Patterns of aggressive behavior in experimentally created social climates. *Journal of Social Psychology* 10:271-99.

Likert, R. 1961. *New patterns of management.* New York: McGraw-Hill.

———. 1967. *The human organization.* New York: McGraw-Hill.

Lowin, A. 1968. Participative decision making: a model, literature critique, and prescriptions for research. *Organizational Behavior and Human Performance* 3:68-106.

Lowin, A., and Craig, J. R. 1968. The influence of level of performance on managerial style: an experimental object-lesson in the ambiguity of correlational data. *Organizational Behavior and Human Performance* 3:440-58.

McGregor, D. 1944. Getting effective leadership in the industrial organization. *Advanced Management* 9:148-53.

Maier, N. R. F. 1955. *Psychology in industry.* 2nd ed. Boston: Houghton-Mifflin.

———. 1963. *Problem-solving discussions and conferences: leadership methods and skills.* New York: McGraw-Hill.

———. 1970. *Problem solving and creativity in individuals and groups.* Belmont, Calif.: Brooks-Cole.

Mann, R. D. 1959. A review of the relationship between personality and performance in small groups. *Psychological Bulletin* 56:241-70.

March, J. G., and Simon, H. A. 1958. *Organizations.* New York: Wiley.

Marrow, A. J. 1964. Risk and uncertainties in action research. *Journal of Social Issues* 20:5-20.

Messick, S. J., and Jackson, D. N. 1957. Authoritarianism or acquiescence in Bass' data. *Journal of Abnormal and Social Psychology* 54:424-25.

Miles, R. E. 1965. Human relations or human resources? *Harvard Business Review* 43:148-63.

Mitchell, T. R. 1969. Leader complexity, leadership style, and group performance. Ph.D. dissertation, University of Illinois.

Morse, Nancy C., and Reimer, E. 1956. The experimental change of a major organizational variable. *Journal of Abnormal and Social Psychology* 52:120-29.

Mulder, M. 1959. Power and satisfaction in task-oriented groups. *Acta Psychologica* 16:178-225.

Mulder, M.; Veen, P.; Hartsuiker, D.; and Westerduin, T. 1970. Cognitive processes in power equalization. *European Journal of Social Psychology* 1:107-30.

OSS Assessment Staff. 1948. *Assessment of men.* New York: Rinehart.

Patchen, M. 1964. Participation in decision-making and motivation: what is the relation? *Personnel Administration* 27:24-31.

Sales, S. M. 1966. Supervisory style and productivity: review and theory. *Personnel Psychology* 19:275-86.

Shaw, M. E. 1964. Communication networks. In *Advances in experimental psychology*, edited by L. Berkowitz, vol. 1, pp. 111-47. New York: Academic Press.

Simon, H. A. 1960. *The new science of management decision.* New York: Harper.

Stagner, R. 1958. The gullibility of personnel managers. *Personnel Psychology* 11:347-52.

Stogdill, R. M. 1948. Personal factors associated with leadership: a survey of the literature. *Journal of Psychology* 25:35-71.

Stogdill, R. M., and Coons, A. E., eds. 1957. *Leader behavior: its description and measurement.* Columbus: Ohio State University, Bureau of Business Research, Res. Monogr. No. 88.

Strauss, G. 1963. Some notes on power equalization. In *The social science of organizations*, edited by H. J. Leavitt, pp. 39-84. Englewood Cliffs. N.J.: Prentice-Hall.

Tannenbaum, R., and Schmidt, W. 1958. How to choose a leadership pattern. *Harvard Business Review* 36:95-101.

Vroom, V. H. 1960. *Some personality determinants of the effects of participation.* Englewood Cliffs. N.J.: Prentice-Hall.

_____. 1964. *Work and motivation.* New York: Wiley.

_____. 1970. Industrial social psychology. In *Handbook of social psychology*, edited by G. Lindzey and E. Aronson, vol. 5, pp. 196-268. Reading, Mass.: Addison-Wesley.

Wagner, H. M. 1969. *Principles of operations research.* Englewood Cliffs, N.J.: Prentice-Hall.

Whyte, W. F. 1955. *Money and motivation: an analysis of incentives in industry.* New York: Harper.

Wirdenius, H. 1958. *Supervisors at work.* Stockholm: The Swedish Council for Personnel Administration, PA Council Report NR 20.

Wood, M. J. 1974 (in press). Power relationships and group decision making in organizations. *Psychological Bulletin.*

Yetton, P. W. 1972. Participation and leadership style: a descriptive model of a manager's choice of a decision process. Ph.D. dissertation, Carnegie-Mellon University.

Author Index

227

Subject Index

Absolute distance from feasible set (ADFS)
  defined, 150
  reliability, 151–52
Absolute distance from normative model (ADNM)
  defined, 150
  reliability, 151–52
Acceptance of decision, feedback cycle in, 47–48
Acceptance requirement
  coding instructions, 214–15
  defined, 26–27
  effect on decision process, 81, 83–84, 86–87, 108–14, 118–19
  errors in coding, 46–47
  individual differences in effects, 127–28
  nesting principle, 96–97
  in recalled problems, 76–77
  in rules, 33–34, 219–20
  rules protecting, 32–38
  See also Problem attributes
Acquiescence response set, 84–85
Agreement with feasible set (AgFS)
  defined, 150
  reliability, 151–52
Agreement with normative model
  defined, 150
  reliability of measures, 151–52
Attitudes toward management practices
  described, 124
  relation to problem set, 132–33
Autocratic leadership
  actual behavior vs. normative model, 138
  effectiveness, 202
  short-term benefits, 45

subordinates' perceptions of superiors, 70–71, 79–81

Coding of problems
  accuracy, 45–48, 142–45
  agreement with experts, 50–51
  description of study, 49–50
  errors analyzed, 51–56
  instructions to coders, 213–17
  internal consistency, 50–51
  need for training, 51, 55–56
  subjective factors, 45–48, 142–45
  validation of experts, 99–101
Communication networks, 26
Computer printout
  example, 163–73
  reactions to, 173–81
  utility of, 162
Concern for people, 61
Conflict among subordinates
  coding instructions, 216–17
  defined, 30
  effect on decision process, 82, 106, 109–10, 112–14, 116, 118–19
  individual differences in effects, 127
  in recalled problems, 76–77
  in rule, 34, 219
  See also Problem attributes
Consideration, 61, 62, 202

Decentralization, 209
Decision method. See Decision processes
Decision processes
  actual behavior compared with normative model, 135–54
  assigning scale values, 65–71, 91